Harlequin in Hogtown
George Luscombe and Toronto Workshop Productions

Toronto Workshop Productions was Toronto's first 'alternative' theatre, and for thirty years, from 1959 until its closure in 1989, it introduced audiences to a radically new form of theatre. Neil Carson's in-depth history of TWP traces the fortunes of many of its actors, writers, designers, and technicians – but the troupe's colourful artistic director, George Luscombe, is its central character.

George Luscombe brought Toronto a new form of theatre based on the techniques and theories he developed during the four years he worked with Joan Littlewood's Theatre Workshop in London. Toronto Workshop Productions began its activities in a small theatre in the basement of a factory in 1959 with Luscombe as artistic director. He presided over a program of collective play creation that fostered cooperative collaboration among all the contributing artists. A series of original works and plays from the European repertoire in innovative productions won the company increasing critical acclaim. The company acquired its own building in 1967, establishing its reputation as the most exciting theatre in the city. By the early 1970s, however, a growing atmosphere of Canadian nationalism caused TWP to be overshadowed by a number of new alternative theatres. Luscombe's and TWP's vision of an ideologically committed, technically experimental theatre remained strong for a number of years, but in the end a combination of internal and external problems overwhelmed the company.

TWP's productions provoked radically different responses among audiences, and Luscombe's particular style of drama – a combination of documentary, stylized movement, and music – remains controversial. As a pioneer and as a stimulating teacher, however, George Luscombe has provided inspiration for countless actors and directors. Carson's book is an invaluable addition to the history of Canadian theatre.

NEIL CARSON is a professor of English at the University of Guelph, and author of *A Companion to Henslowe's Diary* and *Arthur Miller*.

Our job has to be to draw the raw material of the theatre from the community, interpreting it in our own way and giving it back to the community, not as real life but like an image in a purposely distorted mirror.

George Luscombe

Harlequin in Hogtown

George Luscombe and
Toronto Workshop Productions

Neil Carson

UNIVERSITY OF TORONTO PRESS
Toronto Buffalo London

© University of Toronto Press Incorporated 1995
Toronto Buffalo London
Printed in Canada

ISBN 0-8020-0680-9 (cloth)
ISBN 0-8020-7633-5 (paper)

∞

Printed on acid-free paper

Canadian Cataloguing in Publication Data

Carson, Neil, 1931–
    Harlequin in Hogtown : George Luscombe and
    Toronto Workshop Productions

    Includes index.
    ISBN 0-8020-0680-9 (bound)   ISBN 0-8020-7633-5 (pbk.)

    1. Toronto Workshop Productions. 2. Luscombe,
    George, 1926– . 3. Experimental theater –
    Ontario – Toronto. I. Title

    PN2306.T62T673 1995   792′.09713′541   C95-930446-0

Unless otherwise stated, all photographs are from the Toronto Workshop
Productions Archives in the Archival Collections of McLaughlin Library,
University of Guelph.

University of Toronto Press acknowledges the financial assistance to its
publishing program of the Canada Council and the Ontario Arts Council.

This book has been published with the help of a grant from the Canadian
Federation for the Humanities, using funds provided by the Social Sciences
and Humanities Research Council of Canada.

TO ALL THOSE WHO MADE IT HAPPEN

Contents

viii   Contents

Preface

Toronto Workshop Productions is the stepchild of the alternative theatre movement. Born a decade before its better-known Toronto rivals, it saw its own early achievements ignored or undervalued by a new generation of critics who, like doting parents, exclaimed over every faltering step of its younger siblings. The ten-year period during which TWP provided the most vital theatre in the city was dismissed as the 'Dark Ages' before Theatre Passe Muraille discovered collective creation.[1] Its highly acclaimed productions of the 1970s, such as *Ten Lost Years* (1974), *Les Canadiens* (1977), and *Ain't Lookin'* (1980), were considered somehow peripheral to the significant developments in the city. Historians of Canadian theatre continue to distinguish TWP from what they call the 'major alternative theatres,'[2] seeing its work as somehow both less 'collective' than theirs (because the actors were subordinated to the director)[3] and less 'Canadian' (because its Canadian writers and actors did not deal with 'indigenous' material).

This conventional assessment of TWP has always seemed inadequate to me. I remembered having been overwhelmed by the energy and imagination of TWP productions in the early 1960s, and I felt that the excitement of those productions had never been adequately communicated. What was missing from the usual historical accounts was a sense of the novelty of the enterprise. Before TWP, most people believed that original Canadian plays would never be popular in the country. Luscombe and his actors proved them wrong. In effect, they demonstrated the viability of Canadian drama.

In following the story of the company, I have been struck by its ambiguous outlines. TWP was unusual in having a clear aesthetic vision to which it remained faithful for almost thirty years. If it was distinctive artistically, however, it was subject to the same political and economic forces that affected all arts organizations in the 1970s and 1980s. TWP's story, therefore, is both singular and typical, representative and unique. Though it marched to a different drum, TWP was caught up in the same battles that engulfed all the alternative theatres in Toronto.

The task of reconstructing those battles has been more complex than I anticipated. In spite of the existence of extensive archives (including playscripts, photographs, audiotapes, and critical reviews), the spirit of many of TWP's productions is almost irretrievably lost. Fortunately, I was assisted in my archaeological undertaking by many individuals who, in different capacities, had been connected with the company. Foremost among them was George Luscombe, who in a series of interviews in 1987 and 1988 provided me with the basic information out of which this history has been woven. In the months and years following those interviews, I have spoken to a number of performers, administrators, civil servants, and others who were themselves involved in the events I was chronicling. Without exception, they have been generous with their time and have provided me with details and anecdotes with which to enliven this story. To construct a solid foundation for the account, I have also consulted the records of related organizations such as the Canada Council, the Ontario Arts Council, and the City of Toronto. I am grateful to the staffs of the several libraries holding this material, including the National Archives of Canada, the Archives of Ontario, McMaster University Library, the Metropolitan Toronto Reference Library, and the McLaughlin Library of the University of Guelph.

I owe a special debt of gratitude to the late Norman Walford and to Robert Sirman, both formerly at the Ontario Arts Council, for granting me access to records in the Council's possession. But my main appreciation goes to the many individuals who were willing to share with me their memories of their impressions of and relations with the company, including Lou Applebaum, Maja Ardal, Michael Ayoub, Anne Bermonte, David Bolt, Carol Bolt, Jeff Braunstein, Lee Broker, Steven Bush, Tom Butler, Calvin Butler, David Clement, Suzette Couture, Larry Cox, Linda Desjardins, Len Doncheff, Diane Douglass, Arnold Edinborough, Norman Endicott, Ronald Evans, Peter Faulkner, June Faulkner, Joan Ferry, Alan Filewod, Barry Flatman, Bill Glassco, Milo Ringham Gold, Diane Grant, Robert Green, Tom Hendry, John Herbert, Karl Jaffary, Astrid Janson, Urjo Kareda, Nancy (Jowsey) Lewis, Olga Kershaw, Derrick Kershaw, François Klanfer, Sonja Livingston, Doug Livingston, William Lord, Mona Luscombe, Peter McConnell, Catherine McKeehan, Richard McKenna,

Leslie Mendelsohn, Jack Merigold, Peter Millard, Victoria Mitchell, Tony Moffat-Lynch, Kathleen Crawford-Patterson, Tom Patterson, Len Peterson, Walter Pitman, Susan Puff, Geoffrey Saville-Read, Brooky Robins, Grant Roll, Robert Rooney, Toby Ryan, Oscar Ryan, Rick Salutin, Edward Sanders, David Silcox, Florence Silver, Ross Skene, Cedric Smith, Anna Stratton, Paul Thompson, Frances Walsh, Herbert Whittaker, and Jack Winter. Finally, I would like to thank the University of Guelph for financial support during a sabbatical year, which enabled me to work full time on the project.

George Luscombe playing for a group of CCF Youth Club members in Toronto in the 1940s.

Relaxation exercises during a training period at 47 Fraser Avenue. Note the final shape of the stage, with double pillars, projecting platform, and minuscule 'inner stage.'

Rehearsal for *And They'll Make Peace* (1961) at 47 Fraser Avenue. The cast and Jack Winter (in the checked shirt) listen to Luscombe (off camera) give notes. Note the bleacher seating and the use of ramps.

Hey Rube! (1961). *Left to right:* Barbara Armitage, George Sperdakos (with back to camera), Glen Reid, Tony Moffat-Lynch, Joan Maroney (Ferry), Hal Sheftel. Note the clown make-up, which was the inspiration for the company logo.

Nancy (Jowsey) Lewis. Courtesy of Nancy Lewis.

The automobile routine from *The Mechanic* (1964), at the University of Waterloo. *Left to right:* Larry Perkins (Lee Broker), Lyndsay Punchard (seated),
Yvonne Adalian, Gregson Winkfield, Edward Kelly, Victoria Mitchell.

The Death of Woyzeck (1965), at Fraser Avenue. *Left to right:* Larry Perkins (with back to camera), Don Meyers, Gwen Thomas, Yvonne Adalian, Edward Kelly, Victoria Mitchell.

The Golem of Venice (1967), at Fraser Avenue. *Left to right:* Geoffrey Read, Mark Stone (with guitar), Frank Norris, Frances Walsh, Milo Ringham. Note the elastic 'pages' through which the performers entered. Photo by Robert van der Hilst.

The Captain of Köpenick (1967), at Stratford. Note the stylized movements of the actors and the pavilion theatre.

The company in 1967–8. *Left to right:* (back row) David Clement, Ray Whelan, George Luscombe, François Klanfer, Peter Faulkner, Tom Fisher; (front row) Jack Boschulte, Diane Grant, Milo Ringham, Durango Coy (Larry Martin), Barbara Walther, June Faulkner, John Faulkner. Photo by Robert van der Hilst, courtesy of June Faulkner.

The theatre exterior, 12 Alexander Street.

The theatre interior, 12 Alexander Street.

Ray Whelan, Calvin Butler, and Mona and George Luscombe relaxing in Venice, 1969.

Che Guevara (1969). *Left to right:* Cedric Smith (with back to camera), Keith Dalton, Jack Boschulte (kneeling), Mel Dixon, Gay Rowan, Ray Whelan.

The Good Soldier Schweik (1973 revival; first produced 1969). *Left to right:* Ross Skene, Len Doncheff, Jeff Braunstein (in front), Allan Royal, Peter Millard, Grant Roll, François Klanfer (seated), Milo Ringham, Sonja Livingston.

Ten Lost Years (1974), western tour. *Left to right:* Ross Skene, Rich Payne, Michael Burgess (with banjo), Sandy Crawly (with guitar), Rosemary Dunsmore, Iris Paabo (on stool), Peter Faulkner, Diane Douglass, Frances Walsh (sitting on the piano), Peter Millard.

Mr Bones (1972 revival; first produced 1969). *Left to right:* Errol Slue, Don Meyers (partially hidden), Ron Weihs, Suzette Couture, Michael Marshal, Maja Ardal, Allan Royal, Jeff Braunstein.

Summer '76 (1975). *Left to right:* Rich Payne, Diane Douglass, Grant Roll.

George Luscombe at 47 Fraser Avenue. Courtesy of George Luscombe.

HARLEQUIN IN HOGTOWN

Prologue

On a chilly evening towards the end of 1958, a number of young actors gathered at the Parliament Street Library in the Cabbagetown district of Toronto to discuss the founding of a 'group theatre' in the city.[1] As the room filled, the group was welcomed by a gaunt, bespectacled young man who spoke softly but with great intensity of his plans to establish an acting ensemble which would produce Canadian plays and introduce audiences to some of the new European drama then practically unrepresented on Toronto stages. His name was Tony Ferry, and as he described recent developments in British theatre, he spoke of his hope of someday seeing a similar dramatic renaissance in Canada.

Impassioned as he was, Ferry's familiarity with the Toronto theatre scene was still rather narrow. Indeed, he and his wife, Joan Maroney, had only recently arrived in the city after several years abroad. They had met in Quebec, where Tony had come as a young refugee from England during the war, and where Joan had grown up in a theatrical household, the daughter of an actor and director. They married in the early 1950s and went to London, where Joan studied at the Central School of Speech and Drama, and Tony worked as a journalist for a London newspaper and, in his spare time, served as editor of the theatrical journal *Encore*.[2]

Discussion following Ferry's introduction was animated. There was no disagreement about the need for such a theatre, and one of those present stood up to say that he would be willing to devote ten years of his life to the project. But no one seemed to know how the dream could be realized in the absence of any immediate source of financial support. As a first step, they agreed to present playreadings at the Library in an effort to keep interest in the project alive.

The first of these readings was deemed a success, but it brought the vision no closer. Accordingly, Ferry began to plan a summer school to train the kind of actors they would need. He contacted Carlo Mazzone, the Italian mime and former partner of Marcel Marceau, who was to be in Stratford, Ontario, during the summer; he wrote to Carl Weber, a director with the Berliner Ensemble; he approached the actor Powys Thomas and the voice teacher Esme Crampton; and he phoned George Luscombe, the ten-year volunteer of the Parliament Street meeting, whom the Ferrys had known briefly in England.

By the end of February, Ferry had rounded up a number of interested instructors and obtained ideal quarters, to be supplied rent-free by Toronto Industrial Leaseholds Ltd.[3] They consisted of eight rooms in the basement of a printing plant on Fraser Avenue, in an industrial area just north of the site of the Canadian National Exhibition. Finally, he was ready to announce his plans to the press. The newly created 'Theatre Centre' would be a combined teaching and producing organization whose primary functions would be to develop Canadian plays and bring small mobile productions to libraries and schools. An important part of the project, Ferry said, would be the development of Canadian playwrights. 'Drama can't be written in a vacuum,' he told Denis Braithwaite of the *Toronto Star*. 'Playwrights should be intimately associated with the theatre the way Clifford Odets and Eugene O'Neill were. They need to associate with actors and other members of the craft.' Until suitable scripts were available, classical plays might be adapted to Canadian settings to give actors an opportunity to learn to act 'naturally' in environments with which they were intimately familiar. Ferry hoped to be able to finance the work of the Centre through the fees charged the student actors during the summer. Then, in the fall, the group would start with barestage productions suitable for touring.[4]

Towards the end of March, Ferry got a call from an excited Powys Thomas to say that their money problems were over. A group of individuals who had been negotiating to set up a National Theatre School in Canada had contacted Thomas to explore the possibility of combining their efforts. The one condition they had made was that the proposed school not be involved in production. Both Ferry and Luscombe found this restriction unacceptable since, as far as they were concerned, the whole point of the Centre was to integrate training and production. When Thomas accepted the position of director of the National Theatre School a few days later, Ferry and Luscombe decided to go ahead on their own.

Not surprisingly, Ferry's enthusiasm for his new project began to be reflected in the articles he was writing for the *Toronto Star*. In one of these, he launched an attack on the Stratford Festival. Far from stimulating Canadian performers to develop a style out of their own experience, Ferry fulminated, the Festival had simply perpetuated imitation British acting, producing no new work and making no visible effort to assemble 'a permanent troupe of actors developing year by year toward an ensemble.'[5]

It is unlikely Ferry could have anticipated the outrage his attack would provoke. A letter from David Peddie, the son of the CBC radio actor Frank Peddie, to the editor of the *Star* captured much of the feeling of the time:

In 15 years of Canadian playgoing I have yet to see an audience especially interested in Canadian plays ... It seems to me a good case could be made on evidence of the success of the Stratford Festival, for maintaining that the spirit abroad in Canada today has a closer affinity and affection for the spirit of the Shakespearean theatre than for the spirit of the plays written by contemporary writers. If our young writers ... could capture some of the large sounds and colourful images of Shakespeare's plays they might be treated with equal reverence ... What is new and different in Canadian theatre is being done by the actors and directors. When the writers can equal the performers ... then they will be given equal rank in the theatre. As yet, no Canadian writers of any significance have emerged.[6]

It was clear to Ferry and Luscombe that the transformation of the Toronto theatre would never be undertaken by those currently active in the city. The fight against fashionable West End bourgeois drama would have to be carried on by a generation of actors and writers trained in the new European ideas and techniques.

It was the aim of the Theatre Centre summer school to produce such actors. In July, twenty students gathered for classes in movement, voice, and acting in the basement of 47 Fraser Avenue. Exercises in mime and commedia dell'arte were held outdoors in High Park, and rehearsals begun on a production of Goldoni's *A Servant of Two Masters*, which, it was hoped, the group would perform in Toronto parks. Not unexpectedly, the enterprise proved too ambitious. By the end of the summer, the partners had run out of money. Tony Ferry rejoined the *Star*, Carlo Mazzone went back to Italy, and George Luscombe prepared to resume his career as a freelance actor.

1

Don Valley Quixote

But if Ferry and Luscombe seemed ready to allow the Theatre Centre to die, the students were not. For them, the experience had been exhilarating and the acting classes unlike anything they had previously encountered. Six of them approached Luscombe and asked him to continue his teaching into the fall. Though understandably flattered, Luscombe was initially hesitant. He had long dreamed of forming a theatre, but he had recently married and had responsibilities to others. Indeed, he had been considering moving to the United States, where he felt there were better opportunities for a freelance career. Attractive as the prospect of a school of his own might seem, he was reluctant to make a commitment he could not honour.[1]

Luscombe's hesitation reflected a scrupulous nature, but it was also a product of his upbringing in the Todmorden district of East York. Tucked into a sweeping curve of the Don River, East York is separated from the rest of Toronto by a broad ravine, which forms something of a physical and psychological barrier between it and the surrounding regions. In the early years of the century, the area developed a distinct personality reflecting the character of the first settlers, mostly Anglo-Saxon immigrants, who formed a relatively homogeneous community secure in their sense of themselves and strong in their loyalty to the British Crown. Like many of their neighbours, the Luscombes had arrived in East York following the First World War. George's father, Edward, was from Devon; his mother, Ann, was of Irish descent but had grown up in Liverpool. With their daughter, Kaye, born in 1919, they moved into a modest house on Westwood Avenue. A son, Jack, was born in 1923, and George, the youngest, in 1926.

During the thirties, the solidly conservative complexion of the area began to change. At the height of the depression, 47 per cent of the working population of East York, some twelve thousand individuals, were on relief. In those hard times, political convictions began to shift to the left. Speakers at political rallies debated the ideas of Karl Marx, and a group known as the East York Workers was formed to speak for the interests of unorganized labour. Although the communist fringe of the political left never gained control, the period produced a hard core of CCF support in East York which coloured the politics of the region for many years.[2]

In comparison with their neighbours, the Luscombes suffered relatively little. Edward, who worked in the Canadian National railway shops, never lost his job, so the three Luscombe children were protected from the worst effects of the depression. Today, George recalls quarrels about money but no actual deprivation. What sticks in his mind are isolated impressions – the walks with his father down Pottery Road; the brick works where the migrant unemployed would sleep in the lingering warmth of the ovens; the friend too poor to own shoes who appeared at school on cold days in a pair of his mother's.

George's school, Chester Public, was probably not untypical of the Ontario educational system in the 1930s. Its curriculum was patterned on British models, and its approach to pedagogy coloured by English ideals of class and self-discipline. It was an atmosphere George found particularly unstimulating. After his initial delight at finding all his friends in his class, his mind began to wander; he found himself unable to understand what the teachers were talking about or to grasp the relevance of the lessons, and so lost interest in learning. Finding no outlet for his increasingly active imagination, George went to the bottom of the class and stayed there.

His extracurricular activities were scarcely more successful. The Luscombes had managed to acquire a piano in the years before the depression, and although George admired his sister's ability on that instrument, he harboured an ambition to master the Hawaiian guitar. Not surprisingly, his parents would have preferred that their son might find an outlet for his musical talent on the instrument they happened to own. George, however, was not to be distracted. Finally, his parents promised that if he learned to swim, they would get him a guitar. Doggedly, George began classes at the YMCA. His first day at the pool is one of his clearer childhood memories:

There was a great big iron door and we stripped naked, shivering in the cold. They opened the door and there you were facing the tank. The swimming instructor was dressed in nice warm clothes while we were like earwigs with our lips turning blue with the cold. Here we were going to learn to swim fifty yards. When you'd learned that, you were no longer a beginner. If you didn't succeed in the tests, you were punished by being given a 'sinker,' a great heavy washer, very, very heavy, which you had to wear around your neck. In explaining this, the instructor pointed with great glee to a retarded boy in the class and said, 'This boy won ALL the sinkers one day.' We all laughed, of course, but I thought to myself, 'Oh my God, I don't want to get a sinker.' Well, on that first day of instruction, I managed to collect all five sinkers. Every one of them. Every one of them! I can't tell you how devastated I was to go home. And I was so honest that I wore them home. I was ashamed, but I felt obliged to tell the truth. And this was the YMCA – the Young Men's *Christian* Association!

George learned to swim his fifty yards and even became a lifeguard. But he never got his guitar, and in the end he settled for lessons on the piano.

During his last year of public school, the long-expected war in Europe broke out. It was to alter the Luscombes' lives drastically. Although Edward had served in the merchant marine in the First World War and had many unpleasant recollections, he felt obliged to enlist once again. He was driven not by any political ideology but by an inbred loyalty to Britain, inherited along with his rural and conservative prejudices from his Devon family. So, in spite of the fact that he was over forty, he joined the army and was almost immediately posted overseas.

But if he was absent in body, his influence was still strong in the house. Edward Luscombe was a taciturn, quick-tempered man who felt deeply but had difficulty expressing his feelings. Though undemonstrative himself, he had a keen sense of injustice and would act impulsively in the defence of those more vulnerable. His decision to come to Canada had been such an impulse, made on the spur of the moment, as he listened to his father complain about the food his daughters were serving him. Having been in the navy, Edward knew the deprivation many people had suffered during the war, and suddenly he could stand his father's selfishness no longer.

In Canada, that same sense of fairness resulted in Edward's being somewhat isolated. Persuaded against his better judgment to join a union, he stood up at his first meeting to complain about the way in which he had been recruited. When he was ridiculed for his objections, he left and never returned. In arguments with his elder son, Jack, an ardent CCF supporter, about the 'rights' of the East York Workers, he could be heard to mutter that there wasn't a 'worker' among them.

His sense of propriety was equally well developed, so much so that sometimes it was at odds with his instinctive fairness. Once, on a visit to the Art Gallery of Toronto with his two young sons, he was embarrassed when Jack was rebuked by a guard for sliding down a banister. Later, at home, he took his rambunctious son to the basement for a hiding. Wide-eyed George, spared the corporal punishment administered to his brother, was suitably impressed both by the way the Art Gallery was set up to discourage the very kind of creative exuberance that produced the painting, and by the extent to which his father's rigid code supported that repression. Edward Luscombe was, as his son remembers, 'a very honourable man in the awful English sense of that word.'

The transition from Chester Public School to East York Collegiate was not as liberating as George had hoped it would be. Here too the dead hand of discipline held back any expressions of enthusiasm or revolt. The school was run on the 'prefect system,' whereby certain students were recruited to spy on their fellows. This English technique of 'turning little boys into informers' was an abomination to George Luscombe, who rapidly found himself at odds with the new set of teachers. The matriculation subjects were no longer of interest to him – English literature least of all – so of course he failed miserably.

At home, it was decided that if George couldn't work with his brain, then perhaps he should be enrolled in a technical school, where at least he could learn to work with his hands. Accordingly, he was sent off to Danforth Technical Institute with the idea that he would follow his father into the shops. He dutifully registered in the first year of industrial arts, but with no clear idea of what he wanted to do.

At the end of his second attempt at grade nine, George was very little farther ahead. In desperation, he applied to be transferred into the second year of the commercial art option and was accepted. There the academic atmosphere was much more congenial. Not only was the art class a relatively small group, but the teachers left the students alone, according to George, 'because they weren't important to the war effort.' The students were taught a little art history and taken to churches to look at stained-glass windows. But if the program lacked something in intellectual rigour, it provided George with scope for his rebellious and exhibitionist tendencies. He discovered the French impressionist painters and would take his sketching pad into the Don Valley to daub away for hours. When he emerged at the end of the day, covered with paint and with his hair unfashionably long, Westwood Avenue mothers would regard him apprehensively and move to protect their children as he passed by.

It was not only his painterly talents that found an outlet during those years. His skill as a drummer and pianist won him a place in the school band and even got him some jobs playing with groups at night. But perhaps the most important development was his discovery of the Co-operative Commonwealth Youth Movement. His brother, Jack, had founded the East York CCF Club while still in his teens, and that club, like others of its kind, provided entertainment and political education for young people. George was attracted to the group because it was made up of individuals who, like himself, were beginning to question the world and to look for more satisfying answers than the ones provided by entrenched authority. No hotbed of revolutionary intrigue, the club offered discussions focusing on the visionary ideas of George Bernard Shaw or Edward Bellamy rather than on the dialectics of Karl Marx. Communism was seen as a threat to the ideals of socialism, which, at the East York CCF Club, tended to be anything but ideological. For George as well as for his friends, politics was a matter of active involvement – producing shows, singing union songs, or entertaining workers on a picket line. From a young age, Luscombe came to think of politics and entertainment as two sides of the same impulse.

Towards the end of the war, George's father returned to Canada in ill health and, before he could be demobbed, suffered a sudden heart attack and died. His death was a shock. For George, it meant the loss of a stern and emotionally remote man whom he had never really known. When he thought of him, he remembered the walks they had taken in the Don Valley and details of his appearance – the well-worn overalls, his invariable weekday costume; the blue Tip Top Tailor Sunday suit; and the strong, rough hands, permanently curled from a lifetime of manual labour.

For Jack, the tragedy had graver consequences. Because of the strain and the time he spent arranging his father's affairs, Jack failed to attain the 75 per cent average he needed to continue his studies at the University of Toronto. That meant that he became subject to the draft, and some months after his father's death he received his call-up for military service. After a brief basic training, he was sent to Belgium into the last stages of the war. From there, he wrote to George, telling him not to follow him into the army. The advice was unnecessary. George had come to his own conclusions about patriotism and the international struggle against fascism. His circle knew that fascism was not confined to Hitler's Germany: they had friends whose houses had been raided by the RCMP. So he felt that while his father and brother had been right to follow their consciences, he would fight fascism in his own way.

His decision was shatteringly reinforced one afternoon early in 1945. George had gone with his class to see *Hamlet* at the Royal Alexandra Theatre and was enjoying the first professional theatrical production he had ever seen. Part way through the performance, an usher tapped him on the shoulder, signalling for him to follow. After making his way up the dark aisle, George emerged from the auditorium to see a neighbour waiting to speak to him. There was no need for explanations; even before a word was uttered, George knew his brother had been killed.

Jack's early death left George struggling to determine what direction his own life would take. Drawn towards a career in the arts but unsure just how he should proceed, he was tempted for a short time to join a dance band on a cruise ship plying between Toronto and Port Dalhousie. In the end, he made what he thought was a more practical decision and joined the art department of the *Toronto Daily Star*. Such modest success in the world of commercial art, however, did little to satisfy his deeper creative needs, and when he heard that the Toronto CCF Club had started a drama school he decided to enrol. There he met Ann Marshall, whose approach to theatre was to change his life. Marshall not only taught her students the rudiments of drama, introducing them in the process to the ideas and methods of Stanislavski, but also inspired them with a new vision of art. For her, theatre was not an escape; it was a means of engaging with the world, a means whereby true socialists could feel their socialism as well as think it. Here was what George had been looking for – a value system that embraced both politics and art; an aesthetic that joined theatre to life.

In the spring of 1946, after several months of training and preparation, the club presented its first public performance. Marshall and a few other professional actors performed Noel Coward's *Fumed Oak*, and the students played in a piece she had written about a young pianist (performed by George). The event was successful enough to encourage the group to repeat it. The next year they did a second program of one-act plays. *The Lonely* by Ann Marshall, *Sweet Twenty* by Floyd Dell, and *Possession* by George Middleton, a play about divorce, were presented for a single night at Jarvis Collegiate. Soon George was seeking out other opportunities to act. He played a small role in the New Play Society production of *The Time of Your Life* with the CBC radio actor John Drainie, and he auditioned for the CBC. The real turning-point in his career, however, came in 1948, when he heard that E.G. Sterndale Bennett of the Royal Conservatory of Music needed additional actors for his People's Repertory Threatre, a touring company he had formed to give his drama students some practical experience. Luscombe auditioned and was accepted.

This unexpected turn of events presented Luscombe with some hard decisions. His salary at the *Star* was something like $75 a week, soon to rise to $145 under a union contract. As a member of the People's Repertory Theatre, he would be working for his board and a share of any profits left over at the end of the week. Not unexpectedly, most of his friends thought he was crazy. As Luscombe remembers: 'People in Todmorden thought that for someone to get a job as an artist downtown in the city of Toronto was a tremendous accomplishment. But I couldn't see being tied to a desk. And after a while even an art board becomes a desk. So I quit my job – burned my bridges. Everybody advised me against it including every member of the art staff at the *Star*, because once you quit you never get hired back again. But I said, "No, I'm going," because you've only got one time around, you know. To me the opportunity to become a professional actor, to spend all day working at theatre was fantastic, a mind-boggling thing.'

So the group worked all that summer preparing three plays. The actors put $100 into a pot, and since he had been working, Luscombe contributed double that amount. They bought an old army truck for $800, and Mrs Sterndale Bennett doled out the balance of the money to enable the group to eat until the first box-office receipts were collected. In the fall, the student actors and George Luscombe, ex–commercial artist, climbed into their converted van, the scenery on one side and the actors on the other, and set out.

They travelled through rural Ontario, sleeping in cheap motels or, sometimes, in private homes arranged for by their sponsors. By spring, the company was broke and had to dissolve. The students set out to look for other work; Sterndale Bennett left the Conservatory and established his own academy, which he called the Canadian Theatre School; and George Luscombe began to contemplate the vagaries of life as a professional actor.

It was obvious to him that if he was ever going to make a living from acting, he would have to learn more about the craft. Accordingly, he went to the Royal Conservatory of Music and signed up for lessons in voice. He recalls: 'Of course I believed that I didn't speak correctly. I couldn't possibly since I came from the east end of Toronto. So twice a week for about fifteen weeks I tried to correct these things.' But the Conservatory was not teaching him what he wanted to know, and gradually he became convinced that if he was serious about making a career in the theatre, he would have to go where the theatre was – New York or London. Since George's parents were British and he still had relatives in England, the choice seemed obvious. By late 1949, therefore, he had made up his mind.

In December, however, another misfortune struck the family. George's sister, Kaye, never an outgoing girl, had lately become more and more withdrawn. Now her behaviour was becoming erratic to the point where her mother could no longer control it. On New Year's Eve, George asked the family doctor to commit his sister to a mental institution, where she could be properly cared for.

Kaye's illness and his mother's inevitable loneliness made Luscombe's decision to leave Toronto seem even more heartless. But he knew that his life was at stake too. He kept remembering a CBC radio play he had heard while on tour with the People's Repertory Theatre. It was a work entitled *Burlap Bags*, by Len Peterson, that dealt with the situation of people chained to desks, lathes, kitchen stoves, and other machines. Although the chains were not locked, the people were unable to escape because of 'duty.' George knew that if he was ever to realize his talent, he would have to get away from Toronto. He would have to resist the appeals to his sense of filial responsibility and the 'reasonable' arguments of friends and neighbours. However painful it would be, he would have to break those chains. So with the kind of resolve that would characterize his actions throughout his life, he bought a one-way boat ticket to Liverpool, packed his belongings in a trunk, and took the train to Montreal. As he set sail from there for England he didn't know when he would be coming back.

2

Strolling Player

Upon his arrival in London in January 1950, Luscombe began to explore the English theatrical scene. British theatre in the immediate postwar years was in the doldrums. West End stages presented a seemingly endless round of mindless farces or drawing-room comedies of wearying predictability. Playwrights such as Terence Rattigan focused narrowly on the psychological problems of members of the upper middle class and rarely dealt with controversial subjects such as politics or religion. Theatre had become an industry and in the process had lost contact with the community. Luscombe missed the seriousness of purpose he had admired in Ann Marshall. He was beginning to learn that theatre was much more varied in expression than he had previously imagined.

He was also discovering that it was more competitive. As he laboriously went through *Spotlight*, the actor's 'Bible' which listed the various repertory companies in the country and the openings available, he was impressed by the résumés of an alarming number of experienced performers, all infinitely more qualified than he was. Never one to be daunted by unfavourable odds, however, Luscombe diligently sent out hundreds of letters of application and sat down to wait. The silence was overwhelming.

Just as he was beginning to despair, he received a telegram from the manager of a company in Nayland, Wales, called the Midland Repertory Theatre. It read 'Come. Be here by Monday morning and do not accept this letter as a contract.' Puzzled by the noncommittal gist of the communication, Luscombe nevertheless decided he was hardly in a strong bargaining position. Accordingly, he packed his bags, said goodbye to London, and boarded the train to Wales.

Settling into his seat, he reread the letter, which told him to come prepared to play the role of Clive in Philip King's *See How They Run*. Ever conscientious, he took out the script he had bought before leaving and began to memorize the lines, keenly aware of how badly he needed this job. Unfamiliar with British geography and afraid of passing his stop, he spent the night peering at the dimly lit, unpronounceable names on deserted Welsh railway stations. As morning broke, the train finally pulled into Nayland. With a mixture of dread and excitement, he gathered up his possessions and descended to the platform. It was the end of the line.

After passing through the ticket barrier, he found a member of the company, who greeted him warmly and took him to meet his new employer. Jimmy James was a bright-eyed Dickensian figure even shorter than George himself. But if there was a twinkle in his eye, it did not hide the toughness which had enabled James to survive in the hard and demanding world of theatrical touring. After starting as a vaudeville clown, James had married an actress and founded his own theatre company. In the years since then, he, his wife, and their daughter had become virtual gypsies, continually on the move through Wales and the Midlands without ever settling down into a real home. He had earned an adequate living, but since the war the competition of television had been driving companies like the Midland Repertory Theatre out of business and erasing the last vestiges of a theatrical tradition going back to medieval times. At the moment, however, business in Nayland was thriving.

Surveying his new Canadian recruit, James enquired jovially, 'Well, did you study your part?' 'Yes Sir,' replied Luscombe, 'I spent the night on the train memorizing Clive's lines.' 'Clive,' said James, looking puzzled. 'No, no, my boy. Lionel is your part.' In some consternation, Luscombe produced the letter assigning him the wrong role. James was momentarily nonplussed but quickly regained his composure. 'Well,' he said, 'you've got tonight to learn it, so sit down and have a cup of coffee.'

After a fitful sleep, Luscombe rose the next morning at five and studied until ten. Rehearsal was a walk-through with the actors simply mumbling at the pages, incomprehensible to a young Canadian convinced of the social importance of drama and accustomed to the methods of Stanislavski. As he was getting ready to go on for his first performance that evening, Luscombe's hand shook so badly he could not apply eye liner. When he made his entrance, he felt he was stepping off a cliff; with no prompter in the wings, he had nothing upon which to rely but his own ability to ad lib and the willingness of the other actors to help him out. Somehow, he got through the performance, but his initiation into the rigours of provincial stock had only begun. The company stayed in Nayland for eight weeks, and every day

Luscombe had to prepare a new role. By the end of the period, he found that he could memorize a part after a couple of readings.

Travelling up and down Wales brought Luscombe into contact with audiences of a kind he had never before encountered. The Welsh are a passionate people who love melodrama, and the Midland Repertory Theatre gave them what they wanted. They played *The Sign of the Cross, Maria Martin at the Red Barn*, even *Sweeney Todd* – nineteenth-century pot-boilers that were creaky in the 1890s when George Bernard Shaw was trying to drive them from the London stage. What astonished Luscombe was the power these pieces still had to move an unsophisticated crowd. Spectators from the Welsh valleys, who had seen nothing of television and relatively few films, felt no need for elaborately detailed and realistic settings. To them, the reality was in the performance and in the simplicity and directness of the emotions portrayed. When a clergyman came backstage after *The Sign of the Cross* to tell Luscombe what an inspiration his performance had been, the compliment was more than a tribute to the acting of a rather brash Toronto atheist; it was testimony to the emotional openness of the audience. Luscombe learned to cherish that openness.

Because few of their venues had proper facilities, the actors had to bring in virtually all the equipment they needed. Backdrops consisted of a series of rolls about twenty feet in length suspended on a frame and rolled down like window blinds for different scenes. Footlights were portable two-by-fours with sockets nailed into them; lights and cables had to be transported and hung; costumes and properties were packed in hampers so large that it took four men to wrestle them in and out of the school and church halls where they performed. In addition to playing, the actors had to work like circus roustabouts, hauling the scenery from station to hall, setting up, and then dismantling everything for the trip to the next town. The work was physically exhausting and seemingly endless.

The old-timers in the company treated acting as a craft, not an 'art'; a job, not a means of ego gratification or a substitute for psychoanalysis. For Luscombe, who hated the social aspects of amateur theatre in Toronto, this attitude was refreshing. He began to understand the 'working' tradition of theatre, which centred on the actors and stretched back in an uninterrupted line through the Edwardian and Victorian periods to the Elizabethan clown, the commedia dell'arte performer, and the Roman mime. Suddenly, he saw Jimmy James, the clown-turned-manager, as one of the last links in this long chain. And he realized that there were important lessons to be learned from such actors, lessons about professional attitudes and, above all, about methods of survival.

After a year and a half of travelling in Wales, however, Luscombe began to think about moving on. Valuable as he had found the experience, he did not plan to spend the rest of his life in 'fit up.' Not only was the life too demanding physically, but it was becoming too ingrown. Isolated in their vagabond life, the players tended to see themselves as outcasts and the rest of the world as 'yabos.' For Luscombe, a further complication was the close link he had formed with Jimmy James. He had already become almost a member of the family, and there was an unexpressed but growing feeling that perhaps he would marry the James's daughter. One day, Luscombe discovered James reading one of his letters and in a fit of anger wrote a note of resignation, which he presented to James with the words 'Here, you can read this while you're at it!' The incident passed off, but clearly the time was fast approaching when he would have to leave.

A little later, when the air had cleared, James helped Luscombe get a job in Manchester with a larger repertory theatre. The Manchester company performed only one show a week, for which he would be paid the princely sum of eight pounds. Now, Luscombe thought, it would be possible for him to get his teeth into his parts. His first role, the Black Sheep in the pantomime *Bo Peep*, was anything but complex, and he had to admit that the actors around him were doing some shoddy work. But he took his performances seriously and felt that he had attained a level of relative luxury.

In the Manchester company was a gentle man by the name of James Lovell, who was to be instrumental in redirecting the course of Luscombe's career. Lovell had had his own repertory company until a new board of directors had fired him, whereupon he was forced to turn to scene painting in order to survive. The two struck up a friendship and began rooming together. On free afternoons, they would huddle over a coal fire and talk about theatre. It was Lovell who gave Luscombe his first understanding of Shakespeare, by introducing him to the rudiments of textual criticism and showing him how the plays were printed in the seventeenth century – without stage directions and frequently without marked act divisions. In this format, Luscombe could see how the drama was intended to flow uninterruptedly from scene to scene.

Lovell also explained the nature of the Elizabethan theatre, with its projecting stage and encircling audience. For Luscombe, who had had no experience in anything but a proscenium theatre, Lovell's insights provided a glimpse into a new world. He comments: 'The architecture of Shakespeare's theatre had a social context. It was an age of popular theatre and it's that social content which you have in the plays and in the building which became so important to me in the creation of new work. The TWP stage is a result of those conversations around the fire.'[1]

It was Lovell too who in 1952 told Luscombe about Joan Littlewood's Theatre Workshop and urged him to get in touch with her. So when the company's season ended in August, instead of going to London with the other out-of-work actors, Luscombe journeyed north to Edinburgh, where Theatre Workshop was performing in the Festival. There, in the Oddfellows Hall, he watched a rehearsal of *The Travellers* by Ewan MacColl and was dazzled by the skill and intensity of the acting. This, at last, was what he had been looking for – an ensemble with total commitment to a socialist view of life which could nevertheless produce work that was entertaining and interesting. He knew then that he had to get into that company.

Talking with Littlewood and the actors after the show, he expressed an interest in joining them, but no commitments were made on either side. Back in London, full of enthusiasm and hope, he waited in vain for further word and at last reluctantly joined another repertory company. Then one day a telegram arrived, asking him if he still wanted to work with Theatre Workshop. By that time, he was making seven or eight pounds a week (a very good living), and he knew that with Littlewood there would be no security and hardly any wage. But he also knew that working with Theatre Workshop was what he had to do. He replied that he would come as soon as he could get free of his current contract. Not long after, having borrowed the fare from a fellow actor, he boarded the train for Glasgow, where the company was staying.

Theatre Workshop had been formed in 1934 (first as Theatre of Action and later as Theatre Union) by Ewan MacColl and Joan Littlewood.[2] MacColl, the son of a radical Scottish ironworker, had grown up in poverty in the Manchester suburb of Salford. There, humiliated by the condescending charity of the women for whom his mother worked as a charwoman, he had developed a passionate hatred of the British social system along with a keen sense of identification with the industrial working class. Littlewood had come to Manchester from London and was working as assistant stage manager with a local repertory theatre when she met MacColl, who by then had formed his own theatre group. The two discovered that they shared many interests, and they began to work together exploring new theatrical ideas. What began as a part-time collaboration on a 'living newspaper'–style production of an American play called *Newsboy* developed into a thirty-year artistic partnership.

From the beginning, MacColl and Littlewood wanted to create a political theatre which would comment on contemporary social and economic problems from a Marxist perspective. In the pursuit of this aim, they turned for inspiration to developments in Europe, especially to the political theatre that had emerged in Russia and Germany after the First World War. In Russia, the twin catastrophes of revolution and civil conflict had given rise to unprecedented experimentation in all the arts. In the theatre, this experimentation had taken the form of a radical questioning of the very foundations of the drama.

Ever since its advent in France and its subsequent development in Germany and Russia, naturalism had come under increasing attack by those who felt that its attempt to create a 'slice of life' on the stage was wrongheaded. Dadaism, surrealism, symbolism, and expressionism were various manifestations of a widespread impulse to broaden the scope of the drama to embrace fantasy, dreams, and other irrational or psychic phenomena. In Russia, naturalism had found its most powerful practitioner in Konstantin Stanislavski, whose work at the Moscow Art Theatre had been one of the glories of tsarist theatre. To the new directors of the revolution such as Vsevolod Meyerhold, Alexander Tairov, and Evgeni Vakhtangov, however, naturalism was moribund, synonymous with the despised bourgeois life. They wished to create a theatrical style more appropriate for the new, classless society then coming into being.

To achieve this, they felt, required a complete rejection of the bourgeois naturalistic theatre on ideological as well as aesthetic grounds. Where naturalism strove to separate actor and audience, the new approach would bring them closer together; if naturalistic stage designers emphasized the oppressive limitations of environment, the new designers would eliminate all traces of realistic illusion; where the old dramatists had focused on the psychological problems of the individual, the new playwrights would deal with the political concerns of the group; where previously actors had appealed to the spectator's emotions, in the future they would call for a critical understanding of them. To help them effect this revolution in dramatic style, directors and designers not only drew on recent anti-illusionist movements but also ransacked the history books, borrowing conventions from Greek, Elizabethan, Italian, and oriental theatre in an effort to discover the fundamental laws of the art.

By the mid-thirties, when MacColl and Littlewood had begun their own search for new forms, experimentation in political theatre had largely come to an end in Europe. Russian authorities had started to curb the work of anti-illusionist directors in the name of 'socialist realism,' while in Germany the Nazis had initiated their own ruthless purge. In England, MacColl and Littlewood were free from such extreme state repression.

Nevertheless, they faced obstacles of a different kind in their efforts to achieve social change through their productions. Not the least of these obstacles was the peculiar complacency of the British public. Nowhere in the country was there the kind of discontent or factionalism which had led to revolution in Russia and Germany. Polarization along class lines was more evident in the industrial north, where the company performed, but even there a combination of reticence and apathy militated against prolonged social violence. In the period before the Second World War, therefore, the work of Theatre Union caused few ripples on the British social or theatrical scenes.

In 1945, however, the revived troupe, now operating under the name of Theatre Workshop, began to attract critical notice through such works as *The Flying Doctor* (an adaptation of Molière) and *Johnny Noble* by MacColl. In 1946, the company had another hit in MacColl's *Uranium 235*. During the next six years, convinced that their aims could be accomplished only if they performed to working-class audiences, the company staged their productions in union and mining halls throughout England, Wales, and Scotland. They also travelled to Norway, Sweden, West Germany, and Czechoslovakia. By 1952, many of the actors were beginning to weary of this exhausting itinerant life. When Luscombe arrived in Glasgow, he found the company settled in a large house outside the city, rehearsing a production of *Twelfth Night* for schools. Luscombe had been cast as Sebastian, a role he loathed, and was immediately flung into the busy routine of the group.

Theatre Workshop had been established as a combined production unit and training school; rehearsals alternated with sessions designed to enlarge the technical and imaginative scope of the actors. During the mornings, the company worked on exercises derived from Stanislavski to develop concentration, memory, and adaptation and improvisation skills. These exercises would be followed by movement training based on the theories of Rudolph Laban, a Czech dancer and inventor of a system of ballet notation, who united a practical method of analysis with an almost mystic vision of movement as the fount of human spiritual life. Luscombe found the sessions exhilarating.

Afternoons were given over to rehearsals, and there Luscombe began to founder. The ordinary difficulties of fitting into a new company were compounded by the fact that the Theatre Workshop actors had evolved a distinctive and characteristic style of acting, the result of nearly twenty years of work and thought on the part of the company and its founders. The style combined Russian psychological realism with a variety of non-realistic techniques inspired by commedia dell'arte, oriental theatre, and agitprop.

Luscombe had little trouble coping with the physical demands of his role, but he was confused by the director's approach to the play. Unfamiliar with the works of Shakespeare (having had only a short series of classes at the Royal Conservatory of Music in Toronto), Luscombe was unprepared for Littlewood's radical interpretation, which treated the servants as the heroes of the work. Her interest in the aristocratic lovers, by contrast, was perfunctory at best, and the time she spent with Luscombe correspondingly brief. To make matters worse, Luscombe had trouble with his lines and often had to resort to ad libbing. At the end of his first performance in front of a school audience, there was an ominous silence from his fellow actors.

Shortly after the opening of *Twelfth Night*, members of the company met to discuss an issue of critical significance to their future. Gerry Raffles, the business manager, had rented a theatre in London for six weeks to explore the feasibility of setting up permanently in that city. It soon became evident that the company was split on the issue. MacColl strongly opposed the move, which he felt would betray the company's original ideals. He was convinced that the theatre would lose its spirit if it lost its contact with a working-class audience. Others argued that they would be drawing a similar audience from the working-class neighbourhood surrounding their new theatre, in London's East End. Settling into permanent quarters would enable the company to escape the relentless rigours of touring. When the vote was taken, a majority favoured the move.

Early in the new year, therefore, Luscombe and several others packed themselves into a station wagon and drove from Glasgow to London. Their new headquarters, the Theatre Royal and Palace of Varieties, was situated in Angel Lane, not far from the Stratford underground station in east London. The building, which had been partially cleaned up by a small advance party, still bore evidence of years of neglect. The auditorium was dingy and musty, the workshop under the stage damp and dirty, the dressing-rooms cramped and in need of a coat of whitewash. But for the first time in their history the company had a permanent home with reasonably adequate production facilities.

Luscombe found the first couple of weeks at the new theatre in Stratford East hardly less hectic than his days in 'fit up.' Mornings were still given over to exercises in movement and voice, afternoons to rehearsals, and evenings to performances. After unsatisfactory experiences with one or two designers, the company began building their own sets under the direction of John Bury, who was later to become head of design at the National Theatre. That meant further labour, in the dungeon-like atmosphere of the subterranean scene shop, sometimes until two or three in the morning. Every second weekend involved a 'changeover,' the dismantling of one set and the putting up of another. In recompense for these fourteen- and sixteen-hour days, members of the company shared the box-office profits, which in the first year provided each actor with a weekly salary of about two pounds.

Fortunately, Luscombe had learned how to cope with poverty. He bargained for bruised tomatoes at the local market and, in contravention of the city's fire regulations, slept in his dressing-room. These inconveniences were, in his opinion, more than compensated for by the rewards of the work. What he particularly enjoyed was the political commitment of the company. Most of the actors felt they were more than entertainers. They were prophets, the vanguard of a social and cultural revolution, and therefore responsible for understanding the issues of the day and conveying their understanding to their audiences through their work.

In this politically charged atmosphere, it was inevitable that Luscombe would begin to examine his own convictions. The socialist ideas he had picked up from Jack and others in the CCF Youth Movement began to seem a little naïve when compared with the profound radicalism of MacColl and Littlewood. He began to wonder if he should become a Communist: 'I didn't like the idea of being wishy-washy. I was pretending to be a socially concerned person, but I wasn't putting it on the line. I felt bad being part way. But I didn't want to make a foolish commitment. Because where was I going to get the money to pay the dues? As it turned out, I never did sign a card or pay any dues, but my intention was firm. Everybody in the theatre knew that I had made a decision, whereas some of the others had not and were not going to. Making a commitment gives one a sense of values and the strength to take action, in a strike for instance. It eliminates the grey areas. You know which side you're on.'[3]

He also began to broaden his ideas about acting. In the light of his disastrous début in Twelfth Night, he knew that his days as a member of Theatre Workshop might well be numbered. The possibility of being dismissed was something he could hardly bear to think about, having finally found what he considered his theatrical home. As luck would have it, however, he was able to show himself to better advantage in the second production, Molière's The Imaginary Invalid. He recalls: 'I played the ingenue, and evidently I did such a good job that Littlewood had a change of heart about me. And she went to Jobie, who I was working with, and asked him, "How is this young fellow?" Jobie was very pleased with our scene together. It required me to do extraordinary physical things which I was very good at. So she came to me and said, "Would you like to stay with us?" So I won my spurs in Molière.'

At the end of the first season, having produced ten plays in twenty weeks, the group was barely solvent and consequently unable to pay the actors for the summer. Nevertheless, Littlewood resolved to try another season in London and told the players to report back in the fall. Luscombe got a job in the theatre as janitor and so had a place to sleep, and a base from which to eke out a meagre living painting houses in the area. During any free time, he retreated to the prop room over the stage, from which there was access through a skylight to the roof. He remembers: 'In that room, I was surrounded by the history of art and the history of theatre – a whole pile of books. So I slept there and read all day long. Some days I never got down into the theatre; I could live just in that room and on the roof. That was a real education. High school for me was not a place of education, but where I learned a trade called commercial art. I tried to learn what I could, but that stopped at about grade seven. I got my real education at Theatre Workshop.'[4]

The company reassembled in August and took productions of *The Imaginary Invalid* and Chekhov's *Uncle Vanya* to the Edinburgh Festival. On their return to London, Littlewood continued her attempts to revive the classics of world theatre in ways that would be relevant for the working-class audience of the Stratford East district. She did a mordant production of Jonson's bitter satire of bourgeois greed, *The Alchemist*, in October, and early in January 1954 mounted an anti-establishment *Richard II*. In all these productions, Littlewood and her actors were more concerned with the inner action than with the poetry. Her intention was to explore the fear, oppression, and hatred of the fourteenth century. The Richard played by Harry Corbett, one of the older members of the troupe, brought out the arrogance, cruelty, and ultimate self-pity of the king.

What Luscombe found fascinating was the way in which Littlewood led the actors through improvisations to help them understand social and political realities:

Richard II was a real milestone for me in my career. We used to get on the stage in the morning and form two rows. Improvisations consisted of trying to get through people trying to stab you in the back. We did a lot of that in order to get that sense that God was resting on your shoulder, but there was also someone right behind you ready to stab you. I remember Joan trying to point out to us that men who spend their life on horseback or on foot would be different physically. The costume ladies were in on these conversations too, since it would affect the way you wore your clothes. Clothes were not decorative, but had special functions. We could invent our own costumes in keeping with the interpretation. That kind of inventiveness was encouraged all the time.[5]

By 1955, some of the older members of Theatre Workshop, like Harry Corbett and George Cooper, had been with the company for eight or nine years and were beginning to think that their pioneering days were over. Luscombe too was starting to weary of the communal living and the endless scrounging for money. He had heard that things had started to change in Canada and that it was now possible to earn a living in theatre and television in Toronto. Perhaps the time had come to return to his own country and to explore the meaning of political theatre in a more familiar environment.

3

Building a Company

Early in 1956, therefore, Luscombe packed his few worldly goods and set sail on a return voyage to Canada. In Toronto, he auditioned for CBC television and settled down to await results, which were not immediately forthcoming. Meanwhile, he had ample opportunity to renew his acquaintance with his native city. On the face of it, little had changed. True, there was a new professional theatre, the Crest, operating in a converted movie-house in a prosperous residential area, and Toronto theatre-goers spoke enthusiastically about the recently established Shakespearean Festival in Stratford, just one hundred miles away. But when Luscombe visited these institutions, his heart sank. The repertoire of the Crest was indistinguishable from that of any English provincial repertory company, and the acting seemed nothing but a pale imitation of the most mechanical West End attitudinizing. In Stratford, the productions moved gracefully over a boldly conceived thrust stage, but the performers lacked the energy and the critical perspective that made Littlewood's angular and abrasive productions of Shakespeare so exciting. Luscombe was particularly disappointed by the actors' movement, which he found stiff, awkward, and without a sense of period.

So when the possibility of creating his own acting school arose in the autumn of 1959, Luscombe was more than a little intrigued. The short summer training program had demonstrated just how difficult it would be to build the kind of theatre he was interested in. Not only was there nothing in Canada comparable to the traditional English touring company or to such enduringly popular European entertainments as variety, pantomime, or puppet theatre, Canadian actors were unaccustomed to using their bodies, many of them having performed almost exclusively either in front of a microphone in radio or in the constricted settings of realistic drawing-room comedy. Furthermore, there was practically no conception of drama as anything but escapist entertainment. The idea that theatre could challenge audiences, enlighten them, *change* them, had hardly occurred to his students. It was clear that a proper theatre school would have to do more than teach acting; it would need to provide an extensive cultural and political education. Resolving at last to accept what he recognized as a major challenge, Luscombe notified the students that he would be willing to begin further acting classes in September. But, he emphasized, such classes would be closely integrated with a program of public performances. To underline that intention, he called the new organization Workshop Productions.

The actors who gathered at 47 Fraser Avenue that autumn all worked at jobs during the day, so classes were held in the evening, three times a week. The sessions began punctually and were highly disciplined. Stretching, bending, and relaxing exercises were followed by more concentrated work on the body. 'Impersonating a dramatic character,' Luscombe explained, 'consists of more than simply speaking the lines. It means showing us the personality of that character through body language. You can't create the world of Hamlet or Othello if you move like a modern business executive.'

To help the actors develop greater flexibility and control over their bodies, Luscombe returned to exercises based on Laban's theories. Like Schopenhauer and the symbolists, Laban postulated the existence of a deeper level of reality. Messages from this world of silence were carried not by words (which touched only the fringe of existence), nor by music (which was more penetrating than words), but by sequences of move-ments.[1] At the heart of the human search for values, Laban maintained, are primitive impulses, which he called 'efforts.' These impulses give shape to movement (or what he preferred to describe as 'effort expres-sions') in three strata: the motions of everyday life, conventional gestures, and the arts of dancing, singing, and acting. He maintained that even speech and thought were manifestations of these basic efforts.

Luscombe explained to his students that all action, according to Laban, could be analysed in terms of its fundamental components – space, time, and weight. Thus, movement could be described as direct or flexible, sud-den or sustained, firm or gentle; the various possible combinations of these components produced eight 'pure efforts.' For example, a gesture that is firm, direct, and sudden Laban called a 'thrust.' Luscombe's work with the 'efforts' not only strengthened the actors physically but provided them with a vocabulary of movements out of which to create their own body language.

After the physical workout, Luscombe would move on to exercises designed to stimulate and liberate the actors' imaginations. As all teachers of acting have realized, the major challenge for the performer is to re-create a previously rehearsed action as though for the first time. The problem is how to make the action *new* (that is, not conventional or clichéd) and how to keep it *fresh* (not mechanical). Like most of his contemporaries, Luscombe based his own teaching on the pioneering work of Stanislavski. But whereas American teachers of 'the method,' based on Stanislavski, emphasized emotional memory and the need to experience the subjective emotions of a role, Luscombe had been conditioned by his work at Theatre Workshop to focus on what Laban called 'movement thinking.' Laban taught that whereas naturalistic acting captures the surface, interpreting character through dancelike mime movement penetrates to the individual's essence.[2] Luscombe's exercises in improvisation led the actors from the external 'given circumstances' to the internal feelings, from the verbal to the sub-verbal, from the rational to the intuitive, from the realistic to the essential.

Moving among his students in stocking feet, Luscombe would spur them on by giving them the circumstances of a situation. 'You're in Union Station. A boat-train full of immigrants has just come in. Doug, you're an immigration man. Let's have two more in this, two relatives waiting. Okay, go on.' As the actors created a scene based on the situation described, Luscombe would watch them with a kind of glazed intensity, circling them, twitching his body in sympathy with their movements. He would sometimes stop them or suggest other possibilities, but he never told them what to do. Not infrequently, he would explode in frustration. 'Hold it! You're losing the spirit of the thing by thinking up words. Words are only the surface layer.'[3] Then he would try to force the students through that layer by getting them to do a scene in an invented language. Or he would pile a number of chairs on the stage and tell them to imagine that they were cavemen just emerging into a prehistoric jungle. Describing his methods Luscombe would explain: 'The imagination is not static. It can grow. The ability to see further, to see clearly, so see well – these are things that can be learned. So you have to create an atmosphere in which the actors can develop their imaginations.'[4]

In Luscombe's idea of theatre, the imaginative contribution of the actor was paramount. His experiences with Theatre Workshop had persuaded him that the most exciting performances were those produced by the collaboration of creative individuals among whom none was supreme. Theatre Workshop had been run as a collective in which actors, designers, playwrights, directors, and technicians all worked together at all stages of rehearsal and shared equally in the fashioning of the final product. This did not, of course, mean artistic anarchy. Success depended on a precarious equilibrium between the opposing tendencies of democracy and dictatorship. Not the least of Joan Littlewood's talents as a director was her ability to cajole, browbeat, and inspire her actors to levels of achievement they could never have reached on their own. Luscombe had formed his ideas about leadership, loyalty, hard work, and dedication during his time with Jimmy James and Joan Littlewood and from their example, and he held those ideas with an intensity which continually surprised those who did not understand him.

An example of what some people regarded as Luscombe's 'fanaticism' occurred in December 1959. During rehearsals for the one-act plays the company was preparing for presentation at the end of their first season of classes, the actor playing the lead role in García Lorca's *The Love of Don Perlimplin and Belisa in the Garden* brought some friends to 47 Fraser Avenue to see the facilities. Luscombe arrived to find them walking across the stage. 'You can't walk on my stage,' he shouted. 'Get out.' Considerably nonplussed by this red-faced and evidently berserk individual, the friends left. But feeling that he had been insulted, the actor confronted his director and threatened to quit unless Luscombe apologized. Knowing that the play was to open in a short time, the actor no doubt thought he had the upper hand. He was astonished, therefore, when Luscombe said simply, 'Fine. Go ahead,' and promptly hired a replacement. Recalling the incident years later, Luscombe said, 'I don't know what hit me, but I had a bad feeling seeing them laughing on the stage. I felt it was important to show the other actors that you have to have reverence for the place you work in.'[5]

At the end of the first year of evening classes and after the production of four one-act plays, Luscombe was pleased with what his students had accomplished. Nevertheless, he realized that as long as his actors were unable to devote all their time and energy to the theatre, the company would be able to make only limited progress. Lacking material and financial resources, Workshop Productions seemed doomed to relative obscurity. But in 1961, just as Luscombe was beginning to resign himself to the status quo, representatives of the executive of the Arts Theatre Club approached him with a proposal that seemed heaven-sent. They suggested an amalgamation of the Arts Theatre Club and Workshop Productions, and invited Luscombe to be artistic director of the merged companies.

At the time of the proposal, the Arts Theatre Club had been in existence about two years and was under the direction of Basya Hunter. In that time, it had grown to nearly three hundred members, each of whom paid an annual fee of $12.50, which entitled a member to tickets to professional productions sponsored by the Club and provided an opportunity to attend study sessions and act in studio shows. The Club had staged several plays, including Ibsen's *An Enemy of the People*, Eugene O'Neill's *The Iceman Cometh*, and Brecht's *The Great Scholar Wu*, most directed by Basya Hunter. By the end of 1960, however, Hunter had decided that her health would not let her continue as artistic director of the Club, and it was her position that the executive was offering to George Luscombe.

From Luscombe's perspective, the plan had much to recommend it. The Arts Theatre Club had succeeded in getting support from the Canada Council where Workshop Productions had failed, and their executive implied that they would be able to obtain such assistance in the future. Furthermore, the Club had built up a secure financial foundation based on membership fees. The executive felt that those could be increased, and spoke of revenue in the region of $5,000 a year. There was also the prospect of moving productions from the Fraser Avenue basement theatre to the centrally located and more prestigious Central Library Theatre, at College and St George Streets, where the Arts Theatre had presented their work. The amalgamation seemed tailor-made.

In his open letter agreeing to the merger, Luscombe wrote glowingly of his hopes. What Toronto needed, he asserted, was a 'theatre unafraid to experiment ... a theatre where young actors, writers and directors [would be] trained.' Even in his earliest pronouncements, however, Luscombe could not refrain from preaching. 'You do not pay your membership fee to see shows,' he declared. 'You pay to sponsor shows. You do not participate in the art for what you can get out of it, but what you can give into it.' He reassured his readers, 'The more you give of yourself, the more you receive.'[6] Such idealism was inspiring, but not all the members had thought of their relationship to the Club in quite that way.

Early in September 1961, work began in earnest on the first joint production of the amalgamated Workshop Productions/Arts Theatre Club – Aristophanes' *Lysistrata*. Luscombe had appeared in a Theatre Workshop production of the play in 1953 and had prepared a preliminary script based on what he could remember of Ewan MacColl's adaptation. Now, however, he wished to expand the work by having the actors contribute through improvisation.

As rehearsals got under way, however, it became increasingly evident that the marriage between the Arts Theatre Club and Workshop Productions was in trouble. The original agreement specified that Luscombe would have complete artistic freedom and that Arts Theatre would provide a producer. This seemed a reasonable arrangement, but when the producer insisted that funds should be placed in a bank account in his name, Luscombe became uneasy. Further problems arose when the producer objected to the painter Joyce Wieland's highly graphic poster for *Lysistrata*, in which she had depicted characters as Greek comic actors with prominently displayed phalluses. Wieland solved the problem by adroitly changing all the phalluses to swords, but not before Luscombe had overreacted to what he considered interference with his prerogatives. The situation was one designed to exacerbate his natural pugnacity, and he recalls with some embarrassment that 'he may have thrown the producer out of the theatre.'[7]

To complicate things still further, the 1961–2 membership campaign had been a disaster. Of some 288 members, barely 20 had renewed their membership, so that, instead of the subsidy originally mentioned, the Arts Theatre Club could provide no more than $300 plus a guarantee of $650 in personal loans from the executive. By mid-November, it was clear that the merger was benefiting no one and that the proposed production was in serious jeopardy. At the eleventh hour, a grant from the Canada Council enabled the company to proceed with their plans, and on 28 December 1961 Luscombe opened his most ambitious production to date, a collectively adapted version of *Lysistrata* retitled *And They'll Make Peace*.

Peace closed on 3 February 1962, having brought in almost $2,000 at the box office. These receipts along with a Canada Council grant of $1,250 enabled the company to show a modest profit of $415. But the figures were not representative of the group's true financial situation, since the actors were still not being paid and there was no immediate prospect of income with which to pay the rent on their basement theatre. The security Luscombe had hoped for through the amalgamation with the Arts Theatre Club had failed to materialize, and it was evident that to survive, let alone grow, he would have to come up with some new ideas.

In order to keep a nucleus of actors together over the summer, Luscombe planned a tour of the Haliburton cottage country north of Toronto. Three brothers he had known on Westwood Avenue, the Martins, had acquired a farm near Huntsville, Ontario, and he persuaded them to let him use the property as his base. With money donated by the actors and contributions from well-wishers, the group bought an old truck and some army surplus parachutes, which they shipped up to the Martin farm. With this material, the brothers constructed a tent theatre that would seat three hundred on their property on Hall's Lake. By the end of July 1962, five actors (Barbara Armitage, Eleanor Beattie, Douglas Livingston, Marian McLeod, and Tony Moffat-Lynch) had resolved to try to survive the summer on what they could earn from acting. During June and July, they prepared a repertoire of three one-act plays, Chekhov's *The Marriage Proposal* and *The Boor* and a Pirandello adaptation entitled *The Evil Eye*. The company gave a 'preview' performance of their summer program at the Fraser Avenue theatre, for which the admission price was canned goods instead of money. The next day they packed their supplies, piled into their truck, and set off north to the Martin farm on Highway 35, after which they called themselves 'Theatre 35.'

The troupe played to local residents and vacationers, many of whom had never seen a live play before, over the next month. They carried a minimum set – black drapes – which the actors mounted and struck at each location. Tuesdays they performed in the Fenelon Falls Arena, Wednesdays in the Minden Recreation Centre, Thursdays and Fridays in the tent theatre at Hall's Lake, and Saturdays in an open-air theatre built specially for them at the Red Lion Inn in Bobcaygeon. Their first night in Minden they played to one spectator and a dog.[8] Although audiences improved thereafter, the actors eked out a frugal existence, living precariously on slender box-office receipts. They ate porridge and bought gas for the truck on Luscombe's credit card.[9] Gradually, however, as news of the company spread by word of mouth, audiences began to increase. By the time the company returned to Toronto in September, they had only a modest deficit, which Luscombe was able to pay off with part of his Canada Council grant.

The tour had hardly been a commercial triumph, but it confirmed Luscombe in his belief that he should be reaching out to a popular audience. 'Theatre is not real life,' he told a reporter in Haliburton, 'nor is it a religious rite. Bad theatre pretends to be one or the other. When people [have not been spoiled] by bad theatre, their sense of what is true and theatrical is that much stronger. And their enthusiasm ... communicates itself to the actors.'

Feeling that the tour in many ways had been the most exciting thing the group had done, Luscombe was determined to reach a similar audience in Toronto. With that goal in view and to put the theatre on a sounder legal basis, he decided to incorporate the organization under letters patent. Henceforth, the company would be known as Toronto Workshop Productions and would dedicate itself to a number of general aims: producing plays; training actors, directors, designers, stage managers, and production technicians; operating a permanent repertory company; encouraging Canadian playwrights; and promoting public interest in the arts generally. While mere incorporation did not make the newly envisaged company a reality, nevertheless, the official-looking document, with its impressive seal, seemed quietly reassuring.

4

Finding a Voice

From the beginning, Luscombe envisaged his new company as part of an international contingent of artists determined to further the cause of socialism through art. He saw himself as part of a tradition which sought to bring about change by 'educational' rather than political or revolutionary means. The function of the artist was not to get out on the hustings or to man the barricades; it was to demonstrate the social and economic laws governing society. Unfortunately, Canadian audiences, unlike their counterparts in Russia, Germany, or England, appeared to be stubbornly indifferent to live theatre.[1]

The challenge facing the new company, therefore, was how to break through that indifference and make their audiences look at themselves and their country with new eyes. Ideally, what was needed was original Canadian plays that would rip away the familiar surface of life to throw light on the ignored and unexamined corners of the Canadian experience. Until such new works were available, however, Luscombe and his actors would have to make up their repertoire from the existing stock of world dramatic literature. But instead of treating these 'masterpieces' of bourgeois theatre with the respect normally paid to them, Luscombe intended to follow the example of Vsevolod Meyerhold, Erwin Piscator, Bertolt Brecht, and Joan Littlewood. Those directors had shown how the classics of earlier periods could be made relevant to contemporary audiences.

For his first program, Luscombe selected two one-act plays, one of which was Chekhov's farce *The Boor*. Chekhov had been the principal dramatist of the Moscow Art Theatre, where Stanislavski had developed an intimately realistic style of acting to convey the playwright's subtle mixture of ridicule and compassion. Following the Russian Revolution, however, producers such as Vakhtangov had taken a very different approach to Chekhov's works. The new Soviet audiences, they argued, could hardly be expected to sympathize with the ineffectual representatives of the upper middle class that made up Chekhov's dramatis personae. Such characters should be presented on stage as laughable, contemptible examples of an evil society. Accordingly, a more objective, satirical style of acting was developed, to make clear that the Chekhovian figures were deserving of ridicule rather than sympathy.

To achieve the critical perspective he thought necessary, Luscombe introduced a number of 'estranging' techniques which had been developed by Russian and German directors but were practically unknown in Toronto in 1959. The production was staged on a small proscenium stage built in the largest of the basement offices at 47 Fraser Avenue. But instead of using the resources of the theatre to reinforce an illusion of reality, Luscombe highlighted the artificiality of the play. Nathan Cohen of the *Toronto Star* described the scene: 'The set shows the backstage with the actors waiting to go on. A property girl is present too. When the suitor pulls a rope to be admitted, she swings a bell in harmony with his gestures. When a hat rolls off the table, or a glass falls down, she picks them up.'[2] Cohen was entranced by these distancing effects, which he felt enriched the nature of the audience's enjoyment and paradoxically brought them into closer contact with the idea at the play's core.

In a second program of one-act plays produced a few months later, in May 1960, Luscombe mounted another Chekhov farce, *The Marriage Proposal.* Continuing his experiments with audience alienation, Luscombe tried to get his actors to achieve a Brechtian disengagement from their roles. In this, he faced more intractable obstacles. Tony Moffat-Lynch, who played Lomov, recalled his efforts to capture the style Luscombe was after. Convinced by his previous work in the theatre that the actor's task was to 'feel his role,' Moffat-Lynch had worked hard on creating a detailed psychological profile of the character. One night after the show, Luscombe came backstage in a rage, proclaiming loudly that if Tony ever gave a performance like that again he was out. At a loss to know what he had done wrong, Moffat-Lynch asked Luscombe to explain and was informed only that he had been 'acting.' No further enlightened, Moffat-Lynch so exhausted himself with worry over the next two days that his emotions seemed to disappear. On stage, he felt he was somehow standing aloof watching himself perform. After the performance, Luscombe came round to tell him he had been brilliant. Moffat-Lynch realized then what Luscombe had been after, and saw that in previous performances he had allowed his emotions to gain control of him on stage.[3]

Having tested his company on one-act plays, Luscombe felt they were ready to move on to more ambitious fare. Towards the end of 1961, in association with the Arts Theatre Club, he selected Aristophanes' sardonic comment on male warmongering, *Lysistrata*. Several international developments made the choice seem especially relevant. The Berlin blockade, the construction of the Berlin Wall, and the Cuban missile crisis had raised the Cold War tensions to almost unbearable levels and brought the threat of nuclear war closer than ever before. He asked Jack Winter, a playwright who by then had taken Tony Ferry's place as Luscomb's associate in the summer sessions, to help him and on 28 December 1961 opened the collaborative adaptation *And They'll Make Peace*.

The audience sat on three sides of a series of platforms rising from a ramp to an altar-like structure designed by Joyce Wieland. As the house lights dimmed, the theatre was filled with the sounds of drums and eerie birdlike noises coming from behind and beneath the seats. Nathan Cohen described the effect of the scene on him:

At first the voices seem far away and alien: then they are closer and familiar; at length they have the awful, awesome impact of a whole world of women shrieking their grief, as it were, softly into our ears.

A muted thunder of drums begins shortly after the female sobbing, and issues at first from far away and long ago (establishing for us, as does the weeping, that this is something that deals with yesterday but affects us now, today) then rises in volume and emotional power, until it blots out the women's cries. Signifying war, the drumming heralds the advent of two bands of men in uniform armed for combat. And then, the women's voices extinguished, the drumbeat stops. For an instant there is dead silence, the silence that is the prelude to the fight to the death. [There ensues] a stylized battle in semi-darkness ... between four men in headbands and nose guards and loose-flowing burlap shoulder capes ... and four other men in exactly the same uniform except that their shoulder capes are blackish green in colour. Two pair off in turn, matching shields and broad sword-blades, execute their short stylized dance, freeze into immobility while another two take over to go through the same beautiful and ghoulish manoeuvres.[4]

After the battle, shadowy figures move onto the stage foraging among the bodies for the spoils of battle. They are the women of Athens, who begin the play.

Unfortunately, the rest of the production failed to live up to its early promise. There were probably many reasons for that failure. Not only was Luscombe working with fairly raw performers, but his most experienced actress was wrong for the leading role in which she was cast. An even more damaging shortcoming, however, was the earnestness with which Luscombe and Winter had approached the script. Their introduction of contemporary allusions and songs tended to be preachy and heavy-handed. Lysistrata herself was turned into a modern sloganeering revolutionary. 'When the house is dirty,' she admonishes her followers, 'sweep it out – when the walls are rotten, tear them down. We need not live forever in the house of yesterday.'

Herbert Whittaker of the *Globe and Mail* generously praised a certain 'nimbleness of wit' in the writing but felt the collaborative creation of some scenes resulted in a 'blurring of essential fact.' Apart from these reservations (and a definite faintness in his praise of the acting), Whittaker admired Luscombe's ability to inspire his performers, to draw them into the situation presented and help them believe in it. He called Luscombe himself 'very likely the most dedicated and original creative talent working in our theatre.'[5]

Nathan Cohen was less charitable. Apart from his praise of the opening moments, he dismissed the entire production as 'feebly adapted, radically miscast and incompetently performed. If it were to be put on by professionals in a commercial house, it would immediately be recognized for the claptrap it is.' Then, in the avuncular tone he adopted when lecturing those he felt had strayed from the path he wanted them to tread, he went on: 'With this ferociously misguided production [Luscombe is] being unfaithful to his principles as an artist and a human being, to his company, and to the true needs of theatre in this community and the country.'[6]

Cohen's review was a serious set-back to the company. Nevertheless, it forced Luscombe to re-examine his work and to conclude that, in his preoccupation with the socialist and pacifist message of the play, he had not sufficiently explored the satire. Working with Jack Winter, he tried to salvage the production. They eliminated some of the contemporary references and introduced a number of new scenes. A month after the première, the play had undergone considerable revision, with the introduction of a balletic dream sequence, several surrealistic battles, and the near assassination of a warmonger. In a column in the *Toronto Star*, Winter promised that, in the revised version, 'the serious and the jocular blend into a curious and naive power.'[7] But his formulation of the play's underlying theme – 'that peace may be won by fools but can only be maintained by men' – gave little indication that the company had come any closer to the ribald and fantastic spirit of Aristophanes.

When Luscombe looked at the work objectively in the light of the negative criticism, he came to the conclusion that he had, in fact, been carried away by his own ingenuity in the staging. Too often, he saw, he had filled the stage with exciting behaviour without making sure that each actor contributed to the overall picture.[8] And in a similar way, he had allowed his own political convictions to lead him into oversimplifications. In rehearsals, conducted during the Cuban missile crisis, the importance of the play's message had seemed overwhelming. But that very urgency had given rise to an earnestness probably less effective than a more ironic approach would have been. Nevertheless, Luscombe felt that, in *Peace*, the company had developed 'a new style of acting and theatre.'[9]

And They'll Make Peace raised several practical problems of dramaturgy and staging. The new open stage of the company's basement theatre demanded a new relationship between actor and spectator. Furthermore, the adaptation of classic works for Canadian audiences was fraught with difficulties stemming from the thinness of the theatrical tradition in the country and the resulting ignorance on the part of Torontonians of the major works of world theatre. Techniques of irony, parody, or estrangement were doomed to misinterpretation where the originals being modified were unknown. The difficulty of finding a theatrical metaphor through which to express Canadian realities was significantly increased by the naïvety of the audience. To overcome some of that difficulty, Luscombe decided to work on a more recent play. Sometimes called the first proletarian tragedy, Georg Buchner's *Woyzeck* was written in 1837 by a twenty-four-year-old medical student, who was inspired by the real-life story of a German barber-soldier who murdered his mistress in a fit of jealous rage. The soldier was tried, condemned (despite legal and medical contentions that he had been insane at the time of the murder), and publicly executed in Leipzig in 1824, in the first such execution in that city in thirty years. Just what drew the young Buchner to the story is not clear. His attitude to Woyzeck is remarkably sympathetic, but there are also clear indications in the drama that Woyzeck is mad (he suffers from hallucinations), and the story ends with the protagonist's death by drowning rather than execution.

Luscombe was attracted to the work because of its spare but evocative dialogue and because its fragmentary nature – the play remained unfinished at Buchner's death – allowed scope for improvisation. He also felt drawn towards the central character, whom he saw not as a madman but as a victim of society. In December 1963, he began working on improvisations, with a script based on a new translation from the German by two of his students.

One aim was to strengthen the story line, which in the original moved confusingly from scene to scene without transitions or explanations. To bridge one such transition and to emphasize the militarism of Woyzeck's society, Luscombe introduced a number of army drills. Douglas Livingston, a member of the company, had acquired a stereophonic sound system for the theatre and placed speakers around the auditorium and even under the stage. By controlling the various channels, he was able to give the effect of a military band moving from place to place.[10] The drills emphasized the power and even sadism of the officers and the dehumanization of the enlisted personnel. Luscombe was influenced in these scenes, and in other scenes involving an army doctor, by what he had seen on a visit to Auschwitz during a trip to Poland in 1955.[11] But he also recollected his own experiences of regimentation as a child in public school and could identify with the way in which authority could intimidate and crush imagination. The schoolyard, as he remembered it, was not that different from the parade ground.

Sympathy for Woyzeck was also evoked in the production by emphasis on the viciousness of the world around him – a world of arrogant captains and lecherous drum majors. Even the treatment of Woyzeck's mistress, Marie, was brutal. While the press release described her as 'the only creature who ever loved [Woyzeck],' the production tended to stress her infidelity, her impatience with her child, and the generally sordid life she lived amid prostitutes and poverty.

One of the most striking features of the production was Luscombe's creation of a raucous world of brothels and fairground out of the meagre materials at his disposal. The setting consisted of no more than several platforms and a row of doors at the back of the stage to serve as the houses of prostitutes or the entrances to carnival tents. Luscombe believed that whatever illusion of environment was required on stage should be created with bodies rather than with paint and canvas. He wanted his actors to convey by their movements the difference between walking on grass and walking on concrete, between standing in a jungle and standing in a desert.

Perhaps his greatest triumph was his staging of Woyzeck's drowning. In the script, the action moves from a tavern, where Woyzeck falls under suspicion because of blood on his hand, to a river bank, where he tries to get rid of the murder weapon. In Luscombe's staging, as Woyzeck rushed from the room, the actors playing the characters in the tavern suddenly began to move in the stylized 'efforts' of Laban, giving the impression of weightlessness and collectively representing the water. As Woyzeck moved into the 'river' among them, his clothes were seized by the 'waves.' His hat was taken by one actor and passed to another's arm and a third's shoulder and finally to the floor. Suddenly, all the actors, including the one playing Woyzeck, moved off, leaving only a pile of clothing on the stage.[12]

In addition to helping the actors improvise individual scenes and bits of business, Luscombe sometimes divided the action in order to juxtapose certain characters or themes. For example, he counterpointed the off-stage love-making in the brothel with Marie's arguments with her neighbours, and opposed the drunken philosophizing of two apprentices to the anguished despair of Woyzeck. By breaking up the play in that way, Luscombe hoped to prevent the audience from being completely seduced by the surface considerations of the work and to force them to contemplate deeper impressions and meanings.[13]

Woyzeck opened at the Fraser Avenue theatre on Friday, 29 May 1963, and attracted considerable critical attention. In a generous gesture of support that was as characteristic as his acidity, Nathan Cohen commented on the production in his column in the *Star* even though the show had already been reviewed in the paper. He called it 'a stunningly conceived and dynamically executed venture in the resources of total theatre ... a complete marriage of theme and treatment ... It is quite the finest thing Mr Luscombe has done.' He saw Woyzeck as a kind of universal man, 'an apotheosis of a desire for material security and spiritual certainty.' He especially admired the staging as 'bursting with life and color ... tremendously concentrated in its interdependent leaves of experience and entertainment ... a truly passionate work of art.'[14]

Woyzeck marked a particularly satisfying triumph in its thorough vindication of Luscombe's conviction that actors could find truths in a dramatic text that could make it especially relevant for contemporary audiences. The success of the production strengthened him in his belief that the author was merely one member of a creative team whose contribution could, and should, be modified by that of the other collaborators in the production process. In his search for original Canadian works, he was to draw increasingly on the creative input of his acting company.

5

Collaborative Creation I:
Hey Rube! and *The Mechanic*

The importance of improvisation as a tool for teaching acting was first recognized by Stanislavski, who passed the technique on to followers such as Meyerhold and Vakhtangov. Whereas Stanislavski had directed his early exercises inwards, encouraging students to recall and explore their own emotional life, however, Vakhtangov focused outwards, on physical action and atmosphere. He would participate with his students at the Third Studio of the Moscow Art Theatre in improvised scenes on the theme of a play in order to build up the necessary creative atmosphere or to find the 'grain' of a scene.[1] Often these 'études' were undertaken to work out the best way of conveying the company's attitude to an author's characters – for example, to show that Chekhov's speeches of hope were really the vain dreaming of deluded bourgeois landowners. At other times, they were used to eliminate peripheral detail and allow concentration on the core of a problem so that the 'mirror' of the stage reflected essences rather than merely the surface of life.[2]

Luscombe was particularly attracted to Vakhtangov's 'fantastic realism,' which combined inner truth with powerful stage images. He looked to improvisation in his teaching, therefore, to do two things. One was to give the actor a better understanding of his or her own nature and of the social context of a play. The other was to find the concrete gesture that would best project an emotion or an idea to the audience. During the autumn of 1960, the company had spent several weeks remodelling their basement theatre at 47 Fraser Avenue to increase its capacity and enlarge the playing space. They had decided to remove yet another of the partitions, and in doing so they had exposed two steel pillars with obvious structural significance. Afraid of bringing the building down around their ears, they decided to leave the pillars where they were and design an open stage that would surround and incorporate them. Over the next seven weeks, the company constructed a raised playing space from an old revolving stage acquired from the defunct Jupiter Theatre, removed the proscenium and exposed the lighting equipment, and scavenged the Spadina Avenue garment district for salvageable lumber, out of which they built tiered seating on three sides of the stage. The finished auditorium, with seating for one hundred spectators, surrounded a three-quarters-open stage with two prominent pillars.

The redesigned performance space soon began to affect the group's work. One night, during an improvisation exercise, one of the actors began to juggle. Soon the others responded, and a brief circus act materialized. Later, one of the actresses, who had been eating at the theatre to cut down on expenses, improvised a cooking scene.[3] It suddenly occurred to Luscombe that their new quarters would be perfect for a play about circus life. He had known circus performers in Wales while travelling with Jimmy James, and he understood their way of life.[4] Furthermore, the circus milieu provided a perfect context for the exploration of that physicality which was so much a part of Luscombe's idea of theatre.

Tony Moffat-Lynch had also been very interested in clowns during his youth in England and fell easily into their comic mode. Many of the actors, however, had little knowledge of the circus, and Luscombe sent them out to do research on the various clown traditions and to investigate juggling, high-wire, and trapeze routines. As the work progressed, Luscombe pushed his actors to imagine the circumstances of itinerant circus life. He told them of the acrobats' need for continual practice, the bickering brought about by long and close association, the strain of living on the fringe of an indifferent or hostile society. Some of these aspects of circus life Luscombe knew by report; others he could vouch for from his own experience of touring in Wales. The Canadian actors too had little difficulty in responding, because they themselves felt threatened: the company had recently received an eviction notice from their landlord, Industrial Leaseholds, who had at last found paying tenants anxious to move into 47 Fraser Avenue in December. As the actors contemplated their own desperate circumstances, their improvisations took on a heightened urgency. To add to his problems, Luscombe soon discovered that improvisation and collective creation had certain limitations. While the actors could interact with one another to develop isolated scenes, they found it much more difficult to agree on an overall shape for the drama or to collaborate in the construction of a story line with focus, compression, and significance.

Accordingly, Luscombe asked Tony Ferry to attend rehearsals and work
with the company in the development of the script. Ferry found a book
about English circuses[5] and transcribed the actors' dialogue during
improvisations. After rehearsals, Luscombe and Ferry would go over the
scenes looking for ways to provide continuity. Gradually, a series of
vignettes was developed, focusing on the conflict between the performers
in a run-down circus and the local citizens, or 'rubes,' of the town in
which they were playing. A young tough comes to take out one of the
high-wire artists; a boy from the town wants to join the circus; news arrives
that a local girl is missing and that one of the clowns is suspected of having seduced her; the clown confesses under cross-examination; the new
boy is killed attempting a high dive; and local hoodlums attack the performers, triggering the circus emergency cry of 'Hey Rube!'

As they worked together, Luscombe and Ferry disagreed about the significance of the script. Ferry, writing out of a sense of 'personal artistic
doom,'[6] saw the beleaguered performers as typical victims in a society hostile to the arts; Luscombe, somewhat more optimistic, was excited by the
circus as offering an essentially theatrical language. He captured that feeling in the speech he wrote to begin the play:

A hundred years ago this night
A tent was raised and people entered
Paid the price, laughed at clowns
And understood the meaning of a show that never closed.
A hundred years before that time, another place another town
A child laughed when a clown fell down
And in that moment he learned more than all his books could tell.
Time is nowhere, all is present
Past and future both combined
A world of madness, songs and stories
Fools and wisemen, which is which?
Who but you can tell us that?

The lines illustrate Luscombe's conviction that the core of theatrical
meaning is in gesture and that the responsibility for interpreting stage
images lies with the audience. It was a conviction that Ferry, himself an
aspiring playwright, did not share.

As the end of November approached, the company worked out an
agreement with Industrial Leaseholds that allowed them to remain in
their basement theatre for a nominal monthly rent. To pay that rent, they

needed to perform before the public, however, and the new circus play was in trouble. By the end of December, much of the work still remained rough, and Ferry thought the plot needed further development and polish. But Luscombe wanted to get the actors in front of an audience. In the end, Luscombe prevailed, and on 6 February 1961 the company opened its first original play, *Hey Rube!*.

During the initial week, they drew audiences of fewer than a dozen. Those who found their way to Fraser Avenue descended a flight of stairs to a wide hallway decorated with posters of European theatrical productions. Passing through the doors at the end of the hall, they came into an area with bleachers on three sides. The ceiling was covered with a draped parachute resembling the underside of a big top, and on-stage were two 'tent poles' painted a brilliant red. As they entered, the spectators were greeted by various members of the circus already busily engaged in sweeping up or in putting on their make-up. By the time everyone was seated, there were often fewer spectators in the auditorium than actors on the stage. When the newspaper critics finally attended a performance a week after the opening, they did so in the company of just seven other people.

Nathan Cohen reported that he found the story of *Hey Rube!* weak and the characters incompletely drawn. Much of the dialogue, he felt, was bereft of colour and psychological perception, and the theme got lost in murky symbolism. Nevertheless, he was impressed by the actors' dazzling use of pantomime: 'To an ear-splitting, pulse-pounding, blood-tingling fanfare of drums and trumpets, two girls perform a high wire act. Gracefully they make their ascents, gingerly each puts a foot forward to test the wire's slack, confidently the journey is made. (But, in fact, neither has left the ground. The acrobatics are simulated.)'[7] He also liked the way in which Luscombe and his performers had integrated all the elements of performance into what he called 'total theatre,' thereby achieving a 'genuinely meaningful relationship between playmakers and playgoers.' With an enthusiasm wholly uncharacteristic of Toronto's most acid theatre critic, Cohen described the production as 'an exhilarating adventure among the theatre arts ... [a performance which] stands heads [*sic*] and shoulders above most drama productions shown in Toronto, or likely to be shown, this season.'[8]

Herbert Whittaker was no less enthusiastic, but for different reasons: 'It is the skill and sensitivity of Mr Luscombe's method of teaching theatre and its meaning which invests these [scenes] with a completely absorbing reality ... These are not ordinary actors. They are almost inconspicuous as personalities, but are nonetheless convincing for all that. Their life is the life of the circus people with whom they have so thoroughly identified themselves. In fact, when a more practised actor, George Sperdakos, has the stage to deliver the rich lines of the ringmaster, one finds oneself curiously resentful of his carefully developed theatricality.'[9]

With this endorsement from the critics of the major Toronto dailies, *Hey Rube!* ran for five weeks. At the conclusion of what had been their longest season to date, eighteen actors and technicians each received $37.83 as their share of the profit on thirty-one performances.[10] The show played to more than two thousand people and established Workshop Productions as the most forward-looking theatrical group in the city. Whittaker linked it with other recent developments such as the opening of the O'Keefe Centre, the five-week season of the National Ballet at the Royal Alexandra, the Crest's revival of Willis Hall's *The Long, the Short, and the Tall,* and the ten-week run of Jack Gelber's *The Connection* at the House of Hambourg. It appeared that, at last, a truly indigenous theatre was taking root in English-speaking Canada.

The circus milieu of *Hey Rube!* had provided Luscombe with the ideal context in which to explore his ideas. The backstage scenes could be played with a psychologically based realism in a style which tacitly ignored the audience. But these scenes were interspersed with circus acts of a flamboyant theatricality in which acrobats and clowns played directly to the encircling crowd. The disjointed and episodic method of storytelling enabled Luscombe to juxtapose the public and private worlds of his characters. In that way, he could avoid the sentimental or the mawkish and at the same time illustrate the economic and social forces at work in the characters' lives. The structure of the work was rhythmic rather than logical, and the story remained open-ended instead of moving to a pat conclusion. The central situation was a metaphor for the precarious position of the artist in a society driven by greed and ignorance. But this serious point was made deftly with the 'sword of laughter.'

The success of *Hey Rube!* prompted Luscombe to investigate other forms of collaborative play creation. To obviate the need to invent a plot, he decided to adapt a Renaissance comedy by finding modern equivalents for the original characters. The play he chose was Molière's *L'amour médecin* (*Love, the Best Physician*), itself an adaptation of conventional commedia dell'arte motifs. The Molière work tells the familiar story of the daughter outwitting her obtuse father to marry the man of her choice. With the help of Lysetta, her maid, Lucinda convinces her father, Sganarelle, that she is dying because she cannot marry. Sganarelle brings four physicians to examine her, but they cannot agree on a treatment. Lysetta, meanwhile, has arranged for the young lover to disguise himself as a doctor and brings him to the house. He persuades Sganarelle that it is Lucinda's mind that must be treated, and that she will be cured by being made to go through a simulated marriage contract. Sganarelle agrees, only to find out too late that the contract is legally binding.

Luscombe and his actors searched for modern equivalents of these archetypical comic figures. They found them among the conventional characters portrayed in films and the contemporary world of jazz. The obtuse father became the modern businessman worried about his health, the mother was represented by the society matron, and the rival lover was transformed into a cool hipster. The most original insight, however, was that the chicanery which Molière had attacked in the medical profession was now to be found in the world of mechanical appliances. In a society of relentless consumerism, the indispensable witch-doctors are the repairmen. So in the hands of the actors and their dramaturge, Jack Winter, Molière's disguised doctor became an automobile mechanic.

For Luscombe, the exercise provided an opportunity to explore the conventions and practices of commedia dell'arte. Luscombe was attracted to the professional Italian comedy of the sixteenth century because it represented a style of acting diametrically opposed to that of the Shakespearean tradition. Whereas Richard Burbage, Edward Alleyn, and other Elizabethan actors played a dazzling array of different parts, the commedia actors spent their lives perfecting a single role. Shakespeare's colleagues spoke the lines he provided for them; the Italian actors improvised their dialogue following only a brief outline of the plot. Every commedia performance was unique, with each of the performers contributing new *lazzi* or allusions to contemporary scandals or political events. The commedia actor, therefore, was more than a performing puppet; he was an alert, widely read individual whose every performance was a demonstration of skill and intelligence.

The new work evolved slowly during the spring of 1964 as the actors built up their characters, improvising incidents and bits of business suggested by the original play. Much of the comedy was physical, inspired serendipitously during rehearsal and often only tenuously related to the story. Some of the gags, such as Lucinda's father's getting stuck in a tuba, seemed pointless and extraneous. Others were riotously surrealistic. One *lazzo* that regularly brought the house down was a routine in which Donald Meyers as the mechanic tested and repaired a 'car' played by the other members of the company. An ingenious combination of physical actions suggesting tires, pistons, and other mechanical paraphernalia, together with sound effects produced by such unlikely instruments as a sewing machine, a tin whistle, and pots and pans, created a brilliantly comic pantomime which regularly stopped the show.

Winter would take notes during improvisations and then work them into a final script. He described the process as follows: 'After consultations between director and dramaturge, certain broad lines of character, theme and situation were discussed with the actors and technicians. Then, within given circumstances suggested to them, improvisations began. Some led nowhere and were dropped. Some led to insights and were built upon. And slowly ... characterization deepened, inter-relationships developed meaning and ... a narrative line began to emerge [and] dialogue began to be written: at first closely related to what was being suggested in the improvisations, and then gradually freer and wider until the script began to suggest scenes and characters which had not yet been introduced.'[11]

In spite of some signal successes, the process of collaboration employed by the company proved exceptionally time-consuming. After two months of rehearsals and preparation, the show was little more than a one-act play. To stretch it into a length suitable for presentation at the University of Waterloo, where the company had contracted to perform in July, Luscombe got a friend to make a short film of street action to be screened as a second act prior to the improvised automobile routine. Even with this addition, the play came down early, so Luscombe devised a curtain-call, using the five doors in the permanent background of the Waterloo stage, which went on almost as long as another act.[12]

The Molière adaptation, now called *The Mechanic*, opened at the University of Waterloo on 27 July 1964 and was, according to Herbert Whittaker, 'more of a happening than a play ... concentrating on action [rather] than on words.' Whittaker felt that staid audiences might find it frivolous or even facetious, but he admired the energy of the production, saying that it had 'all the bounce of early silent film comedy,' and thought Luscombe's use of the Waterloo thrust stage was inspired.[13]

The company continued to work on the production over the next fifteen months and presented an expanded version in Stratford in the summer of 1965 prior to bringing it to Toronto as the opening play of their winter season. Ronald Evans of the *Toronto Telegram* welcomed the irrepressible high spirits of *The Mechanic*. He particularly admired the setting by Nancy Jowsey, a 'tube, bottle and bulb-strung back-wall, that could be either the stockroom of a garage or a cross-section of a human body.' The car repair routine he called 'one of the most magnificently hilarious scenes I've ever seen,' and he urged his readers, if they had ever wondered what had happened to fun in theatre, to see the production.[14]

Herbert Whittaker, the only Toronto critic to have reviewed the play out of town, feared that Winter's script was in danger of 'being swamped by the accumulated comic business.' 'Almost every second word,' he remonstrated, 'is a cue for the Luscombe stock company to improvise funny things to do.' Many of these, he admitted, were highly inventive and 'a fine demonstration of the mimetic and rhythmic accomplishments of the group.' But at times, 'the rushing about to words comes close to tedium.'[15]

Nathan Cohen also complained of ennui brought about by a 'fast-paced kaleidoscope of impressions' that was nevertheless 'flat and drab.' He compared the company's style to that of an animated cartoon and praised the way in which every ingredient of theatre had been brought into synchronized play. At the end of the first act, for example,

eight members of the cast evoke an uproariously nightmarish picture of traffic in a state of anarchy. Without moving from their places at the back of the three-sided stage, they mount an effect of ear-splitting tumult and vehicular pandemonium. To pursue the cartoon comparison, the cars become a flock of birds of various size and wing strength. Thrown into a sudden panic, the birds swoop up and down and across, threaten to bump into one another and miraculously miss collision, but nevertheless try by some kind of collective unconscious to continue on their given direction. As the actors execute their physical gesturings, there is the accompanying roar of wheels sliding and slithering and turning. The jangle of traffic signals changing from 'stop' to 'go' with ever-increasing frequency is coupled with lights spangling the players at the same pace with every color of the spectrum.

But for Cohen such effective entertainment was not enough. Convinced that drama is fundamentally a verbal art, Cohen deplored what he saw as the usurping of the writer's role by the actors. 'What Jack Winter started to develop as a serious dramatic statement complete with vision and power,' he wrote, 'turns, in the circumstances, into a lively but lifeless spectacle. The language loses its muscularity and clarifying meaning. The characters dissolve into objects in a mirage. The trouble is not that they are symbols, but that they have been removed from Mr. Winter's authority and poured into a group-think, a spiritually mechanized and spook imprint.'[16] Not for the first time, Cohen had put his finger on a weakness in the TWP method which Luscombe had to acknowledge. Improvisation alone could not produce the ideal combination of words and actions that constituted the best drama; actor and writer had to work together. But in Luscombe's experience the alliance was a difficult one.

6

Adding the Language:
Before Compiègne

The early development of TWP reflects the interests and differences of three of its first architects, Tony Ferry, George Luscombe, and Jack Winter. Ferry provided the initial impetus for the creation of the group and first articulated the company's aims. Understandably, those aims reflected his own experience in England with the new British drama and the so-called Angry Young Men. Winter was a later arrival, but he rapidly established a strong presence as dramaturge, drafter of grant applications, and general spokesman. His background was academic (he was working on a PhD thesis on Bernard Shaw), and he was attracted to some of the newer dramatic theories of figures such as Antonin Artaud and the experiments in the small off-off-Broadway theatres such as Caffe Cino and Cafe La Mama (the La Mama Experimental Theatre Club) in New York. Not surprisingly, tensions developed among the three friends, each of whom had unique strengths, and each of whom tended to underestimate the importance of the others' contributions. Ferry and Winter, both aspiring playwrights, were better educated than Luscombe and had a wider familiarity with the theory and literature of theatre. But Luscombe had the practical experience (along with the leadership ability), and the two writers recognized that he was the key to the realization of their own artistic ambitions. It was Ferry, the original partner, who argued that TWP should produce Canadian plays, and it was Ferry who persuaded Luscombe to stage the Canadian *Burlap Bags*, an adaptation of Len Peterson's radio play, along with Chekhov's *The Marriage Proposal* in 1960. But his efforts on his own behalf were less successful. *Gropius*, a play he had submitted for consideration, had been rejected, and he had come to a bitter falling out with Luscombe over the script for *Hey Rube!*

Following his disagreement with Luscombe, Ferry left the company to

help establish a legitimate theatre in a former burlesque house on Queen
Street. The Civic Square Theatre opened on 2 January 1962 with the help
of a $10,000 grant from the Canada Council. After just two productions,
the company ran out of money and the scheme collapsed. In the mean-
time, Ferry's place at TWP had been taken by Jack Winter, who had
approached Luscombe after seeing *Hey Rube!*. Realizing that he would
need the services of a writer, Luscombe invited Winter to participate in
the Haliburton summer school he and Ferry had organized, and later he
invited Winter to work with him on the adaptation of *Lysistrata*.

The two men rapidly established a congenial working relationship.
Winter was some ten years younger than Luscombe and at first very
much the disciple. He was glad of an opportunity to work closely with the
director and the actors who would be developing his plays, and took naturally to the company's collaborative methods. Far from resenting the
actors' suggestions, Winter seemed to agree with Luscombe that actors
are often better able than a writer to explore the nuances of psychological conflict.

After their work on *And They'll Make Peace*, Winter and Luscombe col-
laborated on *The Evil Eye*, an adaptation of Pirandello's *The License*. Then,
early in 1963, possibly inspired by Shaw, Winter began working on a play
of his own about Saint Joan. The work went slowly but was well advanced
by early spring. The script, about the last days of Joan of Arc, presented an
interestingly sardonic view of the much-mythologized peasant girl. Winter's Joan arrives at Troyes as an emissary of Charles VII, the king whom
she has recently crowned at Rheims. But instead of the saint triumphant,
this is a rough-mannered farm girl who leads a small, dispirited army and
has lost faith in her cause and her voices. In the field before the city, she is
met by Catherine, Countess of Troyes, who offers her supplies left behind
by the English and promises to let her hear her own voices, which she
claims are from the Virgin Mary. Seeking to restore her faith, Joan accom-
panies Catherine, to find uniforms and gunpowder but not the supernat-
ural sign she was hoping for. In an effort to provoke a response from
heaven, she first takes off her masculine attire and then, when she
remains unpunished, seduces Catherine's young servant, François Villon.

When Catherine returns, bringing the crystal ball which is the source of
her 'voices,' Joan breaks the glass, ties up Catherine, and accuses her of
planning to betray her. At this point, François claims that he has seen a
vision of stars in the fields outside their hideaway and that he has heard
voices calling for the Maid. Thinking that perhaps this is the sign she has
been seeking, Joan goes off with François and is presumably killed in an

explosion off-stage. Alone, Catherine exults that she has been successful in destroying her enemy. 'She loosed the shadows and they are everywhere – everywhere. She has gone to meet them – gone to glory – we have led her back to God.'

Luscombe and the actors liked much about the play but thought it seriously flawed. There was a good deal of vigorous writing, and a provocatively materialistic view of Joan which presented her voices as delusions and her God as a cause of exploitation and war. But much of the symbolism was confusing – Catherine's function was not at all obvious – and the conflicts were presented in a rather old-fashioned, even melodramatic, format. Luscombe encouraged the actors to analyse the script in order to find the underlying motivation of the characters, and led them in improvisations exploring the given circumstances of each situation. He encouraged the performers to reach into their own imaginations to flesh out the scenes and to find specific actions to illuminate character. As a result of those exercises, the company moved towards a collective understanding of the play, which was incorporated in revisions of the script.

As it stood, the drama was too subjective for Luscombe's taste. The focus was on individual psychology (Joan's disillusionment, Catherine's desire for revenge, François's ambition to go to Paris to become a poet) rather than on the objective facts and issues behind the characters' private lives. There needed to be more explicit examination of war and the economic basis of war. It was necessary to distance the audience from Joan so that they could see her not only as a suffering individual but also as a pawn in international politics and a dupe of false political and religious ideologies. Accomplishing this would mean rewriting the second half of the play and restaging certain scenes so that the actors would be less immersed in the psychological complexities of their characters and freer to demonstrate the limitations of those characters.

Accordingly, Luscombe hired four additional actors to play soldiers who would serve as a kind of chorus and provide a more objective framework for the personal story. He also persuaded Winter to shift the scene of the play from Troyes to Compiègne, which in its associations with the signing of the Armistice and the surrender of France to Hitler, had resonances Luscombe wanted to bring into the performance. For Luscombe, Joan's experiences illustrated the ideological basis of violence and in that respect were related to events of more recent history.

Winter wrote an opening chorus in which he linked Compiègne with Joan's betrayal and capture as well as with other manifestations of ideological prejudice. He also eliminated Joan's seduction of François and an episode in which Catherine seems as eager to don a soldier's uniform as Joan is to wear a dress. Further excisions removed Joan's rather improbable desire to hear Catherine's 'voices' and her hope that dressing as a woman would, by provoking him to retaliation, establish the existence of God.

On Friday, 13 December 1963, TWP opened its first fully scripted original play, *Before Compiègne*. Most of the critics were gratifyingly enthusiastic. Herbert Whittaker hailed the work as a justification of the company's early promise. For the first time, he felt, TWP had actors talented enough to match Luscombe's imagination. He particularly welcomed the company's new emphasis on language, language which he described as 'strong, poetic, and lively.' 'The play,' he wrote, 'confronts the warrior saint at her lowest ebb with a tempter who is a good match for her. Winter has had the good sense to make the tempter a woman, his extension of a historical figure – a false visionary named Catherine de la Rochelle. Her temptations are those of a woman, including clothes and power over men ... The two women, true and false, circle warily as the chorus of soldiers juxtapose a running documentation of historical events, past and to come.'[1]

Ronald Evans of the *Telegram* was equally enthusiastic. He was struck by the unconventional portrait of Joan, 'a cropped, cocky, cursing Joan in a sweat-greasy, dried cowhide jerkin [whose] ears are tuned to the coarse barracks songs and stories.' Evans saw the story as one of betrayal, in which Joan is tricked and must choose between 'a cynical allegiance to the English-allied Duke of Burgundy or death.'[2]

This relatively fulsome praise left Luscombe and Winter unprepared for the devastating reaction of Nathan Cohen. In the past, Cohen had been particularly generous in his praise of the company, and partly on that account Winter had sent him a copy of the script of *Compiègne* prior to the opening. Now, instead of the encouragement they had hoped for, Cohen meted out savage criticism. Acknowledging that there was wit, intelligence, and the possibility of a good narrative line in Winter's conception, Cohen nevertheless felt that the writer had been 'encouraged' to fatten the play's trim, essentially anecdotal shape.

But he reserved his most scathing condemnation for the director. 'Mr Luscombe,' he proclaimed, 'instead of giving the play the hard, clean, sardonic treatment it calls for, has staged it pretentiously, and with great gobs of artistic vulgarity ... In trying to inflate *Before Compiègne* far beyond its dimensions, Mr Luscombe has done his playwright a disservice, and once again called attention to a chronic failing in his own work, one which he must overcome if his efforts are even [*sic*] to take healthy roots.' Although he acknowledged that the production was not a waste, he felt that it was 'naggingly, harassingly and crucially inadequate.'[3]

Not content to confine his remarks to the play he was reviewing, Cohen surveyed Luscombe's career in order to analyse what he considered the director's shortcomings. These were an insensitivity to speech variation and a focus on the interrelationship of characters rather than on their inner lives. He also maintained that Luscombe's emphasis on ensemble and lack of interest in psychology meant that he was ineffective in his handling of performers, a conclusion he arrived at from the fact that no professional actor associated with TWP had conspicuously improved as a result of the experience. (Cohen ignored the fact that Luscombe had been forced to work almost exclusively with amateurs.)

Cohen acknowledged that with certain plays such as *Hey Rube!* or *Woyzeck* Luscombe could 'blend his effects with a singular resourcefulness and extreme intensity of impact. He can achieve distinguished fusions of sound, light, color (through costumes especially) and movement, leading to flash-flood climaxes. On such occasions too, however murky the material, he registers an acute political consciousness. By defining, sometimes forcefully, sometimes through tender silences, but always clearly, a play's economic and social framework, he makes a cogent comment on life today and the values which characterize it.'

Attempting to explain this apparent paradox, Cohen suggested that Luscombe was at his best when dealing with skeletal scripts. Theorizing that his nature fitted him or that experience had conditioned him to be the creator of prime force in a dramatic presentation, Cohen suggested that Luscombe had difficulty when he approached a text with a strong organization in which the characters, dialogue, conflicts, and resolution were basically fixed. 'In such circumstances,' he pronounced, 'Luscombe is forced to be a translator only, to subordinate himself to the vanishing point, and the conflict produces a contraction of his imaginative faculty and disciplines.' Then 'there is an acute loss of focus. The devices are often banal. The actors flounder about on a landscape without guidelines. The climaxes are reached at the wrong time and have the wrong stress. The effects misfire. That was how it was with *And They'll Make Peace*,' Cohen concluded, 'and that's how it is ... with *Before Compiègne*.'[4]

Luscombe was stunned, not only by Cohen's negative response but also by the vehemence with which it had been expressed. Epithets such as 'vulgar,' 'banal,' 'inadequate,' and 'pretentious' were painfully mortifying to read, especially in the column of a critic he respected. Reluctantly,

Luscombe had to admit that Cohen had been right about *And They'll Make Peace.* Could it be that he was right again? Were there shortcomings in his methods that the other critics did not see? If Cohen was wrong in particular, could he be right in general? Did *Woyzeck* and *Hey Rube!* constitute the company's best work? And if so, was the group now moving in the wrong direction?

Winter and Luscombe had an opportunity to rework the play for revival at the Colonnade Theatre in April. For the new version they explored various non-realistic theatrical conventions such as commedia dell'arte, Chinese opera, and silent film. In place of the four soldiers, they introduced a couple of 'zanies,' a sort of medieval Laurel and Hardy duo who livened the action with various *lazzi* while commenting on the proceedings and occasionally taking over the major roles in the play. Another addition was that of a minstrel figure who, like the orchestra in a Chinese opera, provided musical accompaniment to and comment on the action. Douglas Livingston played a variety of instruments (including drums and ocarina) to supply sound effects and a 'medieval' atmosphere. The result was a radically different handling of the script, which in many respects remained the same. Speeches were taken from some characters and assigned to others so that lines which had been serious or portentous in the original version became ironic or comic.

The changes succeeded in marking a clearer distinction in the play between the 'feeling' and 'detached' sides of Joan's character. Comments which had given a rather cynical slant to the Maid were assigned to the new comic observers. This meant that Joan's disillusionment when she learned of Charles's betrayal was more poignant and her refusal to yield to the blandishments of Catherine and become a mere mercenary more credible. Unfortunately, it also shifted attention away from the central character and put undue emphasis on what seemed like extraneous comic turns. The new version of the play also put slightly less stress on the religious basis of war and introduced a final speech which suggested that Joan gave herself up in an act of something like existential despair.

Not all the critics were pleased by the alterations. Ronald Evans called the production 'not the fine powerful piece it was four months ago ... Some of the strength of the play has been sapped off to sweeten up the production.' He felt there was more laughter but less potency, partly because Joan had been pushed aside and attention switched to the two clowns. Evans preferred what he called the 'sturdy chorus of four soldiers' and deplored the 'Mack Sennett capers.' While acknowledging that Luscombe's staging was the most imaginative and exciting in any Toronto theatre, he thought the play itself needed to be restored to its 'original cogency.'[5]

Oscar Ryan, who wrote under the pen name Martin Stone in the *Canadian Tribune*, was more sympathetic to the new mode. He called the Colonnade production 'a new and very different play.' He admired the extraordinary and brilliantly imaginative staging, in which the actors 'soar on wings of fantasy,' singing, clowning, dancing. While he was beguiled by the comic acting of Donald Meyers and Edward Kelly as the two zanies, Dijon and Muchmore (the latter mischievously named after a Toronto clergyman), he admitted that the central idea of the play tended to become obscured in the fireworks.[6] Ralph Hicklin, writing in the *Globe*, had not seen the earlier production, but he too sensed a lack of focus. The play, he felt, 'did not have the final single impact which its separate moments promised.' Hicklin also noted what other critics were to comment on as a recurring weakness in the company – a 'common tendency to stridency.'[7] Nathan Cohen refused to cover the production on the grounds that it was only a revival of a show he had already reviewed.

Following the Colonnade production, Winter and Luscombe decided to carry out further revision in preparation for performances at the University of Waterloo during a short summer season there. They incorporated some of the comic business of the two clowns into the main action, eliminating Dijon and Muchmore and giving some of their lines to Joan and the Captain. In many respects, this revision represented a return to the original Fraser Avenue staging, except that Joan became more amusing. A further lightening of the effect was achieved by having some of the narrative (such as Joan's final capture and execution) sung in ballads by a minstrel. The ending remained something of a problem. In this version, Joan's capture was reported rather than shown, with the result that the climax was weakened slightly. Kemp Thompson, the Kitchener critic, thought the Waterloo production was 'more effective than the version [he had seen] during the winter.' But he felt the play tailed off rather than coming to a strong conclusion.[8]

Nathan Cohen had been persuaded to attend a special performance given for his exclusive benefit prior to the company's return to the University of Waterloo in October. Sitting alone in the uncomfortable basement theatre watching a performance in which Luscombe had to replace Ed Kelly as the Captain, Cohen was converted. 'In its new form', he wrote, '*Before Compiègne* has become a play entitled to serious critical attention. No longer is it a wasteland of false motives and ponderous verse ... It now has a true verbal and emotional flow ... The whole has point and dynamic sensibility'[9]

As the company prepared to launch its fifth season in its out-of-the-way basement theatre, it could afford to take some pride in its achievements. Not only had it won high praise, it had done so primarily with original Canadian work. In the summer, it had won the Telegram Award for best Canadian play for *Before Compiègne*. And in September Nathan Cohen had included *Hey Rube!* in a list of all-Canadian theatre productions which he considered indisputably first class. Of the productions named – Ray Lawler's *The Summer of the Seventeenth Doll* and Chekhov's *Three Sisters* at the Crest, Molière's *Le malade imaginaire* and Brecht's *The Threepenny Opera* at the Théâtre du Nouveau Monde, *The Fantasticks* at the Red Barn, Tennessee Williams's *The Glass Menagerie* at the Neptune, and *Hey Rube!* – only the last was an original Canadian play.

7

Going Professional

The summer experience with Theatre 35 had convinced Luscombe that he must reach out to a popular audience, one unspoiled by exposure to 'bad' theatre and able to respond naturally, and that the kind of theatre he wanted to create could be produced only by professional actors able to devote all their time to the task. In May 1962, therefore, he and Jack Winter submitted a proposal to the Canada Council to establish a permanent company with a nucleus of six actors, whom he proposed to pay $50 a week. He estimated that, playing from August to March, the company would attract an average of 45 per cent attendance in their hundred-seat theatre, and that, with ticket prices at $1.50, they would face a deficit of about $16,500. Luscombe and Winter asked the Council to underwrite this anticipated deficit.[1]

In August, Luscombe learned that the Council had turned down his application but awarded him an individual arts grant of $4,000, for which he had not applied. What he did not know at the time was that the Council's decision, through an ironic turn of fate, had been influenced by the activities of his former partner, Tony Ferry. Alarmed by the precipitous collapse of the Civic Square Theatre, on which the Canada Council had risked a considerable investment, Peter Dwyer at the Council had made enquiries about the quality of the actors at Workshop Productions and had been told that they were 'not entirely professional.' Once burned, the Council decided to move more cautiously in their support of theatrical enterprises in Toronto.[2]

While the award was less than Luscombe and Winter had hoped for, it represented a mild vote of confidence in their work and enabled them to continue with unpaid actors to produce a season of two plays during 1962–3. In the spring of 1963, however, they approached the Council for

support for a more ambitious program. Their new proposal envisaged setting up a professional company of six actors and producing three new
shows a year. Each play would be rehearsed for ten to twelve weeks and
then played for about the same length of time. June and July would be
given over to revivals of the most successful productions of the season.
Such a program, they estimated, would run up a deficit of $10,800, and
they asked the Council to make them a grant of that amount to cover
their anticipated losses.[3]

While he waited for a reply from the Council, Luscombe conducted a
number of acting workshops in different parts of the province. Towards
the end of August, he returned to Toronto to the welcome news that the
Council had awarded Toronto Workshop Productions a grant of $3,600.
In a state of jubilation, Luscombe contacted Winter to tell him the news.
Once the initial euphoria had subsided, however, he began to consider
some of the implications of his new, state-subsidized status. As he reread
the Council letter more carefully, several facts began to trouble him. At
first the sum of $3,600 had seemed a welcome bonanza, but the amount
awarded was in fact just one-third of the sum he had requested. That
meant that the original plans, which had called for the year-round
employment of a core of professional actors, would have to be abandoned. The salaries he had budgeted for his actors were already minimal,
and it would be out of the question to reduce costs by cutting the
amounts any further. Furthermore, the grant was earmarked for the
production of a Canadian play, and it was evident that a professional production of Winter's work would consume the entire subvention. Consequently, the funds provided by the Canada Council would cover no more
than a third of the year.

Upon still closer examination, it appeared that the sum mentioned in
the letter was not an outright grant at all, but a basic grant of $1,800 plus
an equal amount payable only if the theatre was able to raise a matching
$1,800 from sources other than the box office. That meant that the ener-
gies of an already understaffed and overworked administration would
have to be stretched further in the search for alternative financing. While
these limitations were explained logically in terms of a decrease in funds
available to the Canada Council and the need for TWP to begin private
fund-raising, Luscombe felt that far from freeing his hands to devote his
full time to directing, the Council had, in Dr Johnson's phrase, merely
'encumbered him with help.'

Nevertheless, in spite of his reservations, the prospect of establishing a
fully professional acting company was too enticing to let slip. By Septem-

ber 1963, Luscombe was auditioning actors and negotiating with Actors' Equity to draw up a special studio contract. According to its terms, the actors would receive $30 a week during ten weeks of rehearsals and $50 a week for performances. After a series of auditions, Luscombe selected seven actors (Joan Maroney Ferry, Tony Moffat-Lynch [later replaced by Will Albert], Geraldine Douglas, James Beggs, Len Doncheff, Wilson West, and Larry Perkins), who became the first professional TWP company. Several members of the earlier troupe who failed to qualify as actors in the professional group agreed to stay on as volunteers. Sonja Livingston and Eleanor Beattie, both veterans of earlier Luscombe productions, agreed to do props, and Joe Hatt-Cook tried his hand at publicity. Brooky Robins, the young wife of a rising Toronto lawyer, offered to act as business manager.

In addition to these TWP veterans, the new company included four important newcomers whom Luscombe had met as a result of his summer teaching at the Quetico Centre in Atikokan, Ontario. John and June Faulkner were an English couple who had been active in Little Theatre in Atikokan. To allow more time for his theatrical interests, John had given up a job as surveyor with a steel company, turned to teaching, and worked for a year in an Indian school in the north. In Toronto, he got a position at a high school in Don Mills, but he spent all his spare time at the Fraser Avenue theatre, and after three and a half months he resigned to work full time for Luscombe at $25 a week.[4] Faulkner was quiet in manner and a genuine bohemian; described as the black sheep of an aristocratic English family,[5] he had spent a couple of summers with the circus in Sweden before coming to Canada. Passionately interested in the technical side of theatre and an artist of considerable ability, he brought a painter's eye to the art of stage lighting. His wife, June, as devoted to the theatre as her husband but forced by circumstances to spend most of her time supporting the family, helped where she could – washing floors, preparing publicity, and working in the office. A friend of the Faulkners', John Jowsey, who had also just come to Toronto to work for Ontario Hydro, was helping John with lighting. June suggested that Luscombe meet his wife, Nancy, a graduate of the Ontario College of Art who had worked with the New Play Society in the 1940s. Nancy Brown Jowsey had grown up in Toronto and moved to the Lakehead with her husband; now returned to Toronto with a young family, she wanted to get back into theatre as a designer. Luscombe asked her to do an inventory of the company's wardrobe and suggested that she prepare a few costume sketches for *Before Compiègne,* assuring her that there were 'hundreds' of volunteers to do the sewing.[6] That was the beginning of an artistic relationship that was to last for the next ten years.

By early 1964, with the production of *Before Compiègne*, the newly professional company could begin to savour its success. In the second week of January, Brooky Robins received a letter from the Province of Ontario Council for the Arts announcing a grant of $5,400, of which $3,600 was specifically intended to support the permanent company. The news meant that the company's future was more secure and that it would be possible to extend the run of their current production. When Luscombe broke the news to the actors, however, he was unable to get general agreement on the terms for a longer engagement. Upset by what he considered a lack of dedication and loyalty, he closed the show, fired the entire acting company, and resolved to begin again with a clean slate.

Early in February 1964, therefore, Luscombe held open auditions, which brought some seventy-five aspiring actors to the Fraser Avenue theatre. From them, Luscombe selected one-third to work with him for a month without pay or any guarantee of employment. At the end of that time, he chose seven actors (Victoria Mitchell, Gwen Thomas, Larry Perkins, Donald Meyers, Edward Kelly, Yvonne Adalian, and Edward Sanders), whom he offered two-month studio contracts. Then he began rehearsals for a revised version of *Before Compiègne*.

The four-week season at the Colonnade, an innovative apartment and shopping complex on Toronto's fashionable Bloor Street, was a cruel introduction to the realities of Toronto theatre economics. In spite of unprecedented publicity not only for the play but for the new Colonnade Theatre, audiences reached only about 33 per cent in the first week. They rose to 45 per cent in the third week, only to tail off again to less than 30 per cent. That even with their best-publicized production TWP could not attract more than a hundred spectators a night posed serious questions about the company's future. It was clear that their survival would depend on their ability to find outside support to supplement what they could earn at the box office.

In 1964, funding for arts organizations in Toronto came from three agencies: the federally supported Canada Council (founded in 1957), the Province of Ontario Council for the Arts (founded in 1963), and the Municipality of Metropolitan Toronto (grants first approved in 1956). During the early sixties, the most important figure determining grants policy was Peter Dwyer, arts officer for the Canada Council. Dwyer was an Oxford-educated civil servant who had come to the Council from a position on the Privy Council. He brought with him a passionate interest in the arts, a wide-ranging intelligence, a keen sense of fairness, but an essentially elitist faith in high culture and 'professional' standards. Dwyer's convictions were shared by other Council officers, and their views usually carried the day at Council meetings. Their influence was reflected in the Council policy of denying direct grants to amateur organizations and in a policy of reinforcing success – most usually in the dominant arts organizations in the country, such as the National Ballet, the Canadian Opera Company, the Toronto and Montreal symphonies, and the Stratford and Shaw festivals. Although not intended to be interventionist, such a policy, directing as it did the allocation of substantial sums of money, was to have a significant effect on the development of theatre in the country.

Nowhere was this truer than in Toronto, where, between 1962 and 1967, Council decisions (no doubt reflecting advice received from consultants in the city) literally transformed the local scene. Toronto theatrical life during the previous decade had been dominated by the touring shows playing the Royal Alexandra and the O'Keefe Centre (opened in 1960) and by the local productions of the Crest Theatre (founded in 1953). In the early sixties, this status quo came under attack from critics such as Nathan Cohen, who objected to the attempt of the Crest to impose an alien (British) aesthetic on Toronto audiences.[7] In an attempt to respond to such criticism, the Council had somewhat rashly awarded a grant of $10,000 to the Civic Square Theatre in 1961, only to see that organization collapse within a matter of months. Rather more dramatically, in 1964 the Council suddenly withdrew its support from the Crest Theatre, which action led directly to the demise of that company two years later. As Luscombe launched into the turbulent sea of public subsidy, he was to find out very quickly just how unpredictable were the winds of political favour.

Following the four-week run of *Before Compiègne* at the Colonnade, Luscombe and Winter prepared an application for a grant of $20,000 from the Canada Council to run a forty-four-week professional season in 1964–5. Their plans called for a season of three plays, *Before Compiègne*, *The Mechanic*, and a new work, *The Steambath*, all by Jack Winter. In addition, they intended to operate a theatre school.

In August 1964, members of the Council met to consider the request. They were informed that inquiries made in Toronto on behalf of the Council had suggested it might be impossible for Luscombe to contribute substantially to Canadian theatre because he 'found it difficult to come to terms with other members of his profession and could not be influential if he remained outside the mainstream.' Without naming the anonymous consultants, Dwyer accepted their basic assessment and reported to the Council that Luscombe's 'severe approach to the theatre may have served to limit the number of playwrights and actors who can cooperate with him and ... that there is a real danger of inbreeding in such a situation.'[8] Nevertheless, he noted that in the previous year the company had earned about 42 per cent of its budget from operating revenue and had financed the balance with grants and donations, leaving a relatively small deficit of $140. After some deliberation, the Council voted to award TWP a grant of $10,000.The news was communicated to the theatre on 17 August.

Once again, Luscombe's jubilation at receiving Council support was tempered by his awareness that the grant was only half of what he had asked for. Nevertheless, it represented a substantial increase over the previous year's subvention. With the expectation of a similar increase from the province, Luscombe decided to commit himself to a year-round operation. On the last day of August, he signed seven actors to annual contracts at $25 a week with two weeks of paid holidays. The studio contracts worked out with Equity allowed the performers to supplement their somewhat meagre guaranteed earnings with odd jobs in film or television.[9] But for the first time Luscombe could be assured that his actors would be able to spend most of their time at the Fraser Avenue theatre.

Paradoxically, the work of play development suddenly seemed to run into trouble. An adaptation of Woyzeck scheduled to open in the fall, a late addition to the program, was delayed until the new year, and the new Jack Winter plays (now identified as The Steambath and François) never materialized. Instead, after eight weeks of The Death of Woyzeck, the company was forced to revive Before Compiègne and play it in repertory with The Death of Woyzeck on weekends during March 1965. Attendance at these two productions (averaging 28 per cent and 25 per cent) was disappointing.[10] Undaunted by what they hoped would be a temporary set-back, in 1965 Luscombe and Winter approached the Canada and Ontario Arts councils with their most ambitious plans to date.

They proposed raising the basic salary of the actors to $75 a week and substantially increasing the publicity and administration budgets to allow for the hiring of professional staff. They suggested that the increase in the company's budget should be shared between the theatre and the grant-giving agencies. If the two councils would raise their operating grants to the theatre from $10,000 to $25,000, TWP would undertake to triple its box-office receipts (to $20,000, or 25 per cent of the budget) and double its fund-raising (to $10,000). In view of the fact that a recently appointed board had raised close to $5,000 in donations during the year, Luscombe and Winter felt reasonably optimistic that their appeal would receive a sympathetic hearing. They were to be bitterly disappointed.

When it came in September 1965, the Canada Council's award of $10,000 represented no increase at all over the previous year's grant. The decision to hold the company to that level of funding was based on the feeling that TWP had been less productive than expected and that too small a part of their budget (18 per cent) came from operating revenue. Unless these problems were addressed and the Council given clear evidence that TWP had increased its audience and improved its quality, Peter Dwyer informed the company, further assistance would not be provided.[11]

The response of the Province of Ontario Council for the Arts was even more discouraging. Not only was the total grant ($9,000) less than they had been awarded in the previous year, but it was restricted by crippling conditions. In his letter, after expressing disappointment at the low proportion of revenue coming from the box office and private fund-raising, the chairman went on to say that he hoped the award would serve as 'an impetus for [the company's] financial campaign.' To this end, he explained, the Council grant had been divided into two halves – $5,000 as an outright grant and $4,000 to become available when the theatre had raised $10,000 on its own.

From the perspective of the theatre, the grants seemed perverse. Not only had the councils denied them the resources necessary for hiring the personnel they needed (all the administrative staff were unpaid), but they had added to the workload of the theatre by imposing fund-raising conditions which were well beyond their present capability. To add insult to perceived injury, the letter accompanying the initial grant of $5,000 from the provincial agency informed the theatre that they considered themselves one of TWP's 'benefactors' and as such were most interested in future plans and aspirations.[12] Luscombe and Winter felt they had spelled out those aspirations fairly clearly, and wondered how it would be possible to persuade the cultural mandarins of the importance and difficulty of producing original Canadian rather than previously published plays.

The creation of a permanent, professional acting company, far from solving the theatre's difficulties, had in some ways compounded them. The discrepancy between 'professional' and volunteer staff was beginning to produce tensions in the company. Some means would have to be found to coordinate the creative efforts of the many talented people Luscombe had gathered around him.

8

Collaborative Creation II:
Woyzeck and *The Golem of Venice*

The early collaborative productions of the company – *Hey Rube!* and *The Mechanic* – had been very much orchestrated by George Luscombe. Working with amateur actors and an inexperienced writer, he had found it necessary to keep a fairly tight rein on the creative process. He had drawn on the imaginative contributions of his collaborators, but in most cases those contributions had been developed from his suggestions and incorporated into an overall structure of his devising. In the course of their experiments, the company had learned much about how to combine political ideas with stage images to create metaphors that were both arresting in themselves and symbolically suggestive. Sometimes, as in *Hey Rube!*, scenes of slapstick comedy or acrobatic expertise became emblematic, hinting at the discipline, alienation, and danger that are part of the life of any artist. At other times, the impersonation of inanimate objects such as an automobile, using nothing but the actors' physical ingenuity, conveyed a subtle social criticism.

During the early years, the company had also experimented profitably with the underlying structure of drama, searching for non-naturalistic narrative conventions that would enable them to distil or compress the essentials of plot as Laban had reduced the elements of movement in his identification of the pure 'efforts.' This distillation involved eliminating traditional narrative elements (as found in the novel and realistic drama) and substituting for them techniques borrowed from music and film, such as juxtaposition and contrast, rhythm and pattern. Abandoning the fairly straightforward storytelling method of *Hey Rube!*, the company had experimented in successive versions of *Before Compiègne*, taking the play apart and reassembling it in a number of different forms. In *The Mechanic*, the deconstruction of narrative plot was carried even further as the basic Molière story was displaced into the twentieth century and then broken apart as improvisations based on individual character types took the tale in unexpected directions.

Now that they had succeeded in recruiting a professional company, Luscombe and Winter were anxious to continue their journey of exploration. Both agreed that the function of drama was to communicate a truth about life in quintessentially *theatrical* terms, which meant reflecting the world not photographically but in a heightened, coloured, or distorted fashion. Turning their back on naturalism, Luscombe and Winter sought to return to the primitive origins of theatre.

Implicit in the idea that drama is sophisticated ritual or myth is the notion that the actors must rediscover the sources of their art in the deepest levels of their own unconscious. Luscombe believed that improvisation exercises could uncover truths about human nature and society. Both Luscombe and Winter were anxious to take advantage of the longer rehearsal periods now available with a professional company to explore those deeper strata of improvisation.

Their first opportunity came during rehearsals for *Woyzeck* in the fall of 1964. Several months earlier, Luscombe had received a script about prison life in the Guelph reformatory called *Fortune and Men's Eyes*. The play, by John Herbert, was obviously very powerful, but its stark realism was foreign to the theatre's style, and Luscombe felt personally uncomfortable with the homosexual theme. Eager to develop Canadian writers, however, he had suggested that Herbert prepare an adaptation of *Woyzeck* for his consideration. To his surprise, the script arrived on his desk one day in the summer. He decided to use it as his opening production for the 1964–5 season.

Rehearsals for the new version of the Buchner play, to be called *The World of Woyzeck*, got under way in September. Luscombe began by breaking the script into units and taking the actors through improvisations. When he asked Herbert to incorporate some of the dialogue from these improvisations into the play, however, Herbert refused. His response, combined with Luscombe's increasing dissatisfaction with the realism of the piece and the 'cursing and swearing that meant no more than it said,'[1] gave rise to an atmosphere of tension in the theatre – tension that was only heightened by the silent, morose presence of Jack Winter during rehearsals.

In November, to assess the progress of their work, the company staged a week of unpaid and unreviewed previews.[2] Following one of these, Winter and Luscombe retired to a pub, where Winter persuaded his colleague that the work was taking the company in the wrong direction and that he could do a better job of adaptation. When Luscombe told Herbert he was turning the script over to Winter, Herbert threatened to sue the company if they used any of his work. Undeterred, Luscombe decided to scrap everything they had done so far and start anew.

The new version, which he and Winter produced with the actors over the next six weeks, proved to be one of the company's most radical experiments. Nancy Jowsey redesigned the costumes and properties in a non-realistic style, and Luscombe and Winter broke up and rearranged the sequence of the scenes. Whereas previously they had seen Woyzeck in political terms as the victim of social oppression, now they became preoccupied by the themes of sexual passion and jealousy. What emerged from the new improvisations was a series of startling sexual images often expressed in animalistic symbolism. To link these images, Luscombe and Winter employed a circus motif reminiscent of *Hey Rube!*, alternating scenes from Buchner's play with carnivalesque episodes in what they called 'Lechery Fair.' Characters were sometimes transformed into puppets or animals, and the seduction of Marie by the Major was presented as the mating dance of a couple of birds.

The play, now called *The Death of Woyzeck*, finally opened on 9 January 1965 and played three nights a week to almost universally mystified audiences. Many found the vision of the production, the world as freak show, unduly bleak and failed to grasp the satire. Luscombe had once again in his own mind associated the Doctor's treatment of Woyzeck with the horrors of the Nazi scientific experiments on Jews in the concentration camps. But he refused to explain this in program notes, feeling that the play had to communicate on its own terms. That it failed to do so is, perhaps, scarcely surprising. Many of the scenes, such as those in the tavern, which had given so much humanity and colour to the first version, had been eliminated. In their place, Luscombe had introduced action that was as far from simple realism as imaginable. In some cases, he would have an actor step outside a role to act as circus barker, commenting on the actions of other characters. At other times, he experimented with sound and movement in an almost abstract way.

Some of these novelties intrigued the critics. Ronald Evans found 'quite brilliant' a moment when 'the whole company forms a chorus of creaks, peeps, groans and hiccups while the hero bounces tentatively up and down on the stage.' He also praised Yvonne Adalian and Larry Perkins for their 'mad mating dance' and Victoria Mitchell for her 'marvellous mime interpretation of a skitterish performing horse.' But he objected to the fact that 'none of these impressive turns does a thing to advance the action or reveal character.' He compared the production, which he described as 'an enormous torrent of baffling words and bewildering action,' to a modern painting, lashed and spattered with dark streams of colour, giving an immediate impact but defying pattern or purpose.[3] Like Evans, Nathan Cohen admired certain aspects of the production – the fusion of mime and erotica in Victoria Mitchell's astronomical horse, the carnival setting, and the physical virtuosity and vigour of the actors. But, as a committed socialist, he objected to the fatalism of the piece, which he described as an 'amorphous, chichi dirge of resignation.'[4]

If Toronto critics familiar with Luscombe's work were perplexed, out-of-town journalists were totally baffled. The Montreal critic Don Bell thought the production an example of the absurdity 'abstraction in the theatre has led us [to].' Apparently quite unfamiliar with (or unsympathetic to) experimental movements in European theatre in the twentieth century, Bell thought the cast had not memorized the lines and was improvising them during performance. In spite of, or perhaps because of, his incomprehension, however, Bell gives a vivid account of the style of the production: 'As the play opens, seven figures, four male and three female, trot out on the stage. To the background of regimental marching music, they chirp like birds, squeal, grunt, perform short erotic dances, assume various yoga-like positions, sometimes make utterances on the predicament of mankind. But every scrap of dialogue is an isolated entity, bearing little or no communion with the dialogue immediately before or after it.'[5]

Only Herbert Whittaker retained faith in Luscombe's theatrical investigations, comparing his development to that of Ingmar Bergman in his 'extraordinarily personal group of films.' He recognized that, in such a 'vivid, non-representational creation for the stage,' 'sequence means nothing, atmosphere and satirical comment are all.' He also understood that the style made no concessions to the audience and recognized that the spectators would have found it easier to follow the play if they had been given a rough outline of the plot. But while Whittaker also found the evening puzzling and felt that he missed the significance of some of the stage imagery and dialogue, he thought it 'a fascinating world in which to dip.' Far from dismissing Luscombe's efforts as perverse or wrong-headed, Whittaker thought that *The Death of Woyzeck* showed the director 'at his most creative, most integrated and most experimental ... our only true experimentalist.'[6]

When the 1964–5 season ended in mid-April, the company immediately began working to develop new plays for its repertoire. This time, however, instead of basing their improvisations on an existing script they resolved to explore their own concerns and to let the shape of the work emerge naturally from those explorations. Very soon the difficulties inherent in such a method became apparent. Chief among them was the conflicting interests of the various parties involved. Winter, a Jew, was intrigued by prejudice and its intimate connection with religion; Luscombe, equally fascinated with anti-semitism, of which he had seen plenty in the East York of his childhood, tended to be more interested in the political than the religious dimensions of the problem.[7] The actors, disturbed by stories of bigotry and race riots from the American South and by Western intervention in Vietnam, wanted to trace the roots of violence and racism in their own human nature. Not surprisingly, the company improvisations began to move in different directions. One of these took the actors to an examination of class. Improvisations focused on a steambath, one of the few places where prejudice based on clothing and status does not exist. The steambath suggested to some the horrors of the Nazi death camps, where prisoners were lured to their death with the false reassurance that they were simply being taken for a shower, and led to improvisations on the holocaust. The idea of prejudice prompted a consideration of the contempt being manifest for 'Asiatic human beings' by white forces in Vietnam. In an effort to identify more deeply with the 'enemy,' the company improvised scenes of rural life involving singing songs and working in rice paddies.[8]

Another direction led to the origins of religion. The actors created a primitive tribal society in which the children asked the elders to describe the origin of life. Among the creation myths narrated was one dealing with the differentiation of the races: it told how God had failed in his early attempts to make man from baked clay; only on his third attempt, after producing a burnt black man and an undercooked white man, did God finally achieve his purpose – a golden-yellow human being. Another creation story was from Jewish folklore; it focused on the making of a protector, a 'golem,' who would defend the Jews against their enemies. Gradually, these two stories were combined into a series of ritualistic quests for the purified ingredients (earth, air, fire, and water) necessary for the construction of a defending champion. The various elements became identified with different kinds of movement as expressed through the 'efforts.' Individual actors would lead the improvisations of the separate quests, sometimes with genuine enthusiasm but often with no understanding of where the exercise was leading.[9]

While Luscombe stimulated the performers, providing a context for their work, Winter would make notes of the actors' improvised dialogue. But as the weeks went by, the process seemed to break down. As Luscombe subsequently explained, 'The writing not only failed to keep up with the work on stage, but every attempt to extend the work of the actors into language failed.'[10] When it became apparent that the company's efforts were going nowhere, Luscombe decided to abandon the project in order to prepare *The Mechanic* and *Before Compiègne* for a two-week season in the park at Stratford.

It was 1966, almost a year, before Luscombe and Winter could resume their exploratory work, and when they did it was with an entirely new company. Most of the members of the first professional group had left at the end of the 1965–6 season either in disillusionment or in a move to fresh theatrical pastures such as the newly created Neptune Theatre in Halifax. Their departure had necessitated the auditioning and training of a whole new company of actors, who had to be rehearsed in the repertoire for the 1966 'Theatre-in-the-Park' season in Stratford. Under pressure from the Canada Council, that season was supposed to include a new play.

To give shape to the material developed the previous spring, Luscombe and Winter decided to use the trial scene from *The Merchant of Venice* as a foundation. In constructing their own play about commerce and prejudice, however, they altered their source in the same way they had distorted the plots of Molière's *L'amour médecin* and Buchner's *Woyzeck*. Antonio, the merchant, became a poor tailor; Shylock, the moneylender, was reduced to an indigent pawnbroker; and the Duke of Venice became a spokesman for the city's commercial interests. Portia, in addition to being the chief prosecutor of Shylock, became a champion of the Christian church. Into the Shakespearean framework, Winter introduced two Jewish rabbis, representing Eastern and Western Judaism, along with the story of the golem.

Winter thought of the play as a companion piece to *Before Compiègne* (it was set at about the same time) and as a vehicle for his own sardonic views about the hypocrisy of religions and the triumph of naked self-interest. But Luscombe was primarily interested in the theatricality of the piece and resolute that it should not become a soapbox. Indeed, so determined was Luscombe on this point that the lines were sometimes cut to the point where they were obscure even to the actors. Those who sought out Winter for clarification of his intention had to do so in secret to avoid offending Luscombe, who would have been furious if he had known.[11] As the play took shape, Nancy Jowsey helped to establish the tone of the production through her fanciful designs. She devised a sort of fairy-tale setting consisting of a huge book with elastic pages from which the characters entered into the play. The stage was strewn with large children's alphabetical blocks, and the costumes suggested a combination of Mother Goose and outer space.[12] Characteristic of Jowsey's work was a witty use of materials, such as metal pot scrubbers as wigs. The tone of the whole was underlined by the incorporation of nursery rhymes sung to the accompaniment of a glockenspiel.

The play, entitled simply *The New Show*, premièred in Stratford on 16 July 1966. Critical response was mixed. Nathan Cohen thought the company by far the strongest and most personable Luscombe had ever assembled. He welcomed what he saw as a move away from a 'misguided theatricality' and credited Winter's influence for the company's 'fresh awareness of the value of language.' He felt *The New Show* was the first work since *Hey Rube!* to have a 'genuinely radical temper.'[13]

Work on *The New Show* was discontinued following the Stratford season while the company mounted a revival of *Hey Rube!* to open its 1966–7 season. Once that play was launched, however, Luscombe and Winter returned to the production, which both fascinated and baffled them. In Stratford, one of the highlights of the play had been Len Doncheff's performance as the rather feckless tailor, Antonio. When Doncheff left the company in the fall, instead of recasting the role as written, Winter and Luscombe transformed the part into that of Antonio's widow and gave it to Milo Ringham.

Winter's bitterly ironic view of religion is communicated in the play by a series of outrageous paradoxes. He intersperses scenes derived from Shakespeare with others recounting the creation of a golem by two of Shylock's visiting friends, Rabbi Joseph, fleeing from the Spanish Inquisition, and Rabbi Gerontius, a wealthy Jew from Constantinople. When news of their success in creating the powerful defender reaches the court, Portia and the Magnifico (standing in for Shakespeare's Duke) join in the enterprise for their own benefit. The discussion among these four about how their new-made Frankenstein should be used constitutes a bitter satire on the way in which self-interest and realpolitik subvert ideology. Rabbi Joseph wishes to employ the golem to destroy the Inquisition, while the Christian Portia proposes to set up her own secular Inquisition in Venice, with the golem as Grand Inquisitor, to destroy the foreign investors who threaten to undermine Venice's commercial supremacy. She also suggests that the destructive power of the golem might be tested by directing it at the Jewish ghetto in what she describes as a 'slum clearing project.'

A problem that plagued the development of the work was uncertainty about the symbolic significance of the golem itself, thought of in general terms as a force for good or evil which ultimately turns against its creators. Originally associated with money or the economic system, it gradually became identified with nuclear power. Relatively late in rehearsals, Winter and Luscombe introduced broadcast speeches of the American nuclear physicist J. Robert Oppenheimer and General Groves of the Manhattan project to link the creation of the golem with the building of the atom bomb.

When *The Golem of Venice* finally opened in Toronto on 17 March 1967, it attracted little attention. Only Herbert Whittaker from the major papers attended the première, and he found the revised production a disappointment. 'One senses a schism,' he wrote, 'between directorial and writing achievement. Sometimes the playwright and director seem almost in opposition ... One wishes Winter would trust his audience more and allow the play's perspective – linking his Venice and our world – to develop without the electronic nudge [of speeches through the loudspeakers]. His writing is already so staccato and involuted that we would welcome more opportunity to concentrate on it.'[14] He disliked what he called the 'bodiless documentary commentary' derived from Oppenheimer's writings and testimony and failed to see (or at least comment on) the relationship it implied between Hiroshima and the holocaust. The general public was equally puzzled; most spectators felt that the passion which lay behind the work had not been moulded into a coherent form.

The experience of working on the development of *The Golem of Venice* had been something of a strain on all members of the company. Under pressure, Luscombe could be demanding and ruthless. His obsession with the work often made him oblivious to the concerns and feelings of others, with the result that he frequently, though unintentionally, gave offence and caused suffering. During the long gestation period of *The Golem*, tensions between Luscombe and the actors, and even more between Luscombe and Winter, had reached such a point that by the end of the process Luscombe and Winter were scarcely speaking to one another. In the spring, Winter announced that he was leaving the company, and Luscombe realized he would have to find other ways of forging drama out of the disparate elements of gesture and language.

9

The Search for Audiences

A paradox of Luscombe's method of creating plays was that while he steadily professed an interest in reaching a popular or working-class audience, his style of theatre effectively precluded his doing so. However vehemently he might insist on the political orientation of his work, the fact was that the immediate relevance of the plays was sometimes opaque. If Nathan Cohen could appreciate the 'radical temper' of *The Golem of Venice*, the majority of spectators who sat through that obscure production were at a loss to see a connection between its convoluted narrative and stereotypical characters and their own lives. The very experimental techniques that appealed to sophisticated theatre lovers and left-leaning intellectuals proved an obstacle to the cultivation of a genuinely untutored public. It is an irony of history that, like Meyerhold and Vakhtangov, the Russian experimentalists he admired, Luscombe was to be overshadowed in the 1970s by Canada's own version of socialist realism.

The decline of TWP was many years in the future, but there were some who foresaw the danger in the mid-sixties. Although Nathan Cohen had the highest hopes for the company, he felt that it was failing to realize its potential. 'No other organization in Canada,' Cohen wrote, 'is as fundamentally political in the broad sense. If it took hold ... it could become a truly liberating force. It could open up a vast new world of experience for a genuinely new audience [and] ... force the playgoer to reexamine his society and its values.'[1] He felt that TWP should be going into areas where people were unaware of theatre; they should be organizing regular meetings and exhibitions or mounting 'prickly new interpretations of the classics.' Instead, the company seemed to Cohen to be drawing 'virtually all of its support from the people [they] least want to reach: that sliver of middle class Torontonians of the professional and academic class, who always go to the theatre and who are ever ready to cheer what seems to be socially or aesthetically revolutionary so long as it is rarefied and not publically dangerous.' Luscombe was all too aware of the problem, but it was not as easily resolved as Cohen implied.

The difficulty was getting the proper people into the proper setting. It was not simply a matter of taking plays into a working-class environment. Luscombe had turned down the opportunity to set up a union-sponsored theatre to tour factories for the same reasons that Ewan MacColl had abandoned performing at factory gates: it was impossible to create the requisite circle of enchantment in such uncontrolled circumstances. He had to acknowledge, however, that he had failed to attract a working-class audience into his theatre at 47 Fraser Avenue. He had discovered, as Joan Littlewood had before him, that moving into a working-class neighbourhood does not guarantee that the locals will come to your door.

The company's most consistent effort to reach new audiences took place in Stratford, where TWP organized a series of summer programs which they called 'Theatre-in-the-Park.' The plan was launched on a trial basis in July 1964, with two performances of *Before Compiègne* given free of charge before an audience of passersby not far from the Festival Theatre. The experiment proved successful enough to encourage Luscombe to undertake a more extended program the following year. In January 1965, Brooky Robins began making enquiries about renting the Avon Theatre for the purpose. The negotiations were unsuccessful, but following a suggestion by the Stratford Festival general manager, Victor Polley, the company secured the use of the Sea Cadet building on the shore of the Avon River.

Meanwhile, Nancy Jowsey began to consider the problem of how to mark out a suitable playing space for the performances. Taking her inspiration from primitive 'booth stages,' Jowsey created a complex of three small tent pavilions with scalloped fringes and fluttering pennants which could provide entrances to, and a background for, an open playing space. The stage itself was a platform raised about two feet off the ground, providing sufficient height for the actors to be easily seen by the audience, seated in stacking chairs on the surrounding grass. The whole design had a distinctly medieval or fairground atmosphere appropriate to *Before Compiègne* and the commedia dell'arte character of *The Mechanic.*

In spite of their gay pavilion theatre, however, TPW's first Stratford season proved less successful than they had hoped. The weather was unseasonably damp (two performances had to be called off because of rain), and audiences were small (averaging only about twenty spectators per performance).[2] Some of the actors disliked playing outdoors, feeling that the inevitable distractions of busy park life made a profitable actor-audience relationship impossible. The combination of inclement weather and indifferent crowds proved fatal to the theatre's hopes, and the season lost a considerable amount of money.[3]

Following the financial failure of their 1965 Theatre-in-the-Park season, TWP approached Victor Polley with a request that the Festival include information about their outdoor performances with the regular Stratford promotional material. Polley and the artistic director, Michael Langham, agreed to distribute TWP's material along with their own and even undertook to sell tickets to their productions through the Festival box office. Luscombe therefore had every reason to feel optimistic about the prospects for the next season, which he scheduled to run for four weeks.

The company that assembled in Stratford in July 1966 was one of the strongest Luscombe had developed. Most of the actors stayed in the Fryfogel Inn, near the village of Shakespeare, but some made other arrangements. Len Doncheff slept in the tent until forbidden to do so by the Stratford parks board, and Douglas Livingston played piano and organ at the Dominion Hotel to help subsidize his accommodation there. Luscombe, his wife, Mona, and their two small daughters slept in a trailer in the park. During the summer, they were visited by members of a local circus, who were so impressed by Doncheff's performance as Pandro in *Hey Rube!* that they invited him to take part in their show.[4] In many respects, that Stratford season seemed like the culmination of the company's efforts, the final justification of what they were trying to do.

The actors gave two performances a day, at eleven in the morning and two-thirty in the afternoon, but day after day most of the three hundred chairs they had rented from the board of education remained empty. The promotion of the productions through the Festival's mailing list had produced no more than fifteen tickets per performance in advance sales. The company's own publicity had been curtailed, partly through lack of funds and partly because June Faulkner was not able to help out during the summer. Nancy Jowsey, in addition to her responsibilities as designer, doubled as publicist. On days when *The Mechanic* was performed, Douglas Livingston tried to attract attention on his way to the tent theatre by riding a child's tricycle through the park with his tuba on his back. The jaunty pavilion and the gaily costumed actors attracted crowds of curious children and contemptuous motorcycle gangs, but relatively few paying customers. By the end of the season, including the three mornings they had been rained out, Mona Luscombe, as box-office manager, reported total sales of 2,558, or an average of 17 per cent attendance. Against income of $4,303, she recorded expenses of over $7,000, so that the loss on the summer operation was almost $3,000.

Disappointed but still convinced of the long-range value of the Stratford season, Luscombe resolved to extend the program to six weeks the following year. But developments prior to their opening highlighted how crucially important it is for a company to have complete control over the environment in which it plays. When TWP began negotiations for the 1967 season, they were told that the Sea Cadet building by the river was unavailable, and in spite of interventions on the company's behalf by Victor Polley the parks board failed to come up with a suitable alternative. The only building they were able to rent was the Optimist Club House, located close to the Exhibition Hall on Nile Street.[5] As a result, TWP's 'Theatre-in-the-Park' was reduced to something more like a theatre in the parking lot. The Optimist Club refused to grant them permission to operate a coffee shop on the premises, and the board of education told them that the chairs they had rented in the past would not be available. Noise from passing cars and motorcycles, dust from the road, and rain all contributed to a disastrous season. In a final reckoning, June Faulkner estimated that, in the three years they had played in Stratford, the company had lost close to $15,000.[6] Clearly, the attempt to reach a new audience in Stratford had been a failure.

Much more successful were the company's efforts to arrange for performances for young people in Toronto itself. Luscombe had attempted to interest the City of Toronto Department of Parks and Recreation in sponsoring performances by the company as early as 1963, but it was not until three years later, in 1966, that that body finally agreed to underwrite two free performances in Nathan Phillips Square, in front of the new City Hall. The first of these, a performance of *Hey Rube!*, took place on a Sunday afternoon, on the stage designed for Stratford, before an estimated fifteen hundred spectators.[7] In that setting, much of the play's drama got lost in the vast acoustical voids of the plaza, but the *Star* critic Arthur Zeldin felt the 'play's theatricality gleamed like a jewel.'[8]

The success of the public performances convinced Luscombe that the audience he was trying to reach existed if only he could find a way to bring them to his plays. But getting Mohammed to come to the mountain seemed even more difficult than moving the mountain to Mohammed. Nor was the nature of the difficulty at all obvious. The Fraser Avenue theatre had many disadvantages. It was small and dingy and far from the centre of the city. Nevertheless, the company had not done significantly better business in the new Colonnade Theatre, located in the very heart of fashionable Toronto. Increasingly, however, the limitations of 47 Fraser Avenue were being brought home to Luscombe and his colleagues. The Canada Council had expressed concern about the modest audience figures the theatre had reported, and was beginning to suggest that continued support would depend on the expansion of that audience.[9] It was daily becoming more apparent that the company would ultimately have to find a larger, more centrally located theatre.

Accordingly, Luscombe and June Faulkner began to scour the city. They looked at several warehouses, one or two churches, and a synagogue on Spadina Avenue that appealed to Luscombe because of the working-class history of the area.[10] Then Faulkner remembered watching a rehearsal of the Canadian Players in a building off Yonge Street north of Carlton and took Luscombe to look at it. Originally a hardware store, it had been cut up into 'studio' spaces by temporary partitions. If these could be cleared out, the space available would be just adequate for the construction of a stage and small auditorium, with cramped but adequate dressing-room facilities at the rear. Its location – 12 Alexander Street, between the high-toned ambience of Carman's restaurant to the east and the burgeoning sex shops and body-rub parlours of the Yonge Street strip – was ideal. What better place – just a musket-shot from the home of William Lyon Mackenzie – to conduct a theatrical campaign against the bastions of power and privilege?

Sitting in Luscombe's car outside the building on a September evening in 1967, Luscombe and Faulkner considered their alternatives. The Council's support had been contingent on their finding a larger theatre, and their experience at 47 Fraser Avenue reinforced their opinion that they could not survive and grow in such small quarters. Of course, they had absolutely no money – but that meant they had nothing to lose. So although they had no idea where they would find the necessary funds, they hesitated only briefly before deciding to take out a lease.[11]

Next, they had to consider the design of the new space. Luscombe had become fully committed to the thrust stage, but few architects or builders had experience with such theatres. Then they remembered Gerald Robinson, who had designed the Colonnade Theatre. Robinson expressed great interest in the project, and he agreed to design the theatre for nothing in consultation with Luscombe and John Faulkner. Preliminary estimates indicated that the cost of the undertaking would be in the neighbourhood of $25,000.

At the end of November, John Faulkner began dismantling the partitions in the Alexander Street building in preparation for redesigning its interior. By 2 December, he and his crew had cleared the warehouse back to its walls to reveal a cavernous space covered by a steel-trussed roof. With the help of the architect, the company located a contractor who, once he had ascertained that TWP was supported by government grants, was willing to proceed with the work without an initial down payment. The design called for an open stage backed by two levels of dressing-rooms on one side and a costume room on the other. In front of the stage would be a steeply raked set of bleacher-like seats with the two ends bent around the thrust stage. Two control booths were to be built into the upper corners of the auditorium from which sound and light operators would have a full view of the stage. In what had at one time been a windowed showroom at the front of the building, the architect had designed a box office, two public washrooms, and an administrative office for the theatre staff.[12] Work on the renovations to 12 Alexander Street proceeded at a hectic pace through December. John Faulkner put in twelve- and fourteen-hour days, running the lighting for the production at Fraser Avenue at night and labouring through the day to get the new theatre ready for an opening in late December. Meanwhile, the actors were spending equally long hours rehearsing the second production of the season.

Had members of the company had leisure to reflect on their situation, they might have been struck by a number of paradoxes. In many Canadian cities, such as Vancouver, Winnipeg, and Halifax, theatre was thriving. The Vancouver Playhouse had some six thousand subscribers and had just opened George Ryga's highly successful *The Ecstasy of Rita Joe*; Winnipeg's Manitoba Theatre Centre continued to attract strong support for its program and had included Ann Henry's *Lulu Street* in its Centennial year schedule; Halifax's Neptune Theatre was touring Canada with a highly acclaimed production of Synge's *The Playboy of the Western World* and a less admired Canadian play by Arthur Murphy entitled *The Sleeping Bag*. Elsewhere, Canadian dramatists were receiving new recognition, partly through the requirement that the 1967 Dominion Drama Festival be made up entirely of Canadian plays and partly through the production of a Centennial play sponsored by the Centennial Commission.

By contrast, the situation in Toronto was chaotic. A variety of amateur and semi-professional companies competed for the theatre spaces available, and all those in different ways seemed either inadequate or unaffordable. The O'Keefe Centre and the Royal Alexandra Theatre were booked almost entirely by imported productions; medium-sized theatres such as the Crest and the Bayview Playhouse stood empty as the combined Crest–Canadian Players organization tried to resurrect itself from the ashes of its financial collapse; pocket theatres such as the Colonnade, the Poor Alex, the Central Library, and the Hydro Theatre played host to assorted, usually short-lived, producing organizations.

Fresh from a trip to Europe, where he had found cities of comparable size supporting three and four professional theatres, Nathan Cohen was struck anew by the shortage of theatre facilities in Canada's most populous and prosperous English-speaking city. Because of this shortage, he complained, the city had missed out on many of the attractions available during the Centennial year, including touring productions by the Neptune, Théâtre du Nouveau Monde, Holiday Theatre, and Roland Petit Ballet as well as the Manitoba Theatre Centre's production of Brecht's *Galileo*.[13] The shortage was compounded by the destruction by fire of the Hydro Theatre in August and by the protracted deliberations of the Toronto Arts Foundation, which continued to mire the St Lawrence Centre for the Arts in controversies and delay. Conceived as a Centennial project to house a world-class repertory company, the Centre was still two years from completion.

In the atmosphere of uncertainty, jealousy, and competing aesthetics which was the Toronto theatre scene, Luscombe stood alone. He had created a fully professional company of some twenty members whom he employed between forty and fifty-two weeks a year; he had introduced Toronto theatre-goers to an entirely new repertoire, Canadian as well as European; and he had a very clear notion of the role he thought theatre should play in life and the way TWP would fill that role. He also had a growing sense of alienation from the mainstream and a conviction that whenever the St Lawrence Centre was completed, TWP would not be asked to be the resident company.

As December drew to a close, therefore, it became increasingly imperative in Luscombe's mind to make a gesture that would establish the presence and the nature of his company. The newly formed Theatre Toronto under its imported artistic director, Clifford Williams, was preparing to launch its first season in the Royal Alex. It had chosen as its opening production an English version of a Canadian play written in French by Jean Basile about life in eighteenth-century Quebec entitled *The Drummer Boy*. Resolved to upstage the new manifestation of what he expected would be nothing but a reincarnation of traditional, British-inspired, colonial Toronto theatre, Luscombe determined to open his own new show before the end of the year. Construction continued through Christmas week, but by 30 December the theatre was still not finished. Nevertheless, Luscombe led his actors into the incomplete facilities, where on New Year's Eve, 1967, they gave their first performance in what was to be their permanent home.

10

Political Entertainment:
Mr Bones

It was a small band of loyal followers who struggled through one of the worst snowstorms of the winter to attend the New Year's Eve preview at Toronto Workshop Productions' new theatre. Picking their way through a still unfinished lobby, spectators mounted a flight of steps which brought them to the top of a steeply raked auditorium. The seating extended the full width of the auditorium and was arranged in a three-segmented arc around a protruding thrust stage. No curtain or proscenium arch separated the playing space from the auditorium, so the actors and audience shared the same overarching space. The gloom of the black-painted auditorium was relieved by the light reflected from the brightly coloured setting, already in full view on the stage. That setting consisted of an elevated chair surrounded by a number of boxes painted in red, white, and blue stripes. As the audience grew quiet with anticipation, they were suddenly assaulted by the sounds of guitars, banjos, and tambourines as the performers surged onto the stage in a dazzling burst of colour and movement.[1]

The production with which the company had chosen to open their new theatre was called *Gentlemen Be Seated*, and it was the result of nearly three years of collaborative effort going back to the spring of 1965. Inspired by concern about the Vietnam war, the arms race, and the civil rights movement in the American South, the group had attempted to explore the roots of race prejudice. Their improvisations had focused on two main areas, anti-semitism and the hostility between whites and blacks. The first of these subjects had been developed in *The Golem of Venice*; the second, through several stages, in the present work – a sort of documentary-political-historical-minstrel show.

Early in the evolution of the work, Luscombe had decided to use the

American minstrel show as an informing theatrical metaphor. The original minstrels were black troubadours, social outcasts who entertained their audiences with a combination of music and political commentary. The central characters in every improvisation were Mr Tambo (the middleman), Mr Bones (the radical), and Mr Jethro (the conservative). In their skits, they argued current social or political questions with a sardonic attitude to their self-appointed friends as well as to their acknowledged class enemies.[2]

White imitators of the minstrels perverted its original intention, reducing it to a hideous lampoon in which the black culture was caricatured by performers in black face. The conventional form of this white minstrel show was a three-part sequence in which crosstalk, music, and skits alternated. The principal role was played by a central figure called Mr Interlocutor who acted as master of ceremonies, engaged in comic exchanges with two end men, Mr Tambo and Mr Bones, and generally supervised the rest of the entertainers. This hybrid form, one of the few indigenous American theatrical genres, seemed the perfect vehicle with which to trace the escalating violence of the civil rights movement to its roots in the reconstruction period following the Civil War.

The earliest version of the play drew parallels between the character relationships in the conventional minstrel show and the history of the Civil War. Mr Interlocutor became Abraham Lincoln, and the minstrels represented the slave population of the South. In the early improvisations, a running plot involving various schemes on the part of a number of assassins to do away with Lincoln was alternated with scenes of the President with his wife and members of his cabinet. The original plan called for the action to be confined to a single day, 14 April 1865, during which Lincoln's activities would be traced until his death at Ford's Theatre that evening. This action would be complemented physically by the gradual construction during the play of the theatre box in which Lincoln would finally watch the show (the minstrels) and in which he would be shot. The work was thought of, therefore, as a self-referential structure in which the theatre itself brought together 'real life' and its distorted representation in a complex performance metaphor.

Early in the play's evolution, however, it became apparent that Winter and Luscombe had different ideas about how the work should be developed. Winter's researches turned up a wealth of interesting details about southern bigotry and about the lives of the major figures which he wanted to include in the story. But Luscombe was interested in getting beyond the private fate of the individual. Like Piscator, he believed that 'feelings

must be pressed into service as evidence to support our world view.'[3] Luscombe found that the more individualized the characters became, the
more they were confined to their own period. Accordingly, he wanted to
shift the focus away from the characters' private lives and onto the parallels between the assassination of Lincoln and that of President Kennedy.
In that way, he hoped to compel the audience to see the contemporary
relevance of the historical events.

By the fall of 1966, the script had reached its final form as a minstrel
show with scenes dealing alternately with the schemes of the assassins
and the frustration of their plots through luck or accident. A serious
weakness in the work was that it provided no clear motivation for the
assassination, which was presented not as the act of a demented individual but as part of a mysterious conspiracy being directed from above
through rather cryptic sealed orders. Not improbably, the development
of these scenes grew out of a conviction on the part of the writer and
director that history was a product of economic forces rather than personal grievances. But by the time Winter gave up work on the project,
no satisfactory way had been found to link the operation of those forces
in 1865 with their role in the civil rights movement and the Kennedy
assassination a hundred years later. The necessary connection was provided by Jan Carew.

On his return from Stratford in August 1967, Luscombe was anxious to
find a replacement for Winter, who had resigned in the spring of that
year. He arranged a meeting with several writers interested in working in
the theatre. Among those who attended a gathering at his house were
Tony Ferry, Len Peterson, Hugh Webster, Michael John Nimchuk, Austin
Clark, and Jan Carew. Carew was a West Indian writer living and teaching
in Toronto who had established a reputation as a novelist. But he had little experience of the theatre, and nothing had prepared him for his
encounters with Luscombe and the actors at TWP.

Working with the material left by Winter, Carew introduced the figure
of Thaddeus Stevens, a radical Republican who had advocated sweeping
reforms following the defeat of the Confederate states. Arguing that freeing the slaves would be futile unless the blacks were given the means to
support themselves, Stevens advocated the confiscation and redistribu-
tion of southern property. By giving prominence to Stevens's opinions,
Carew was able to portray Lincoln as something of a reactionary and to
show more clearly how his refusal to take difficult decisions in 1865 had
simply postponed the inevitable. Thus, not peace but escalating black violence was the real legacy of Lincoln's failure of nerve. By implication, the

solution today was the same as the solution then – the repudiation of compromise and the final empowerment of the blacks.

Carew was totally taken aback by the way in which his work was freely adapted and changed in the process of rehearsal. Luscombe's technique was to determine what a scene could not do without and then eliminate almost everything else.[4] Sometimes this technique had the virtue of tightening the action and pruning unnecessary exposition. But Luscombe's conviction that an actor was often the most reliable guide to the emotional heart of a scene tended to distress writers. It is said that after the opening-night performance, Carew was so angry at what had been done to his script that he stormed into the TWP office and tore up the phone book.[5]

Sometimes, Luscombe's success in making action speak louder than words was electrifying; he could sum up in a gesture or sound what would seem laboured or too explicit in dialogue. At other times, however, he simply obscured the meaning. Such was the case with the ending of this play. Presumably, the assassination of Lincoln by John Wilkes Booth, played by a minstrel, was intended as a kind of theatrical endorsation of black militancy. In performance, however, the murder was highly stylized. Instead of being shot in the back of the head, Lincoln was invited to join the minstrels in their concluding dance. When he did so, his place in the box beside Mrs Lincoln was taken by a silent and impassive Booth. The implied conversion of white liberal opinion (Lincoln) to the cause of black power was neatly symbolized by this bit of choreography.

In the show that finally opened at 12 Alexander Street on New Year's Eve, the actor who played Mr Interlocutor and Lincoln was dressed in a black frock coat and sat centre stage during much of the action like a copy of the Lincoln Memorial. The minstrels were dressed in white jump suits decorated with black stars and stripes and wore swirling half capes of black lined in bright pastel colours. These 'minstrels,' none of whom wore black face, doubled as assassins or members of Lincoln's entourage by using the capes as skirts or reversing them to reveal the coloured lining. The transformations were accompanied by changes of lighting – brightly coloured illumination for the minstrel routines and a bare white work light for the conspiracy scenes. The company demonstrated considerable dexterity in these changes, but the absence of black face diminished the central theme of racial conflict and seems to have puzzled some spectators.

Unfortunately, none of the major Toronto drama critics attended the official opening of the play, on 10 January 1968. Their substitutes, for the most part, were baffled by the complex political allegory (for which Luscombe and Carew had provided little explanation in the house program). Jim McPherson of the *Telegram* admitted quite cheerily that he was 'less interested in what the production had to say than the brilliant manner in which it says it.' He considered the performance 'a splendid example of how music and drama, light and design, may be skilfully blended into one splendidly evocative experience ... infinitely more important and satisfactory than what the playwright is saying.'[6]

Not everyone was so indifferent to the ideas. Oscar Ryan speculated that *Gentlemen Be Seated* probably represented the first time the Negro position in United States history had been examined in a theatre through a Marxist perspective. He considered the 'debunking' of Lincoln to be timely and useful in helping audiences 'understand the forces which for a century have prepared today's American crisis.'[7] The production ran for four weeks, averaging about 32 per cent attendance.

While pleased, on the whole, with the company's first presentation in their new home, Luscombe was bothered by their failure to bring the piece to a satisfactory conclusion. As Oscar Ryan had complained, the play 'ends' but 'isn't really over.' This was a continuing problem in their work, related in part to their essentially exploratory method and in part to their avoidance of simple narrative forms. A premise of the play, of course, was that the assassination of Lincoln was indeed not an end but the beginning of the black revolution. Nevertheless, it was apparent from the response of critics and audience alike that the play had failed to make a strong connection between the events of 1865 and the condition of the blacks in America today. Several months later, Luscombe saw a way to make that connection clearer.

The original cast of *Gentlemen Be Seated* was all white, and Luscombe had deliberately avoided the use of black face for the production. Towards the end of 1968, however, two events coincided which made it possible for him to re-examine the problems of the play. He hired two black actors, Mel Dixon and Calvin Butler, and he invited Jan Carew to return to work with the actors to incorporate some reference to contemporary black life into a revival of the play. Carew suggested introducing two slavelike characters, Willie and Bush, representing urban and rural outlooks and roughly parallel to the Bones-Jethro relationship of the original minstrel shows. The actors began improvising around this idea, but neither Carew nor Luscombe was clear about the direction in which they wanted the work to go.[8]

In its focus on the ideological conflict between Lincoln and Thaddeus

Stevens, *Gentlemen* had condemned the half-hearted policies of the reconstruction period but had not shown clearly enough their consequences. With two black actors in the company, Luscombe wanted to juxtapose the real experience of the blacks with the trivialization of that experience by the whites in the minstrel show. The framework for the juxtaposition he wanted was in the structure of the minstrel show itself. Traditionally, such entertainments were divided into three elements – the chorus work of the minstrels, the crosstalk between Mr Interlocutor and the two end men, and the 'olio,' a small playlet, usually a crude farce with a plot taken from a curtain-raiser from the English stage. *Gentlemen* had combined the first two of these to create the two worlds of the minstrels and the assassins. In his reworking of the play, Luscombe introduced a third world, that of contemporary black life. From the perspective of the present, the black actors served as observers, commenting on the actions of the characters in the play. But he found that while this technique gave the necessary contrast between the real and the 'distorted' life in the work, it did not convey the present situation with sufficient force.

One day, Calvin Butler brought Luscombe a book entitled *New Plays of Black Theatre*, which included *Mission Impossible* by the American writer Ben Caldwell. It dealt in harrowing realism with life in the black ghettos in the 1960s. Suddenly, Luscombe realized that this dimension was what was needed to round out *Gentlemen Be Seated*. Just as the original minstrel shows drew on the Victorian stage for the 'olio,' he would borrow from the Black Theatre for the same purpose. If the language and opinions expressed were violent or shocking, that would simply illustrate more graphically the consequences of the policies pursued after the American Civil War.

On 22 April 1969, after a week of previews, the play, now called *Mr Bones*, opened to brilliant reviews. Herbert Whittaker hailed the play as a 'masterwork.' George Luscombe, he wrote, 'is Canada's most improved director.' Whereas in *Gentlemen Be Seated* the focus was on Lincoln and the political arguments, in *Mr Bones* it starts with the Negro. 'The satire on the Civil War attitudes pointing toward their present-day consequences, is now sharpened with the comment of the principal victims. The two Negro characters, Willie and Bush, who open the show, have their individual musical expression burlesqued as the Minstrels take over. They are reduced to being onlookers, or servants, to the ensuing action but their presence is never lost.'[9]

Ralph Hicklin of the *Telegram* admired several features of the production – the quick role changes by which the actors, attired in white coveralls decorated with stars on one leg and stripes on the other, switched from assassins to cabinet members with a simple alteration of hat or cloak; the macabre humour of the assassination scene, carried out in the dark with the only sound after the shot a voice saying 'Good shot Booth!'; and the positioning of the powerful scene of ghetto death to follow upon the warning of Thaddeus Stevens that, without proper reparation, the Civil War will be fought over and over until the land is reduced to ashes. His enthusiasm even caused him to compare the struggling Toronto Workshop Productions with one of the most successful Toronto theatrical fixtures, *Spring Thaw*, which had opened the previous evening. '*Mr Bones*,' he estimated, 'contained in its first five minutes more theatre, more intelligence, more imagination, more social comment, and more entertainment than the entire two acts of the revue at the Royal Alexandra.'[10]

Nathan Cohen was particularly impressed by the skilful juxtaposition of politics and entertainment, what he called 'art and society aptly mated.' He thought the company played with 'a believable sense of individual feeling and vocal clarity' and welcomed their 'unaccustomed' appreciation for characterization and respect for the spoken word. He too was struck by the powerful juxtaposition of the Lincoln assassination scene and the Caldwell play dealing with death in the ghetto. 'That time-smashing conjunction of present and past,' he wrote, 'the coupling of yesterday and now and the bloody prefiguration of tomorrow, is, in every respect – social, aesthetic, political – the highlight of the deeply-felt presentation.' Unlike some of his colleagues, Cohen did not make the mistake of thinking that because the play was set somewhere else, it had no relevance to Canada, or that because it was infectiously entertaining, it could not contain a serious view of life. 'When minutes after the fateful shot, the company springs into the finale, strumming their guitars and banjos, banging their tambourines and spoons, singing and dancing as they connect the U.S. tensions with the Canadian scene, they are not engaging in a hypocritical moment of breast beating. That is rather the indispensable last ingredient in the pattern, a jolting warning that we too have been cultivating a harvest of racial wrath and the day of reckoning is closer than most people think.'[11]

In spite of glowing reviews, attendance during the first few weeks was poor, hovering around 30 per cent of capacity. With the contractor threatening to issue a writ against the theatre to collect the money still owed him for renovations, and the Board of Control (City Executive) delaying a decision regarding its capital grant, the situation for the theatre was desperate. In mid-May, Nathan Cohen took the unusual step of appealing directly to audiences and government in his column. Reviewing the company's history, he commented on the significant strides made in the last year. He noted a 'marked improvement in the standards of the acting [and a] fresh stress upon the importance of the text ... For the theatre to have to curtail its operations after making such progress,' he proclaimed, 'would be ... much more serious in its consequences than the disappearance of Theatre Toronto.'[12]

Whether or not it was responsible, Cohen's plea coincided with a change in fortune. Audiences began to pick up; the City of Toronto came through with a grant for $15,000; and on 29 May, a letter arrived at 12 Alexander Street inviting the company to perform at the International Theatre Festival at the Venice Biennale. Before Luscombe could appear at what Cohen called the 'most important cultural showcase to which a Canadian drama organization has been invited,'[13] however, he had an even more exciting personal engagement to fulfil – his first opportunity to direct in New York.

11

Broadway Beckons

It was a paradox characteristic of artistic life in Canada that while Luscombe and TWP were having difficulty establishing themselves in Toronto, they were slowly building a reputation abroad. Interest in the company was strongest in New York, where several producers had made overtures with a view to sponsoring them in that city. But Luscombe's attitude to the New York commercial theatre, one of wary suspicion bordering on outright hostility, had previously stood in the way of his negotiating successful arrangements. By the beginning of 1969, however, circumstances had altered sufficiently that he was willing to test the waters south of the border.

Luscombe's receptiveness to an invitation to direct in New York in 1969 may have been affected by the failure of similar negotiations some four years earlier. In that case, protracted and ultimately unsuccessful discussions about the appearance of *The Mechanic* off-Broadway had seriously undermined the morale of his first professional company and contributed in no small way to its ultimate demise. Those initial talks had taken place in Stratford during the company's first Theatre-in-the-Park season in 1965. June Faulkner, then working as a volunteer publicity assistant, had managed to arrange her holidays to coincide with the company's Stratford season. There she met Peter Witt, a New York agent in the city to see the Festival productions, whom she persuaded to attend *The Mechanic*. So impressed was Witt that he brought the New York producer Alexander Cohen to a subsequent performance. Cohen initiated negotiations with Luscombe and Winter to include *The Mechanic* in his Nine O'Clock Theatre Series at the John Golden Theatre in New York.

While the negotiations continued, however, Luscombe began to ponder the implications of the invitation. The prospect of a New York appearance was obviously exhilarating, but he had to balance it against other considerations. The kind of creative work Luscombe was interested in could be done properly only by a group willing to devote all their time to it. The company he had built was developing nicely, and he was reluctant to jeopardize that progress. Furthermore, a season in New York would considerably complicate planning. Should he try to run a Toronto season with a second company, or should he gamble that the New York run would be short and that he could return for a Toronto opening in the late fall or early winter? In the end, the decision was taken out of his hands.

By the middle of September, developments in New York had altered Cohen's plans. A newspaper strike had seriously affected the box-office receipts of his current production, *Baker Street*, and his financial commitments to two new shows, *The Devils* and *The Cherry Orchard*, made it impossible for him to proceed with the planned Nine O'Clock series. That meant that the anticipated invitation to *The Mechanic* would not be forthcoming.[1] For the time being, at any rate, the prospect of a New York engagement faded. Nevertheless, the idea of American celebrity, once awakened, was difficult to suppress. Luscombe contacted Peter Witt in New York to see if Paul Libin and Ted Mann might be interested in bringing *The Mechanic* into their theatre, the Circle in the Square. Negotiations dragged on through the fall and winter in an atmosphere of uncertainty and increasing tension between the actors and Jack Winter on the one hand and Luscombe and the general manager, Brooky Robins, on the other.

Towards the end of February 1966, Witt informed the company that he had been successful in interesting Ted Mann in a possible sponsorship of the group and that Mann wanted to come to Toronto to see the show himself. Hopes for a New York engagement, which had been dashed by the termination of the negotiations with Alexander Cohen, were suddenly revived. There was an electric excitement in the air on the final Saturday performance with Mann in the house. At a post-performance meeting, Luscombe, Winter, and Robins decided they would go to New York to discuss the practical details of a short season there.

On 2 March, the trio met Witt, Mann, and Libin at the Russian Tea Room for an extended lunch. The Canadians knew little about the problems of theatrical production in New York, nor were they unanimous in their attitude to the project. For Winter, the prospect of a New York production was understandably intoxicating. But for different reasons neither Luscombe nor Robins was totally committed to the idea. Luscombe feared that the creative work of the group might be jeopardized by commercial success as Theatre Workshop had been damaged by its triumphs in the West End. Robins was worried about the financial implications. The company was rapidly approaching a crisis. The first half of their grants had been spent, and they were nowhere close to raising the $10,000 necessary to claim the balance of their Province of Ontatio Council for the Arts award. Box-office income from a New York run might tide them over, but the chances of financial disaster seemed, on the whole, much greater than the prospects of success. After failing to reach an agreement that afternoon, the three Canadians flew back to Toronto and went directly to a further meeting at Robins's home. After late-night discussions, which this time involved Brooky's husband, a Toronto lawyer, the group decided that they were not yet ready to tackle the jungle of Broadway.

News of the outcome was communicated to the actors in Toronto and undoubtedly contributed to the decision of several of them to leave the company at the end of the winter season. During the next three months, Victoria Mitchell, Yvonne Adalian, and Donald Meyers went to the Neptune Theatre in Halifax; Larry Perkins, Ed Kelly, Ed Sanders, and Gregson Winkfield resigned to find less stressful theatrical employment. To replace them, Luscombe held auditions and began training a second professional company. He promoted three apprentice actors, Peter McConnell, Mary Jess Walton, and Frances Walsh, and welcomed back Len Doncheff, who had worked with him on the original *Before Compiègne*. To this core, he added a number of young newcomers, including David Clement, Geoffrey Read, and Milo Ringham. He persuaded Doug Livingston and his wife, Sonja, to rejoin them for the summer. With this group, he began working on the repertoire for the second Stratford season.

The company's appearances at Stratford were not successful financially, but they brought the company to the attention of a wider audience than they could reach in Toronto. Among the spectators attracted to Stratford for performances at the Festival Theatre were representatives of the international theatre community. During the summer of 1966, Cheryl Crawford, a New York producer and co-founder of the Group Theatre, attended all four productions of TWP's Theatre-in-the-Park season. In a letter to the Rockefeller Foundation, she reported:

Last weekend I saw seven productions at Stratford, Ontario. I thought the Stratford ones were dullish but I feel compelled to write you about a very exciting young group who did four productions in repertory out of doors ... They are very talented actors who also dance, mime, sing and play musical instruments ... They are dedicated and idealistic and serious in a laughing way ... I saw their four shows with audiences about equally mixed between middle age and youth. All were very responsive and I felt the plays and ideas and freshness of presentation really stirred the young in a way that our commercial productions seldom do ... For myself, I found it the most interesting theatre I have seen for a long time.[2]

Gratifying as it was, such privately expressed critical acclaim had little effect on the fortunes of the company in the immediately succeeding months. Successes like *Hey Rube!* were followed by failures like *The Golem of Venice*, with the result that the company found itself on a kind of critical roller-coaster, alternately praised and condemned.

TWP's love-hate relationship with the Canadian critics was put under new strain after the company's move to Alexander Street in the winter of 1967–8. There the inauguration of a subscription series had necessitated a change in programming which at first seemed to alienate the critics still further. The new playing schedule, calling for a different play each month, meant not only that productions would have to be mounted more quickly but also that the company would have to rely much more heavily on the established international repertoire than in the past. Suddenly, the problem of selecting plays took on a new urgency, and everyone in the company was canvassed for ideas.

The first attempts to design a season from existing scripts proved disastrous. A rushed production of *The Alchemist* exposed the performers' almost fatal inexperience with classical drama, as the actors floundered hopelessly through Ben Jonson's tortuous blank verse. Attendance was a pitiful 14 per cent, and the production was withdrawn at the end of three weeks.

To complicate their plans still further, the running expenses for the new building were more than four times the cost of operating at Fraser Avenue. To bring in additional revenue, therefore, the company was compelled to rent the theatre to other organizations, including the Toronto Children's Theatre, the Studio Children's Theatre, the Toronto Repertory Ensemble, and the Toronto Dance Theatre. In April, they brought in an American production of Arthur Miller's *A View from the Bridge* to cover the rehearsal period of their next scheduled production, Ewan MacColl's anti-war allegory *The Travellers*, which had so impressed Luscombe in Edinburgh. The response of the critics to Ewan MacColl was even more hostile than to Ben Jonson, and in dismay the company was forced to withdraw the production after only eleven performances. By mid-May 1968, therefore, just four and a half months after moving into their new quarters and with two successive box-office and critical failures, the company faced imminent financial collapse.

With a sense of desperation, June Faulkner appealed to Nathan Cohen for help. 'We're desperate for a script that will work,' she admitted. Cohen gave her a typescript of a work by the New York writer Norman Kline called *Faces*, a collection of comic sketches about middle-class suburbanites. June read it and concluded that it would never interest Luscombe 'in a million years.' Nevertheless, she showed it to her husband and, later, to Nancy Jowsey, both of whom liked it. 'All right,' she said to Jowsey, 'you take it to George and tell him what you see in it.'[3] Jowsey had recently done a number of slide shows inspired in part by the imaginative photographic exhibits she had seen at the Czech pavilion at Expo 67. She took the Cohen script to Luscombe and described her conception of the production as a kind of animated comic strip using screens and back projections.[4] Intrigued, Luscombe agreed to try it.

The company Luscombe retained to work on *Faces* – Sylvia Tucker, Len Doncheff, Tony Sibbald, Ray Whelan, Diane Grant, and Frances Walsh – included only two of the actors who had begun the season with him. Nevertheless, all the performers had worked with Luscombe before and were familiar with his methods and responsive to his way of directing. The set, devised by Jowsey, consisted of two rows of four translucent panels, one above the other. In front of the upper row was a narrow platform accessible from the ground by a spiral staircase. With the help of a series of rear projectors, the eight panels could be filled with cartoon images or used as screens for silhouettes. The whole was evocative both of the panels of a newspaper cartoon strip and of the honeycomb existence of big-city apartment life.

The actors worked well together, and their physical style seemed ideal for the low-key, Thurber-like comedy of the sketches. Kline's wistful humour and the neurotic self-absorption of the characters seemed at first very foreign to the usual Luscombe mode. But he became fascinated with the way in which Kline moved from what looks like a logical situation into an off-beat development and then back again. In rehearsals, he demonstrated a surprising affinity for the material, and the performers responded brilliantly. To pad out the rather short script, Luscombe and the actors invented a prologue and epilogue involving a group of friends showing home movies. The actors improvised the scene, working out the given circumstances (who owned the house, who were in love, who were new to the group, and so on), and then conveyed all that information in pantomime and in 'dialogue' which consisted of nothing but the names of the characters. The routine became one of the skits most frequently admired by the critics, who, of course, knew nothing of its origin.[5]

Faces opened on 28 May 1968, after a week of previews. Kline himself flew up from New York to see the production – the first professional staging of the piece – and, along with most of the critics, was delighted. Whittaker called the production 'a happy union of two styles': 'That familiar cartoon rhythm, the emphasis on mime and posture rather than dialogue, the chameleon touch of the Luscombe actors – all these have found their most compatible author in the unassuming Kline.'[6] Cohen, understandably predisposed to the script, called the production a 'tantalizing, and often effective entertainment ... a kaleidoscope of short scenes anatomizing life among the sodality of white, middle-class American suburbia. Not exactly a revue, or a vaudeville, or a cartoon strip, it has the qualities of all three. In those frequent moments when there was an imaginative compatibility between the material and the performers,' Cohen felt, *Faces* spun 'a magic web.'[7]

Audiences were equally enthusiastic, and the production ran for nine weeks. It then moved on for a week's engagement at the International Theatre Festival at Brandeis University, where TWP shared the program with theatre companies such as Cafe La Mama from New York and the Traverse Theatre from Edinburgh.[8] The director Tom O'Horgan was there, beginning rehearsals for *Hair*, as was the playwright Megan Terry. June Faulkner felt rather embarrassed that the company was presenting an 'idiotic middle-class comedy' which was not at all representative of TWP's work, but the critics loved it, and not even a case of food poisoning could altogether dampen the actors' sense of triumph.[9]

On his return to Toronto, Luscombe began to plan his next season and soon forgot about *Faces*. Early in February 1969, however, he received a letter from Peter Witt, now acting as TWP's New York agent, who told him that the producer Leonard Sillman was interested in mounting a production of the play in New York and, on Norman Kline's insistence, wanted George to direct. After only a little hesitation, during which he wondered if American actors would be able to adapt to his methods, Luscombe decided that the opportunity was too good to pass up and cabled his agreement.

Prior to setting off on this new adventure, Luscombe collected a letter of reference from Nathan Cohen. If *Faces* succeeded in New York, who could tell what doors might swing open? Testimony from Toronto's leading drama critic might prove useful. Certainly, it was remarkably generous. 'In my considered judgment,' wrote Cohen, 'Luscombe is the single most enterprising and resourceful director in Canada, and his is, overall, the most artistically adventurous company that we have. His every production bears his personal signature in terms of the style of the players, and the pointing out and up of the theme of the play through movement and gesture bordering often on pure dance, but never becoming effete or decadent. It is my further opinion, that, as a theatre figure, Luscombe stands alone. I know no one else in Canada or the U.S., in Broadway, off-Broadway, regional and community theatre who works in the same manner or is able to produce the same exciting results.'[10]

But when Luscombe arrived in New York, he began to wonder what he had let himself in for. The American actors lacked the skill of his Canadian cast, having little ability in movement and no training in or taste for improvisation. Accustomed to being instructed in every aspect of their performance, they were baffled by Luscombe's insistence that they come up with their own ideas. Furthermore, the production budget allowed for only three weeks of rehearsal with a week of previews. Growing more and more despondent, Luscombe had little inclination to meet new people and spent most of his free time in his room.

Meanwhile, the Toronto theatre community watched events in New York with the usual mixture of hope and envy. Cohen, who had been responsible for finding the *Faces* script in the first place, took a somewhat proprietary interest in the proceedings. Three days before the opening, he ran a Saturday column devoted to the achievements of Toronto Workshop Productions and its determined, uncompromising director. The difference between Luscombe and other directors interested in the group theatre ideal, he suggested, was that Luscombe was 'constantly being tempted away from his chase, and steadfastly resisting the enticements.' He was far more interested in the company's trip to Venice than in directing on Broadway. 'With all his mistakes, the difficulties people have working with him, the discrepancy between his commitment to the group ideal and his dominant personality, Luscombe has been giving Toronto the only consistent exciting and meaningful local theatre it has known during the last decade.' With evidence that Luscombe's kind of theatre was finally gaining acceptance from audiences in Toronto, Cohen wondered how success might affect his idealism.[11] He need hardly have worried.

On Tuesday, 16 September 1969, *Faces*, retitled *The American Hamburger League* to avoid confusion with the John Cassavetes film, opened to scathing reviews and closed after one performance. Cohen, who had travelled to New York to attend the event, put the best possible face on it by blaming the cast, which he said was 'empty of quality both as varieties of social types and as entertainers.' The quality of 'gaiety and unassertive irony' which he admired in the Toronto company was lacking, and the performers were heavy and cloying. But he also expressed his disappointment in Luscombe's direction, saying (with his characteristic pungency of utterance) that his effects trailed off into 'substandard television variety program banalities and trivia.'[12]

Understandably, the experience severely undermined Luscombe's composure. As the final rehearsals were falling apart owing to the producer's continual interference, Luscombe had considered patrolling the lobby of the theatre on opening night with a sign The Director of This Play Has Resigned.[13] But now not only was he prevented from expressing his bitter disappointment, both with himself and with the whole New York system, he had to confront members of the Canadian press and actors from his own company, such as Calvin Butler, who had flown down to attend the opening. The next morning, after a grim vigil waiting for the New York reviews, he sat in the hotel lobby trying to explain to Sid Adilman of the *Telegram* just what had gone wrong. Although he never dropped his façade of pugnacious optimism, by the time he arrived back in Toronto his mood was one of black frustration. Never again, he vowed, would he lose control of a production as he had lost control of *Faces*.

12

Chronicling the Revolution:
Che Guevara

Luscombe returned to Toronto just three days before the company was due to fly to Italy for its appearance at the Venice Biennale. Plans called for the presentation of two productions, *Mr Bones* and a play about the Argentinian revolutionary Che Guevara. The second work was of particular interest to the Italians and was the one to which the company owed their invitation to the festival. Mario Fratti, the Italian author of *Che Guevara* (which had had a successful run at TWP in December 1968), was a personal friend of the director of the Biennale. He had suggested that the TWP production of *Che* might be a worthwhile addition to the Venice festival and had contacted the theatre in February 1969, asking them to send information to Venice. It was not until April, however, that June Faulkner finally got around to putting the material in the mail. On 24 May, a telegram asking for an estimate of their expenses had arrived, and three days later an official invitation guaranteed them full board and accommodation in Venice plus a partial contribution to the performers' salaries. Faulkner sent off a provisional acceptance.[1]

With Luscombe in New York, preparations for the Venice trip had been left in John Faulkner's hands. Faulkner was a soft-spoken, mild-mannered man who was extremely popular with almost everyone who knew him. While his commitment both to the theatre and to left-wing ideas was probably as deep as Luscombe's, he was more diffident about imposing his will on others. As a result of a considerably more relaxed atmosphere in the theatre during the summer, the internal dynamics of the company had begun to change.

Because of Luscombe's political orientation, actors attracted to his theatre tended to have strong political convictions, or to develop them fairly quickly after they had been hired. This disposition was particularly true of the 1969 company, which was much more representative than earlier groups of the tensions at work in the society outside the theatre. Several of the actors, including Jack Boschulte, François Klanfer, Steven Bush, and Cedric Smith, had strong leftist sentiments and vehemently opposed American involvement in Vietnam. Mel Dixon and Calvin Butler, both blacks, were as intensely concerned about civil rights. These two issues had profoundly divided American society during the previous year, which had seen the assassinations of Martin Luther King and Robert Kennedy, the police brutality at the Democratic National Convention in Chicago, and, finally, the election of Richard Nixon, generally regarded as an enemy to the left.

As usual, these American concerns overflowed into Canada, where they significantly affected Canadian youth culture and the emergent alternative theatre. Inspired by ideas of the American New Left, the TWP actors saw themselves as political activists working in the vanguard of a revolution that would bring peace, love, self-fulfilment, and universal participatory democracy. Heightening the intoxication of this notion was the more chemical euphoria induced by widespread use of marijuana.

In this atmosphere, while the cat was conveniently away in New York, the actors began to find fault with Luscombe's restrictive style of management. TWP, they felt, was a false collective unduly dominated by the personality of one man. They wanted more say in the choice of plays; they wanted to do more guerrilla theatre; they talked of taking over the company and eliminating the 'dehumanizing' discipline of the 'efforts' and the manipulation of the analysis of a play through the extensive discussion of units and objectives. During August, such sentiments influenced their rehearsals of *Che Guevara* and *Mr Bones*.[2]

By the time Luscombe returned from New York, the actors were anxious to show him the results of their work. In his absence, they had taken the opportunity to 'improve' their roles by adding naturalistic props and bits of psychological realism. They had also introduced a number of realistic back projections, especially into a scene at the beginning in which the CIA explains why Che must be eliminated. Luscombe was furious. He raged at John Faulkner, whom he blamed for changing the conception of the production, and he tried in a single afternoon to restore some of the fantasy which had been lost.

When the company arrived in Venice on Monday afternoon, therefore, they were in an agitated state – confused by apparently contradictory directions and exhausted from the overnight flight and four-hour stop-over in Paris. Undaunted, Luscombe called a rehearsal for that afternoon.

After hastily registering in their hotels, the dispirited actors gathered in a damp and evil-smelling basement, where the combination of foul air and exhaustion soon made most of them ill.[3] Reluctantly, Luscombe gave up the work. He would simply have to hope that the discipline he had tried to instil in the company would enable it to get through the four scheduled performances.

The double bill the company had brought to Venice was representative of two aspects of TWP's work. *Mr Bones* was perhaps the most successful example of a play which had originated with the actors' improvisations and subsequently been given shape by a writer. *Che Guevara* illustrated the company's other way of working – building and shaping a performance on the foundation of a playwright's script.

Mario Fratti was an Italian dramatist and critic living in New York, where he taught play-writing at Columbia University. Fratti had grown up in Italy; there, the defeat of the wartime partisans and the postwar re-emergence of the fascists in positions of power and influence had made him a committed Communist. He emigrated to New York in 1963 and found a country which he thought was on the brink of revolution. But there were features of the American scene which could not be explained by classic Marxist economic theory. The Western Hemisphere seemed to produce a kind of enlightened capitalist quite unlike anything Fratti had encountered in Europe. The middle-class 'drop-out,' the wealthy altruist, the privileged politician such as Robert Kennedy ready to risk assassination for an idea he believed in – these were apparent contradictions. When Fratti read of the death of Che Guevara in the Bolivian jungle, he resolved to dramatize the life of this paradoxical 'new man.'[4]

Che Guevara, an Argentinian revolutionary who had left the security of a position in the socialist government of Fidel Castro in Cuba to foment revolution in Bolivia, had been tracked down by Bolivian and American security troops in the fall of 1967 and finally killed on 27 October of that year. Alive, Che had been something of an embarrassment to his friends; dead, he became a hero and martyr. More than any other contemporary figure, he seemed to embody the selfless devotion to a revolutionary ideal that appealed so powerfully to the youth of the period.

Fratti had sent a number of plays to Toronto Workshop Productions in the early years of the decade without so much as an acknowledgement. In July 1968, however, he received a letter from June Faulkner asking to see more of his work.[5] He bundled up a copy of the newly completed *Che Guevara* and put it in the post. When Luscombe got around to reading the play after returning from the festival at Brandeis University, he liked the subject but thought the script would have to be revised drastically. The original was an almost actionless sequence of lectures on revolutionary theory by a Christlike Guevara, who was finally executed in a symbolic tableau between two co-revolutionaries. Luscombe thought he saw beneath the naïve and clumsy symbolism a story that could form the basis for a strong dramatic production. With the season still not planned and pressure mounting for him to make a decision, Luscombe phoned Fratti in New York to see if he would be willing to rewrite the play.

Like many artists, Luscombe saw life through the prism of his own obsessions. As he explained to Fratti, he was not interested in Che as a Christ figure or saintly martyr. What excited Luscombe was the image of a man, flawed and imperfect, who nevertheless was able to persevere in the course he had chosen by virtue of his resources of courage and optimism. Luscombe's interest was not in the details of Che's biography so much as in capturing the essence of Che's struggle and illustrating its relevance to the present. This essence he saw as the conflict between the visionary individual and the reactionary interests preventing the realization of his vision. Luscombe suggested that Fratti come to Toronto to discuss the matter further.[6]

Fratti arrived in September and found Luscombe in the midst of auditions for a new company. He was excited by the vitality of the young group but somewhat dismayed by Luscombe's method of choosing his performers. Instead of asking the actors questions about their previous experience, he would quiz them about their political awareness. 'Did they read the papers every morning? Who is the president of Bolivia? Who owns the copper mines there?'[7] Following detailed discussions with Luscombe, Fratti returned to New York and began reworking the script. By early November, he had written an additional sixty pages and eliminated several of the original characters.

Rehearsals began in early November 1968, and there was a sense in the company that this was to be something of a novel departure. Luscombe had recruited several new actors and brought back a number of former company members such as Milo Ringham, Jack Boschulte, and Larry Perkins. Daily sessions began with warm-up exercises followed by improvisations designed to help the actors understand the given circumstances of the story. The actors devoted hours to capturing the physical reality of such actions as sitting round a camp-fire, climbing mountainous terrain, digging in rocky soil. Awkward or lazy actors would cringe under Luscombe's fury. 'I don't want any of that CBC acting,' he would shout, bearing down on the hapless offender. 'I want to see sweat. I want to see dirt.'[8]

Within days, Larry Perkins had resigned and been replaced in the role of Che by Cedric Smith, a folk-singer and actor who had recently been deported from the United States.[9]

From the beginning, Luscombe was determined to stage the production in a non-realistic or symbolic way as a counterbalance to the realism of the script. That meant that gunfire and bombs, for example, were not conveyed by realistic effects, but by music; guns were not imitation rifles, but pieces of driftwood and iron pipe. Over the entire stage floor, he had projected the familiar image of Che in his black beret. Nancy Jowsey and John Faulkner experimented with fabrics, shapes, and lights. Jowsey hung ropes and rope ladders from the grid and distributed woven boxes over the stage; Faulkner created a pattern of dappled green light to give the impression of sunlight filtered through leaves. To help establish that the play had a relevance for Canadian audiences, Luscombe got each actor to think up a story about revolution that he or she could relate to personally.[10] Cedric Smith was accustomed to regaling an audience with that kind of anecdote, but some of the other actors found it difficult at first to step out of character in the midst of a performance.

In spite of Fratti's revisions, much of the script remained flaccid: characters were two-dimensional, speeches were too long and abstract, there was little or no conflict or plot development. Luscombe cut great swaths of narration and got his actors to improvise incidents to flesh out the lives of individual characters. As usual, the improvisations often grew out of personal experiences. A discussion of seasickness recalled the food poisoning the actors had suffered following a seafood dinner during the festival at Brandeis; a routine involving Che acting as a dentist reflected Luscombe's own traumatic experience a few months earlier when he had had all his teeth removed.

As the production developed, Luscombe began to incorporate music with the other elements of performance. He chose works by the Beatles as most representative of the revolutionary spirit in North America. The actors began to grow their hair and to assume more of the dress of the youth culture of the time. They also introduced dance, which became an important dimension of the show, both as a symbol of the youthful, revolutionary spirit and as a means of moving from one scene to another.

Finally, the company held a week of preview performances starting on 12 December 1968. Receipts from the previous production had been disappointing, and fund-raising efforts had fallen behind expectations. The contractor was becoming more and more insistent that his bill for renovations to the theatre be paid. Bankruptcy seemed imminent. As the official opening night of 17 December rolled around, the very future of the company rode on the success of *Che*.

Reviews of the production in the principal Toronto newspapers were lukewarm at best. Jim McPherson of the *Telegram* described the play as a compilation of 'biographical and philosophical vignettes ... of Che's last few months in the Bolivian bush.' He felt the work did not reveal the forces shaping Guevara, and thought that Luscombe's efforts to flesh out the rather flat text were not very satisfactory.[11] Herbert Whittaker also faulted the play, saying its blaze of admiration failed to reveal Che's features with great clarity. He acknowledged, however, that 'this rather irregular stage-piece' inspired some of Luscombe's best work as director. He also admired Nancy Jowsey's setting, which 'with a few ropes and lots of dark space beyond effectively suggested the Bolivian jungle.'[12]

The *Star* review was written by Don Rubin, a young American drama instructor from York University, substituting for Nathan Cohen. Rubin felt the play lacked focus. 'It never makes up its mind whether it wants to be a dramatic examination of the psyche of a revolutionary,' he wrote, 'or just a Brechtian-styled biography of Guevara himself.' The characters as written, he felt, were thin and lifeless and were given no extra dimension in the performance. While he complimented Luscombe's direction and Jowsey's design, he dismissed the production as a whole as 'far too soft and sweet to work as anything more than a kind of romantic tribute to a contemporary folk hero.'[13]

The combination of cool reviews and the Christmas season played havoc with the box office. In the middle of Christmas week, Faulkner phoned Nathan Cohen, told him that the show was dying, and begged him to come to see it. On New Year's Eve, Cohen's own evaluation of the play appeared in his regular entertainment column under the headline 'Che, the Best Play Locally in a Year.' Cohen agreed with his colleagues about the merits of the script. 'To understand what director George Luscombe and his company are doing,' he wrote, 'you must realize that Mario Fratti has written an abominable play.' Describing it as 'amateur reportage,' he concluded that Fratti had no ability whatever to probe situation or character. The Che he has created, Cohen concluded, 'is not flesh and blood, [but] an indiscriminate assortment of banal attitudes about the revolutionary hero – loyal, brave, self-sacrificing, a man of the people, patient, fair, a lover of women (but ever so chaste about it), a 100 per cent bore.'

Cohen's admiration was reserved for the production, which he called an 'audacious and invigorating experience.' In working around the text itself, he felt, Luscombe had shaped a performance which established 'an inspiring yet down-to-earth image of Che and what he stood for.' Unlike several of the critics, who mistook the actors' personal experiences for those of the characters, Cohen admired the way in which these remembered incidents connected 'that tiny struggle in Bolivia with other larger struggles.' He found Smith's deliberately jerky and emotionless performance deeply moving, 'steadily growing in force and conviction.' Overcoming, for once, his previously expressed bias towards text, Cohen marvelled that TWP 'could do so much with what is really just a title and a nebulous notion.'[14] Largely as a result of Cohen's enthusiasm, business began to pick up, until, by 14 January, *Che* had become the best-attended and most controversial TWP attraction since *Hey Rube!*.

Now in Venice, Luscombe hoped the company would be able to recapture some of that earlier excitement. Their playing schedule, however, called for two performances of *Mr Bones* to precede the presentation of *Che*. So on the evening of Wednesday, 23 September, the actors gathered in the theatre in the Palazzo Grassi and awaited the nine o'clock curtain for *Mr Bones*. As the hour approached, the three-hundred-seat space, which had been set up in a beer garden with a temporary roof,[15] remained empty, and the actors began to wonder aloud if they would be playing to a vacant house. Overhearing their concern, their hosts assured them that Italian audiences never arrived on time, and indeed, by about nine-thirty the house was full and the performance began.

It was not a great success. The simultaneous translators had difficulty keeping up with the pace of the show, and many of the audience seemed puzzled by the interpretation of Lincoln as a reluctant liberal. To add to the problems, the performance was erratic and generally uncoordinated.[16] Nevertheless, the spectators thoroughly enjoyed the visual effects and the music. One Italian critic, confessing that he had expected (on the basis of unidentified reports) to find Canadian acting to be in the staid British drawing-room tradition, was surprised by the youth and vitality of the company. After the show, eighty or ninety members of the audience stayed to discuss the production, and then the company went off to a reception arranged by the Canadian consul.

It was *Che Guevara*, however, that most interested the Italian theatregoers. Even before the production opened, strong feelings had been generated. Some thought Fratti a lightweight dramatist who had no business writing about Guevara; others felt that a company like TWP, which received the bulk of its funding from government, could not possibly be revolutionary. During the opening performance, the capacity audience became more and more vigorous in its expression of displeasure. The translators, who relied in part on the scripts which had been sent in advance, were baffled by the stage version, which bore little resemblance to what they had in front of them. As the translation faltered, spectators began to hiss the actors, who in their turn became rattled. By the intermission, Calvin Butler feared there would be a riot in the theatre.[17]

Fortunately, things quieted down during the second half, and not surprisingly a record crowd stayed for the open discussion. Very quickly what was supposed to be a debate about the merits of the production became an examination of the reliability of the play. Mario Fratti, who had been unable to come to Venice from New York himself, was represented by others. His German translator denounced the production as a perversion of the author's intention as incorporated in his original script. Admitting that he had made changes, Luscombe claimed that he had cleared all the alterations with Fratti and that the dramatist had seen the show and approved it.

The brief altercation was symptomatic of the gap between the Europeans and the Canadians. The Italian Communists, who had lived through the horrors of the war and its aftermath only to see privilege reinstated in their country, took revolution seriously and found the TWP treatment of Che trivial. The TWP actors might think of themselves as revolutionaries, but the Italians regarded them as little more than innocent children playing at politics. One member of the audience put the feeling into words by saying that the company was wasting its time fooling around in the theatre and that 'the only place for the revolution was in the revolution.'[18]

Luscombe found the experience exhilarating. Here at last was an audience as passionately committed to politics as he was himself. Against those critics who maintained that art was peripheral to politics, he argued, as had Joan Littlewood before him, that the political artist could contribute to social change through a transformation of an audience's awareness. Furthermore, he asserted that it was the theatre artist who, in Canada at any rate, had the most freedom of expression. But Luscombe did not speak for everyone in his company. Many of the actors were drawn from a generation who saw the relationship between theatre and politics somewhat differently. To them, the drama was not so much a 'weapon' in the class war as a vehicle for personal expression. When accused by a member of the audience of failing to get into the character of Che, Cedric Smith had illustrated this ideological difference by saying that he was less interested in getting into the character he was portraying than in expressing his own feelings.[19] Although the ultimate incompatibility of these two ideas was obscured in the general excitement of the Venetian experience, it was to become more apparent when the company returned to Toronto and to the problems of mounting a regular season.

13

Collaborative Creation III:
Chicago '70

In the fall of 1969, Luscombe and the company plunged rather precipi-
tously into the planning of the 1969–70 season. On the suggestion of
Cedric Smith, who thought the play might lend itself to interesting psychedelic effects, the theatre opened with a production of Shakespeare's
The Tempest. It was not well received, and ran for only three weeks. In January, the group premièred an original play by the young Canadian playwright Carol Bolt. Set in the seventeenth century and dealing with the
Indian wars of the period, *Daganawida* proved puzzling to audiences and
critics alike. The total box-office revenue for the two productions
amounted to less than $4,000.

With two flops in a row, the actors began to ask whether the process of
script selection might not be at fault. The question of repertoire had
always presented a problem, and it was compounded by the desire of the
actors in 1970 to have greater say in the operation of the theatre. Inspired
by the self-expressive theories of acting associated with experimental
groups such as the Living Theatre, the TWP performers continued to
chafe under Luscombe's restrictive discipline. Although the threatened
rebellion of the previous summer had not materialized, there was a lingering resentment of Luscombe's autocratic style of choosing plays. Several of the actors felt that the company should be confronting
contemporary political issues directly (rather than obliquely as TWP
seemed wont to do), and they pointed to the success of *Mr Bones* and *Che*
as evidence of an audience for work with a strong political stance. What
the public wanted, they believed, was not reworked classics or historical
plays, but guerrilla theatre that would attack social injustices directly.

While Luscombe and his actors shared a common vision of social justice, they differed in their notions of how the theatre could help to reor-

der the world. Luscombe, deriving his ideas from Brecht and the formalist tradition of the Russians, thought of the theatre as a medium which distorted reality so as to make the audience see it through new eyes. The purpose of drama was revelation, not exhortation. For the performers, most of whom were ten or fifteen years younger than Luscombe, the relationship between politics and theatre was more intimate.

The political consciousness of the actors' generation had been formed not, as Luscombe's had been, on Spain and the Second World War but on American experiences of the sixties. The rapidly developing technology which enabled television news cameras to project images of events, virtually as they happened, into the tranquillity of private homes meant that ignorance of, or indifference to, world events was impossible. Consequently, the imaginations of a large number of the youth maturing in the sixties were formed by images of the brutality and heroism of the civil rights movement or the agony and suffering in Vietnam. The realities of social injustice and military power, which previous generations had been spared through the abstractions of news reports, were brought home to the generation of the sixties with unprecedented clarity.

One consequence of the television revolution was a blurring of the distinction between reality and art. As warfare and police brutality became 'theatricalized' on the evening news, theatre began to take to the streets and to infiltrate political action. Increasingly, organizers began to realize that 'dramatic' protest could exert an influence disproportionate to its size through the creation of images that would be broadcast through the mass media. The alienated young, wishing to change a system which perpetrated racism and military aggression but from which they seemed to be excluded, turned increasingly in the late sixties to what were essentially theatrical or symbolic attacks on the establishment. Attempts, for example, to levitate the Pentagon were not reasonable political actions but dramatic gestures suggesting the failure of 'rational' politics.

From its inception, the youth culture of the sixties was beset by internal, unacknowledged contradictions. Its advocacy of a social revolution and the democratizing of power was fundamentally irreconcilable with the doctrine of self-realization. As David Farber has pointed out, participatory democracy implies a consensual politics inconsistent with 'doing your own thing.'[1] As long as the revolution remained personal, it could be embodied in a more or less innocent hedonism of sex, drugs, and rock music. But as soon as collective action on a large scale was attempted, the inherent contradictions in the movement threatened to break it up.

The demonstration organized in 1968 to coincide with the Democratic

National Convention in Chicago was just such an action, and it marked the end of a phase in the movement. Designed to catch the attention of the national news media, the demonstration brought together a loose confederation of protest groups in an uneasy alliance. Among the most active of them were the Mobilization to End the War in Vietnam (Mobe), the Yippies, and the Black Panthers (a black activist organization which had come to symbolize a new black militancy after the death of the pacifist Martin Luther King). These groups came to Chicago with various motives. Ostensibly, they were protesting not against the Democratic convention but against the very system of which it was a part. To most of those gathered in the parks and streets of the city, who knew how blacks in the South had routinely been excluded from the political process, the convention epitomized the gigantic charade by which a closed system masqueraded as a democracy.[2]

But the more militant leaders of some of the organizations such as the Students for a Democratic Society (SDS) were looking for a showdown in which, by provoking retaliation on the part of the police and the military, they would be able to discredit and possibly shake the structures of power. As the extremists had hoped and predicted, the antipathy felt by the Chicago authorities towards the protesters led to a clash in which police were shown on national television wielding clubs and bludgeoning unarmed young people in an orgy of violence.

In the investigation and national soul-searching that followed the riot, there were conflicting conclusions, which themselves demonstrated how deeply American society was divided. Some commentators felt that the police had been the aggressors and went so far as to describe the incident as a 'police riot.' A Survey Research Center poll conducted following the event, however, found that little more than 10 per cent of all whites polled thought too much force had been used by the police (although 63 per cent of all blacks thought so). Even among those opposed to the war in Vietnam, only 12 per cent expressed 'extreme sympathy' for the protesters.[3]

Immediately following the convention, Attorney General Ramsey Clark was unable to find evidence that the various groups organizing the demonstration had been part of a conspiracy, and refused to prosecute anyone. After the election of President Richard Nixon, who had run on a promise of 'law and order,' however, the administration took a harder line. The Justice Department under its new attorney general, John Mitchell, launched the prosecution of eight of the Chicago protest leaders – Jerry Rubin and Abbie Hoffman, the founders of the Yippies, Tom Hayden, David Dellinger, John Froines, Rennie Davis, and Lee Weiner of Mobe, and Bobby Seale of the Black Panthers.[4]

The trial of the so-called Chicago 8 got under way in September 1969, with the defence attorney, William Kunstler, arguing before Julius J. Hoffman, a seventy-four-year-old judge with a reputation for becoming personally involved in the cases he tried. It rapidly gained national attention. Against the arbitrary and seemingly hostile behaviour of Judge Hoffman, the defendants used all their considerable skill in the techniques of street theatre to disrupt the proceedings. In the face of open disrespect for the authority of the court, the legitimacy of the proceedings, and the dignity of his person, Judge Hoffman was provoked into actions and judgments that called the whole judicial process into disrepute. After repeated outbursts, Bobby Seale was gagged and tied to his seat in the courtroom. By the end of the trial, Judge Hoffman had sentenced every defendant and their two attorneys to terms of from two to four years for contempt of court.

To many of the American TWP actors, such as Steven Bush and Jack Boschulte, the proceedings in Chicago had been of intense interest because they seemed to epitomize the very rigidity and impenetrability of the American system against which the young had been protesting. In the course of rather desultory rehearsals for a Polish play called *The Police* which Luscombe was preparing as the third production for the season, Jack Boschulte brought in a copy of *Ramparts*, a left-wing American journal, which contained an article about the Chicago trial. As Bush read the article, he came to a transcript of some of the proceedings and began to act out the parts of the participants. Soon some of the other actors joined in, and they all moved down to the stage and began acting out a scene.[5] Suddenly, the rehearsal process came alive. Here was material to which the actors felt they could relate directly and which could form the basis of a passionate work of theatre. They suggested to Luscombe that instead of *The Police* they work on a collectively created docudrama based on the Chicago trial.

Cool to the idea at first, Luscombe gradually lent his support to the project. The actors collected whatever material they could find on the trial, but since reporters were prevented from making notes in the courtroom, news was scanty. Jack Boschulte travelled to Chicago to see if he could get more up-to-date information. He attended some of the sessions and began compiling transcripts of the trial from memory. Soon the actors in Toronto were getting almost daily reports of the court proceedings.

By mid-February, the show was beginning to develop, but there was disagreement about what shape it should take. Bush and some others wanted it to be true to the ideals of collective creativity as embodied in the hippie culture. They felt that Luscombe with his attention to dramatic structure was suffocating their spontaneity and liveliness.[6] For his part, Luscombe had little sympathy for creative anarchy and maintained a strong guiding hand. One day, Steven Bush brought in a copy of *Alice in Wonderland*, suggesting that there were parallels between the Chicago trial and that of Alice. The company spread the material they had gathered on the first two rows of seats in the theatre, and the actors picked up their 'lines' when inspired to do so.

Meanwhile, Nancy Jowsey created a versatile unit setting out of metal pipes and shiny tinsel. At centre stage, an elevated platform reminiscent of the scaffolding at a construction site and flanked by stairways on each side served as the judge's seat. Behind it, on a stand, was a huge British judge's wig surmounted by a crown, which was used in the 'Alice in Wonderland' scenes. Beneath it, in a cramped space crammed with electronic equipment, was a broadcast booth. Downstage, a number of wood-and-pipe stools of various sizes served as chairs, tables, or other structures, as the action demanded. The whole was enclosed by a backdrop of aluminium foil, which reflected the stage lights with a kind of garish vulgarity. The actors were dressed in an eclectic mixture of flowered shirts, miniskirts, psychedelic flared trousers, embroidered vests, and headbands, and most had beards and long hair. The visual effect was rather like that of a disco bar.

As the work evolved, the actors combined the literal transcripts of the trial with group improvisations. Those sometimes parodied the events in the Chicago courtroom and sometimes suggested outrageous parallels with schoolroom scenes, fashion shows, or incidents from the trial in *Alice in Wonderland*. Sometimes, Luscombe would encourage the actors to work with particular objects supplied by him. Diane Grant selected a red hat, which she used to play Alice and reversed when she represented the Chicago jury.[7] The result was a characteristic TWP mixture of documentary 'truth,' culled from research into primary materials such as the court transcripts, and a political attitude conveyed by caricature, irony, and deliberate theatrical distortion. There is no question that it was a one-sided vision of reality. But Luscombe and his actors were not interested in objectivity. While they maintained it was the Hellzapoppin' aspects of the situation, the 'complete madness of the trial,' that attracted them,[8] they obviously identified deeply with the defendants.[9] To them, the Chicago 'conspiracy' was a protest against racism and injustice. It was a cause they felt they were a part of and one to which their theatre was dedicated.

The play, entitled *Chicago '70*, which opened on 10 March 1970, featured one of the strongest companies Luscombe had assembled; it included Mel Dixon, Jim Lawrence, Calvin Butler, Neil Walsh, Steven Bush, Peter Faulkner, Diane Grant, François Klanfer, Ray Whelan, Rick McKenna, and Carol Carrington. It played to a sold-out house and a standing ovation. The production was recognizably in the TWP tradition of *Hey Rube!* and *Mr Bones*, but its impact was greater than theirs because it spoke more directly to its audience. The Chicago trial seemed to epitomize a judicial and political system devoid of all credibility. The only rational response to such a system was ridicule.

On the whole, committed leftists and the young praised the play unreservedly. Oscar Ryan called the production 'one of the most colorful and inspired ever mounted by TWP.'[10] Sandy Naiman of *Seneca* compared it with two other productions running in Toronto at the same time, saying that it made '*Dionysus in 69* look like pointed toed shoes of years gone by and *Hair* like a poorly rehearsed kindergarten recital.'[11] Herbert Whittaker agreed that no other production that season had anything like the play's immediacy. '*Hair* describes a five-year old flower culture,' he wrote, '*Striker Schneiderman* [at the St Lawrence Centre] goes back to 1919 and *Spring Thaw* doesn't go anywhere in its topicality.'[12] As for the production as a whole, he thought that Luscombe had contributed some of the 'best, most amusing, original and pointed directorial touches of his creative career.'[13]

But there were other critics who expressed what was to become an increasingly familiar complaint about Luscombe's work – that it sacrificed serious political analysis for sloganeering and cheap effects. Some of this criticism came from the right. Jim McPherson, in the relatively conservative *Telegram*, thought the production 'superficial and obvious' and regretted that Luscombe had compiled such a one-sided analysis from the wealth of material at his disposal.[14] Paul Levine, writing in *Canadian Forum*, objected that the Alice in Wonderland analogy allowed the audience to laugh off the trial as 'nothing but' theatre and quoted Brecht's comment that 'the man who laughs has not yet been told the terrible news.'[15]

But the most trenchant criticism, as usual, came from Nathan Cohen, whose leftist sympathies were apparently not engaged. Starting from the somewhat surprising premise that the avant-garde no longer had any real application in the arts, Cohen argued that *Chicago '70* would have been stronger if the players had let the facts speak for themselves. 'The show is at its best when it is most straightforward – when poet Allan Ginsberg is explaining his concept of spirituality – when Abbie Hoffman is telling how he and a band of others showered the New York Stock Exchange with money – when Mayor Daley of Chicago is talking about the instructions he gave the police on the eve of the convention in 1968 ... when Bobbie Seale is insisting on his right to cross-examine witnesses since he has no lawyer. But these moments are brief. For the most part, the production is adulterated by devices, flourishes, interpolations, and artificialities which blur the issues, stunt the characters, and diminish the drama of the occasion.'[16]

What is surprising about this response is that, after ten years of following the fortunes of TWP, Cohen still failed to understand its aesthetic. For those 'devices, flourishes, interpolations and artificialities' that Cohen deplored lay at the very heart of Luscombe's theatre.

Misunderstandings of that kind were to plague Luscombe and his company for years. As Canadian playwrights turned to what Cohen called the 'theatre of fact' and audiences sought out realistic treatments of Canadian history and social problems, Luscombe's theatre of gesture seemed more and more old-fashioned. Spectators who shared Luscombe's delight in a dance or a pratfall never learned to share his conviction that such things were more significant, and often communicated more 'meaning,' than words.

The success of *Chicago '70* resulted in the company's being invited to perform at the International Festival of Theatre Arts in Wolfville, Nova Scotia, in July. Even more exciting was an arrangement, worked out with Ted Mann and Paul Libin, for TWP to appear in New York. Plans called for the Canadian company to open at the Martinique Theatre on 15 May for two weeks of previews and to play through June, after which an American cast would take over if attendance warranted it.

The New York opening was everything such occasions were supposed to be. After the show, the cast went to the producers' office to wait for the notices. A typesetter at the *New York Times* phoned in Clive Barnes's review, which praised the players' brilliance, vigour, and gusto. He called the work 'an interesting piece of political theatre, imaginatively fashioned, deftly acted, amusing in part, moving in part, that makes no bones about its partisanship.' He concluded with a congratulatory exclamation, 'Right On!'[17] There was euphoria in the office, the producers poured champagne, and the company left for Sardi's.

The other American reviewers were split along the same lines as their

Canadian counterparts. Several objected to the rather manic style, dismissing it as 'mindless' or 'youthful'; some felt the play was nothing but propaganda. Undoubtedly, many of the reviews were coloured by the political leanings of the writers. One who was obviously sympathetic was Martin Washburn of the *Village Voice*. 'Of the several plays I have seen that claim to reconstruct courtroom scenes in order to comment on injustice,' he wrote, '*Chicago '70* seems to me by far the best .... The integrity of *Chicago '70* is such that it does not attempt to hide its satirical inspiration .... They have found a way to legitimately go beyond the confines of courtroom drama (which I think are far too limited to carry any serious theatrical intentions) and to attempt reconstruction, without subverting the aesthetics of the stage.'[18]

Jack Kroll in *Newsweek* made one of the most perceptive comments about the relationship between fact and fantasy in political satire. He found that the use of the Alice in Wonderland parallel and the attendant doubling of roles created a dual focus, the effect of which was 'to sharpen immensely the "existential" outlines of personality ... *Chicago '70* makes you think because it makes you react, whether with laughter or anger, to reality.'[19]

In spite of Barnes's review, business at the Martinique Theatre was poor. One night, Jerry Rubin and Abbie Hoffman, finally free on bail, came to a performance. They took the actors out for a drink after the show. Calvin Butler still remembers Rubin's parting words to the Canadians, 'Don't forget to buy my book.'[20] Finally, after playing to disappointing houses, the play was taken off on 14 June.

During this time, tensions between the actors and Luscombe had increased. The performers felt Luscombe was insufficiently radical, and Luscombe thought the actors were plotting an insurrection. The frictions were intensified at the festival in Wolfville by the actors' efforts to promote *Chicago '70*, which was playing to very poor houses in a five-hundred-seat theatre. Company members attending a Joan Baez concert with thousands of spectators announced a special, two-for-one price on *Chicago '70* tickets. When Luscombe, who had not been consulted, heard of the offer, he was furious and more convinced than ever that the actors were trying to seize 'his' theatre. After the final performance, he went to the performers' dressing-rooms and announced grimly, 'All right, the revolution is over.'

14

The European Repertoire

The tensions which had surfaced in the company during the production of *Che* and *Chicago '70* were a reflection of the time. It was a period when talk of 'revolution' invaded all areas of public discourse, from censorship and drug laws to college curricula and from the role of the military to Quebec nationalism. The aspirations of the New Left, with its emphasis on hedonism and individual self-realization, were ultimately repugnant to Luscombe, brought up on the Old Left principles of discipline in the service of a supra-personal ideal. While he could share his younger colleagues' passion for equality between the races and for individual dignity, he was suspicious of the incipient anti-rationalism among the young, who seemed susceptible to demagoguery and mysticism. In the end, these differences, and Luscombe's inflexible retention of artistic control, split the company and brought about an almost complete turnover of personnel in the summer of 1970.

The new group that assembled in the autumn of that year was attracted by the political reputation of the theatre but unfamiliar with Luscombe's methods of working. Nevertheless, they responded enthusiastically to the physical challenges of his style and the left-wing stance of the productions. A political allegory based on the Pied Piper legend written by Nancy Jowsey and produced under pressure was a critical failure, as was the staging by Geoffrey Read of Brendan Behan's *The Hostage*. Those productions prompted Nathan Cohen to return to a theme that had been an important motif of his criticism from the beginning – the importance of text-based theatre and the need for the company to go beyond the development of original Canadian works to explore the European repertoire so sadly neglected on North American stages.[1]

Because of his convictions, Luscombe was interested in producing only work with a socialist (or at least a humanist) world-view, but over the years he had introduced Toronto audiences to a number of European plays that expressed his own outlook on the world. One of these was Carl Zuckmayer's *The Captain of Köpenick*, the last production the company staged in its tiny basement theatre, in the autumn of 1967. Written by the author of the filmscript for the internationally acclaimed *The Blue Angel*, the play is a genial satire on the German love of military ostentation and unquestioning respect for authority and regulations. It is based on the true story of an almost illiterate middle-aged Prussian who in 1906 succeeded in taking over the town hall of Köpenick by disguising himself as an officer in a uniform purchased from a second-hand shop. Although the historic Wilhelm Voigt's exploit lasted for little more than an hour, he was able to parlay it into something like national fame, and Zuckmayer remembered having seen him as an old man selling postcards of himself in military uniform at a Mainz carnival.[2] The 'uniform worship' satirized in *The Captain of Köpenick* was to lead to national catastrophe twice in Zuckmayer's lifetime – once in a stampede to rally behind a gaudily beribboned Kaiser Wilhelm and a second time, more ominously, in the frenzied response to the Voigt-like figure of Adolf Hitler.

However prescient Zuckmayer may have been when he wrote the play in 1931, he chose to present his ideas light-heartedly rather than in the heavily allegorical and hysterical style of the expressionists of the previous decade. That meant that not only the humour, depending for its effect on a knowledge of German character types, but also the narrative style was difficult to translate into another language. As Zuckmayer himself explained in his preface to the English adaptation produced by the National Theatre of Britain in 1971, 'the composition of the original play moves along two tracks: the story of the hapless man, slowly waking up to the use of his wits, and the story of the uniform's slow degradation. And it begins – a warning signal for the Germany of 1931 – with the birth and the idolatry of the Uniform, while the man looking for work is thrown out as a beggar.'[3] The slow-developing, almost picaresque style of the piece seemed confusing to non-Germans who did not know the story of the inevitable masquerade.

Luscombe's revision of the script, undertaken in the spring of 1967, just after Jack Winter left the company, was fairly faithful to the original, although it reduced the length to allow for the mime sequences that were an invariable component of any TWP production. Notable in the text is the subtlety of the humour and the wide range of tone, from the Dickensian sentimentality of the death of the young girl to the harsh, Gorki-like realism of the scene in the doss house. In rehearsals, Luscombe tended to mute the sentiment and exaggerate the satire. He also focused rather heavily on the injustices suffered by Voigt, so that apart from the central character there were few portraits of any depth or complexity. The show was regarded by many critics as one of the most interesting the company had mounted, although several confessed to being mystified in many places by the tone.

To accommodate the eighteen scenes of the play, Nancy Jowsey created an ingenious playing area consisting of two semicircular platforms with a cagelike structure in the middle of the upper one. This geometrical unit divided the front playing area from a rear space where properties were kept. It served in different ways as background for tavern or jail. The bars of the cage could be removed to serve as clubs or rifles. Basic costumes of plain grey uniforms or blouses and skirts were altered by the addition of hats, cloaks, or other simple adornments. The all-powerful Captain's Uniform, in dazzling red, was shown to have a life of its own by being made to move about the stage without apparent support.

As might be expected, of the two major critics, Herbert Whittaker was more sympathetic to the visual and kinetic approach of the director and designer. He particularly admired the way in which Luscombe had found remarkable physical illustrations of action – an officers' club, for example, in which the members solemnly concentrate on a game of marbles, expressing themselves only in grunts, which reveal both their success in the game and their rank in relation to the other players. In other sequences, the company paraded to the accompaniment of recorded marches, thereby capturing the spirit of German militarism with ten men and a phonograph. To Whittaker, the vivid nature of these cameos made Zuckmayer's verbal message almost redundant. Nevertheless, while admiring the actors' ability to transform themselves instantly into many different physical types, he acknowledged that the concentration on physical movement was at the expense of speech. The vocal monotony of the company palled after a time, but he was willing to forgive it because of the exciting mime sequences.[4]

Cohen, reiterating a frequent complaint, reminded his readers that it was 'a besetting weakness [of TWP] that the shows lacked intellectual substance commensurate with their bustle and theatricality ... [and that] all too often the manner of the presentation turned out to be the only justification.' Too frequently in the past, he complained, the characters had emerged as commodities and objects rather than human beings. In *The Captain of Köpenick*, however, in spite of its 'fascinations and frustrations in general,' Cohen thought he saw an important step forward in the company's artistry. Here there was a successful blend of what he called an 'expressionist approach' and basic narrative. He admired the 'disclosure of the ambitions, interplay and psychological attitudes' of a succession of army and civic officials.

Like other critics, Cohen commented favourably on the mime sequences, including one in which 'a slow motion attack by a soldier on a down-and-outer becomes the prelude to a grotesque, phantom-like ballet with the various actors moving around as though they were mannequins, their arms flopping loosely ahead of them or at their sides.' But in *Köpenick*, unlike in some other productions, he felt that the 'kaleidoscopic fusion of sound, light and music, and ensemble pose and posture' served to reinforce 'emotional and social strength.' The production, he concluded, was a 'statement, not a diversion with pretences.'[5]

Other critics who began to discover TWP frequently found it difficult to respond to the new relationship they experienced in Luscombe's theatre of the physical, the verbal, and the psychological. Overwhelmed by the theatricality of his productions, they often felt the 'meaning' of the play was obscured by pretentious stylization. They complained about diction, or the 'superficiality' of the acting, or that too many things were happening at once so that it was difficult to follow important speeches.

Almost without exception, however, reviewers found *Köpenick* both challenging and enjoyable. Oscar Ryan thought the production illustrated those strengths which set Luscombe apart from all other directors working in Canada – 'his selection of off-beat, provocative, meaningful and contemporary scripts; his imaginative and experimental staging; his economy in the use of stage props, costumes and effects; and his actors' conscientious performances.'[6]

Another example of the company's ability to mount provocative productions of European scripts was the 1969 staging of Jaroslav Hašek's *The Good Soldier Schweik*. Hašek's novel, an account of the adventures of a wily Czech private in the Austro-Hungarian forces during the First World War, had beguiled audiences in Europe in several stage adaptations, including ones by Piscator and Brecht. Luscombe himself had performed in a version of the work by Ewan MacColl. The story was relatively unknown in Canada, however, and Luscombe thought the Soviet invasion of Czechoslovakia in August 1968 provided an excellent occasion to introduce Schweik to Canadian audiences. He decided to use an adaptation by the Canadian writer Michael John Nimchuk.

The original is a sprawling picaresque novel which follows its unlikely hero through a series of adventures beginning in Schweik's Bohemian home town, passing through various parts of Central Europe, and ending at the front lines. Piscator had captured the sweep of the novel by using conveyor belts to move scenery across the stage past marching soldiers. The tone of the production had been established by the projection of cartoon figures by the caricaturist Georg Grosz onto a screen at the back of the stage.

Lacking the resources of a heavily subsidized European theatre, Luscombe and Nancy Jowsey devised a translucent background panel on which to project angular shapes, cartoon locations, or the silhouettes of actors. On-stage, a small unit of vaguely ecclesiastical shape served various functions as the action moved from rooming-house to tavern to barracks. The actors appeared in white terry-cloth coveralls altered by the addition of hats or other accessories – all but Ray Whelan as Schweik played several roles.

The play was greeted by the critics as one of the most successful productions in the company's nine-year history. Oscar Ryan thought the production an advance over past achievements. 'Climaxes are better defined, less ambiguous, more concise,' he wrote.[7] But it was Nathan Cohen who was most fulsome in his appreciation. Having expressed his exasperation with the fact that Toronto theatre reflected almost nothing of the 'political and cultural ferment going on in the world,'[8] he welcomed this play. He had often found the political content of Luscombe-Winter productions naïve and strident, and the new combination of Luscombe and Nimchuk seemed to him better balanced. Luscombe's handling of his actors had become more efficient and cohesive, 'quite at variance with the unfinished, often crude air characteristic of his work hitherto.' He thought the actors spoke clearly and with understanding, and he welcomed a new note of romantic tenderness, even suggesting that the slapstick veered over into soft-heartedness at the end, when Schweik, alone in a pool of light, 'recites the names of all the people he met during the play, all gone now, casualties of war and the follies that go with it.' Indeed, if he had any quarrel with the production, it was that it was perhaps a little bland. He found no clarification of political thought, nor anything to 'disturb, jar, or shock people.'[9]

Schweik played to enthusiastic houses for four weeks and then was held over until 12 April. No doubt, a factor contributing to the play's success was what Cohen called the 'amiable' nature of its commentary on bureaucracy in and out of uniform. But there was another reason for its popularity. Members of the Toronto Czech community flocked to the production, and the company added a special Sunday matinee for their benefit. François Klanfer remembers performing at that matinee, struggling to sing a Czech folk-song he had learned phonetically. As he entered, he was conscious of an eerie silence and wondered if the audience was hostile. Suddenly, as he moved downstage, he realized that many of the spectators were openly weeping. The play became the company's biggest hit, the first to cover running costs from box-office receipts.

In January 1971, Luscombe began rehearsals for a new work by Munro Scott called *Wu-Feng*. Luscombe had been interested in China since the early sixties, but not all the actors shared his enthusiasm for Scott's treatment of the subject, and several were openly hostile. One day, they confronted the director and asked him to drop the play. Luscombe persuaded the company to let him bring in the playwright to see if the script could be satisfactorily revised. When Scott refused to rewrite and the actors remained adamant that they did not want to perform in it, he decided to cancel the show, leaving the company without a play for their next production.[10]

In desperation, they gathered in the foyer of the theatre and read scripts. Diane Grant brought in *Shelley, the Idealist*, a work about the English poet by Ann Jellicoe. It was neither political nor like anything the company had done before, so when Luscombe agreed to stage it, several of the actors, including Phil Savath and Larry Mollin, left, accusing him of selling out the TWP principles. The remaining members of the group worked through what was one of the shortest but also, paradoxically, one of the most pleasant rehearsal periods they had had at TWP. Nancy Jowsey devised a simple setting consisting of a semicircle of seven lattice-work arches behind a white wrought-iron garden seat located in the middle of the stage. The arches served as entrances or, occasionally, as niches in which the actors stood like statues waiting to enter. The performers were in period costumes, with the exception of Ray Whelan, who, as a kind of chorus figure, wore a short peasant smock (which he hated because he thought it looked like a dress).[11]

Several critics expressed surprise that Luscombe could direct a work in which the actors spoke distinctly and quietly and in which there was virtually no singing and dancing. In this production, they found strong acting combined with the touches of theatricality they had come to associate with TWP. In one sequence, Suzette Couture, playing Shelley's first wife, wore a shawl which became the 'baby' she carried in her arms. In the course of an argument with her husband, the 'baby' unravelled and turned into a wave, symbolizing the water in which she committed suicide.[12] At the end of the play, the dead Shelley runs in slow motion towards the audience, crying, 'Come on,' while the others follow at a distance. Oscar Ryan called it 'one of TWP's most satisfying productions,'[13] and Brian Pearl of *Excalibur* thought it 'one of the most competent and well-produced shows of the year.'[14]

As usual, however, Nathan Cohen's comments were the most thoughtful. Having expressed his disappointment with the company's recent productions, *The Piper* and *The Hostage*, he was, perhaps, pleased to be able to reassert his faith in their talent. The subject of *Shelley, the Idealist*, 'the position and function of women in a male-oriented society,' he thought 'most unusual for Toronto Workshop Productions.' The power of the performances, especially the women's, he thought impressive, and he found it 'strange and exhilarating' that you could hear the text.[15] This was to be the last compliment the company would ever receive from their most rigorous critic. Sixteen days later, at the age of forty-seven, Nathan Cohen died while undergoing heart surgery in a Toronto hospital.

Cohen's death was to transform the Toronto critical scene. Through his flamboyant manner, his magisterial tone, his extensive exposure on television and radio as well as in the press, and his wide-ranging interests, Cohen had come to dominate drama criticism in the city. That dominance had had mixed results. In the eleven years he worked for the *Star*, he created an entertainment section in which discussion of the theatre was as good as it was anywhere in North America, outside New York and Boston. But much of that discussion was conducted in a deliberately provocative style. Like Shaw before him, Cohen consciously created a public persona. His affectation of exotic canes, cloaks, and outrageous pronouncements was the visible manifestation of a naturally questioning and combative mind. It was no accident that the title of his long-running radio and television quiz program was *Fighting Words*. For Cohen, language was a weapon, and in an imperfect world he was not happy unless he was fighting to make that world better.

The problem with Cohen's campaign to transform Canadian theatre in his own image was that it was doomed to failure. In the name of integrity and high standards, he attempted to lay down a prescriptive view of the drama which bore no relationship to the realities of the market-place. By condemning such popular hits as *Brigadoon* and *Hair*, he simply alienated their audiences without being able to create a demand for the kind of drama he admired. Throughout his career, he called for the creation of an indigenous Canadian drama and for the elimination of the colonial attitudes inhibiting its development. In the end, he was not to see the realization of his dream. His death came just as the Toronto theatre was beginning to explode.

15

New Perspectives

When the actors reassembled in the autumn to begin rehearsals for the 1971–2 season, it was to a theatre darkened by tragedy. During the summer, while swimming in unfamiliar waters in the Caribbean, John Faulkner had been caught in an undertow and drowned. His death left a huge gap in the company. Not only would it be difficult to replace him as a brilliantly imaginative lighting designer, but his steadying influence on the group would be lost. In stormy rehearsal periods, John had often provided an island of quiet strength. It was shocking to realize that that calm presence was gone. A memorial service and benefit performance at the theatre brought together members of the Toronto theatre community in a final celebration of a kindly and independent spirit. Musicians from Grossman's tavern performed, and Milton Acorn read a poem he had written for the occasion.

Though unobserved at the time, Faulkner's death signalled the end of a phase in the development of Toronto Workshop Productions. The era of pioneer theatre, with its reliance on enthusiasm and Rube Goldberg ingenuity, was passing as the company's financial responsibilities increased. To the pressures of theatre ownership and subscription planning (which had already changed the company from what it had been at 47 Fraser Avenue) were now added the challenge of competition from a group of new theatres just struggling into life.

The early seventies saw an unprecedented upsurge of theatrical activity in all parts of the country, but particularly in Toronto. The most notable cause of this sudden growth was the demographic change resulting from the birth of the so-called baby boomers in the years immediately following 1945. The postwar generation had grown up in an environment very different from that of their parents. The arts had been elevated to a position of more importance and dignity in the school curriculum, and the emergence of institutions such as the Stratford Festival, the National Ballet, and the Canadian Opera Company in the 1950s had provided career models not available in the twenties and thirties. Furthermore, the youth culture of the 1960s put a strong emphasis on creativity (albeit of a rather self-indulgent variety) and stressed the importance of living a life of self-fulfilment rather than one dominated by a sense of duty.

Equally important, however, were recent political developments. In 1971, faced with a dramatic increase in unemployment among young people (a consequence of the postwar generation's beginning to enter the labour market), Ottawa established a summer work program euphemistically called Opportunities for Youth. The program proved so successful that it was followed by a second scheme, the Local Initiatives Program or LIP, which provided employment assistance on a year-round basis. Those initiatives were operated through Manpower offices, and provided salaries for young people employed on locally approved projects.

A probably unforeseen consequence of this sudden government munificence was its effect on the arts in Canada. The majority of the projects undertaken under the program were in such areas as construction, social action, and community development, but a significant number were innovative enterprises in the theatre. In the 1971–2 season alone, some $2.5 million in new money was spent on theatre groups, of which a mere $34,000 went to previously established companies.[1] A particular anomaly of this new form of arts subsidy (no doubt a consequence of its being administered as an employment scheme) was the absence of any aesthetic criteria for determining a group's eligibility for funding. Whereas the old theatre companies had had to meet fairly rigorous standards of professionalism in order to qualify for grants from the Canada Council, no such restrictions existed in the new program. The result was a proliferation of shoestring theatre operations kept alive by LIP grants and unemployment insurance benefits until 1975, when the youth programs vanished as quixotically as they had appeared.

The emergence of so many new theatres in Toronto, a city which had previously felt no shortage of them, complicated tensions which had been building in the artistic community for some years. The tensions were most clearly evident in the sharpening opposition during the 1960s between an ossifying 'establishment' theatre and a burgeoning alternative movement. Nathan Cohen had spearheaded the attack on the stodginess and colonial attitudes of Canada's cultural czars, whether at the Crest, the Dominion Drama Festival, or the organizations that attempted to replace them.

In 1967, fresh from a trip to Europe, he had commented on the anomalous position of the country's most prosperous English-speaking metropolis. Whereas Canadian cities such as Vancouver, Winnipeg, and Halifax enjoyed a thriving theatrical culture, Toronto remained artistically and architecturally impoverished. Lacking adequate venues, the city had missed several of the touring attractions organized for the Centennial.[2]

Meanwhile, the St Lawrence Centre for the Arts, Toronto's Centennial project, which was to have provided the city with world-class theatre and music facilities, remained mired in controversy and delay. Stalled by disagreements and diminished by budget cuts through the late 1960s, the building that eventually opened in 1970 proved to be a mere shadow of the original concept. Cohen, citing insipid and platitudinous productions, dismissed its first season as 'devoid of interest.' What he objected to most, however, was the fact that the Centre was not representative of the new Toronto. Its board of governors, he maintained, included 'all the old familiars from the established senior cultural groups in the city – symphony, ballet, art gallery, Crest, Canadian Players, Theatre Toronto.'[3] He predicted that if the Centre followed the policy of the now defunct establishment theatres and directed themselves towards a Toronto society that had lost most of its influence during the war, it would suffer a fate similar to theirs.[4]

If Cohen was the most articulate and effective opponent of Toronto's establishment theatre, he was not the only one. During the late 1960s, Toronto Workshop Productions was merely the most successful of a number of companies attempting in different ways to provide alternative dramatic fare for Toronto audiences. In March 1969, Trio Productions, in association with Theatre Passe Muraille, staged Rochelle Owens's *Futz* at the Central Library Theatre. It was to cause one of the more amusing confrontations between the self-appointed guardians of establishment morality and the counter-culture radicals beginning to storm the citadel.

The play had already caused something of a sensation when first presented by the La Mama Experimental Theatre Club in New York and later at the Traverse Theatre in Edinburgh. By the time it closed in Toronto, the morality squad had issued more than four hundred summonses to actors, crew members, producers, ushers, and even hat-check attendants for taking part in or associating with an obscene performance. By 15 May, all charges except those against the director and the producers had been dropped. But the Crown doggedly pressed its case against these 'offenders,' and a trial date was set for 4 June. By October, an initial guilty verdict had been appealed, and an unrepentant Theatre Passe Muraille was presenting a second La Mama script, the Tom O'Horgan production of Paul Foster's *Tom Paine*, which had appeared in Edinburgh along with *Futz* in 1967.

Another Toronto group which was beginning to import some of the new experimental work from New York was Studio Lab. Originally established by Ernest Schwarz as a children's theatre, Studio Lab had begun to cater to more mature audiences. In February 1969, they had produced Michael McClure's *The Beard*, a fantasy seduction which had been labelled obscene by the San Francisco police when presented there by the Actor's Workshop. In December, Schwarz and his company opened what was to be the succès de scandale of the year – a local production of *Dionysus in 69*, an experiment in ritual and nudity originated by Richard Schechner's recently formed Performance Group of New York.

Perhaps the most vivid indication of how Toronto theatrical taste was changing, however, was the arrival at the Royal Alex in December 1969 of the rock musical *Hair*. With its celebration of the youth culture and its full frontal nudity, *Hair* played to enthusiastic or curious audiences for a total of twelve months. By the time the *Futz* appeal was heard in the county court on 7 April 1970, it was evident to Judge William Lyon that community standards of tolerance had so changed that confirmation of the lower court judgment could not be justified.

The catalyst for this sudden transformation was the return to Toronto of several young directors fresh from experience abroad and eager to exercise their talents in their native country. Feeling themselves excluded from the established theatres and dedicated to different aesthetic aims, several of these young artists set up theatres of their own. Within a few short years, four companies emerged: Theatre Passe Muraille, founded in 1968 by Jim Garrard; Factory Theatre Lab, founded in 1970 by Ken Gass and Frank Trotz; Tarragon Theatre, founded in 1971 by Bill Glassco; and Toronto Free Theatre, founded in 1971 by Tom Hendry, Martin Kinch, John Palmer, and others. Though these companies came to be referred to collectively as the 'alternative' theatres,[5] in fact they shared no common program or methodology. In general, their inspiration came from New York and Europe rather than England. They looked to the new directors of New York and Poland – O'Horgan, Julian Beck, Judith Melina, Jerzy Grotowski. They read the international theatre magazines and 'modelled their work after *Tulane Drama Review* descriptions of Off-off-Broadway and Eastern Europe.'[6]

This new movement in the Toronto theatre found its voice in August 1970. That month, several young directors, including Jim Plaxton, Jim

Garrard, Martin Kinch, John Palmer, Paul Thompson, Ken Gass, Henry
Tarvainen, and Martin Brenzell, organized the Festival of Underground
Theatre to showcase their work and that of some of the international the-
atre companies they looked to for inspiration. Among the entries were
Passe Muraille's *Ubu Raw*, directed by Paul Thompson; Ibsen's *A Doll's
House*, directed by John Palmer; and Tom Eyen's *White Whore and the Bit
Player*, directed by Martin Brenzell. But the greatest excitement was gener-
ated by the appearances of such international companies as the Bread
and Puppet Theatre from New York and the Théâtre de la Grande
Panique from Paris. Conspicuously absent from the festival was George
Luscombe and Toronto Workshop Productions. Increasingly, Luscombe
was to find himself isolated, not only from the new young directors but
also from a second generation of critics.

During the previous decade, drama criticism had been dominated by
Nathan Cohen and Herbert Whittaker, writing in the two major dailies,
the *Toronto Star* and the *Globe and Mail*. Both men were deeply knowledge-
able, and they shared a passionate conviction that what they did was
important. In that conviction, they seemed to be supported by their newspapers. With Cohen's death and Whittaker's partial, and then complete,
retirement, however, all that changed. The writers who replaced the older
critics were seldom as erudite as their predecessors, and they tended to
regard arts criticism as simply another branch of journalism, like foreign
affairs or sports writing. Their attitude no doubt reflected a change in the
editorial policy of the papers themselves. No longer did arts criticism
enjoy any particular prestige. The concept of drama as an expression of
high human culture was gradually being replaced by the notion of theatre
as entertainment.

An individual who resisted the trend was Cohen's immediate successor,
Urjo Kareda. Kareda had written occasional pieces for Cohen since at
least 1967, when he contributed a sympathetic article on Luscombe and
the working methods of TWP. His recent contributions to the *Star* had
been mostly film reviews, but by the fall of 1971 he had assumed the not
insignificant mantle of his former editor. Kareda's approach to the theatre was, like Cohen's, essentially that of a spectator. His enthusiasm for
the art was boundless and his knowledge extensive, but his reviews tended
to smell of the lamp and the library rather than of sweat and greasepaint.
What Kareda brought that was new was the perspective of a younger generation. Whereas Cohen and Whittaker looked back to the thirties and
early forties as their formative period, Kareda was a product of the sixties.
He was in tune with the new breed of actors and directors just then

appearing in the city. If anything, he identified even more strongly than his predecessors with the new Canadian playwrights, and he did much to promote them in his columns.

Also affecting the critical climate in Toronto during this time was the emergence of Canadian drama as a subject of serious academic enquiry. In the previous decade, discussion of Canadian plays had been confined almost exclusively to the columns of the newspapers, but the seventies saw a proliferation of articles on the subject in periodicals and learned journals. This flurry of interest in a new area of Canadian writing culminated in 1974 with the creation of the *Canadian Theatre Review*, a journal devoted entirely to a subject that ten years earlier could hardly have been said to exist.

As the forum for serious discussion of Canadian theatre shifted from the daily press to the academic journals, the tone of that discussion altered. Comment on the subject became more literary and theoretical than it had been hitherto. Writers began to take more interest in what might be called 'the sociology of theatre' and tried to relate it to larger patterns in the country's cultural development. In an article entitled 'Creeping toward a Culture' in the first volume of *Canadian Theatre Review*, the editor, Don Rubin, gave a heavily footnoted version of the notion that was coming to dominate accounts of Canadian play-writing. Citing the 1889 theory of the French literary historian Ferdinand Brunetière that periods of excellence in the drama coincide with moments when nations are exalted by the expression of a collective will, Rubin argued that the sudden appearance of so many new Canadian playwrights was an expression of a new national self-awareness brought about by the country's participation in the Second World War and furthered by the Centennial celebrations of 1967.[7] In conformance with this theory, Rubin tended to dismiss as insignificant Canadian plays written before 1967 and to regard as quintessentially 'Canadian' plays that dealt with national history and politics.

His rather narrow interpretation – what might be called the 'set in Canada' as opposed to the merely 'made in Canada' doctrine of Canadian drama – rapidly became the accepted orthodoxy among critics and public alike. Audiences began to flock in substantial numbers to the new alternative theatres to watch plays about generational conflict in Newfoundland, the 1837 rebellion of farmers in Upper Canada, or blood-feuds among Irish settlers in nineteenth-century Ontario.

Other developments also contributed to a growing interest in indigenous drama. The Playwrights' Conference, held under the aegis of the

Canada Council in 1971, recommended that funding to theatres should be contingent on their including a certain number of Canadian plays in their seasons. That recommendation, while not adopted in its entirety, influenced Council policy, and theatres felt under increasing pressure to produce original Canadian scripts and to bring new playwrights into the theatre. The following year saw the establishment of the Floyd S. Chalmers Canadian Play Awards and the creation of the Toronto Drama Bench to adjudicate it. To many, TWP seemed out of step with these developments. Its 'Canadian' plays tended not to be regional or historical, and the theatre had acquired a reputation for being inhospitable to writers. Luscombe's dealings with playwrights had been marked by tension, suspicion, and bitterness, and in spite of repeated efforts he had failed to find another author with whom he could work as comfortably as he had with Jack Winter. It was becoming evident that if TWP was to compete successfully for a share of the limited Toronto theatre audience, it might have to modify its strategy.

16

Old Wine in New Bottles:
Ten Lost Years

As he moved to adjust to the new Toronto theatre scene in the early seventies, Luscombe had difficulty adapting to the emerging critical orthodoxy. He was suspicious of nationalism. As a Marxist, he believed that nations were shaped by international forces and that social and political developments in other countries had direct relevance to what was happening in Canada. Indeed, in certain cases, the operation of such forces might be more clearly evident in stories about rural China or allegories based on American politics than in plays on Canadian subjects. Nevertheless, it was obvious that TWP could not go on ignoring the growing interest in Canadian material on the part of local audiences.

One of his early efforts to deal with a Canadian topic straightforwardly (rather than indirectly through allegory or dramatic metaphor) was his attempt to mount a new play by the poet Milton Acorn. The project was first proposed in 1972 by Acorn and Cedric Smith, who had been collaborating on a late-night show at the Alexander Street theatre.[1] With help from the Canada Council, Luscombe had commissioned Acorn to complete a drama about the exploitation of farm workers in Prince Edward Island to be called *The Road to Charlottetown*. On the strength of the commission, Acorn went north to work in seclusion, and during the summer of 1973 he mailed back his play in instalments. When the final draft arrived in December, Luscombe was not happy with the second act, but lacking an alternative script, he began rehearsals hoping to refashion the play with the actors' help.

During these rehearsals, Acorn watched the transformation of his work with a grim stoicism until he could endure it no longer. Finally one morning he appeared in the foyer of the theatre accompanied by a well-dressed stranger whom Luscombe took to be his lawyer, and demanded to know if further changes were being contemplated. When Luscombe muttered gruffly that he would make what alterations he thought necessary, Acorn handed him an envelope, turned on his heel, and walked out of the theatre without a word. Nonplussed, Luscombe opened the letter to find that he was threatened with legal action if the script was altered any further. He reacted with his usual determination. Although he had no immediate alternative to *The Road to Charlottetown*, he informed the actors that rehearsals were suspended.[2]

This was not the first time the company had had to scramble for a last-minute replacement in their program, but the timing of the current emergency could scarcely have been more unfortunate. Not only had they suffered losses on the two opening productions of the season, *Richard Thirdtime*, an adaptation of Shakespeare's *Richard III* by Steven Bush and Rick McKenna, and Jean Anouilh's *Thieves' Carnival*, but they had failed to achieve any of the objectives they had spelled out so ambitiously to the funding agencies six months earlier. It was desperately important that they come up with a production that would vindicate their claim to being the senior alternative theatre in the city and demonstrate their professed commitment to original Canadian drama.

One day, having overcome his disappointment that the Charlottetown play had been cancelled, Cedric Smith walked into the theatre to convey to Luscombe his enthusiasm about a work he had recently seen at Theatre Passe Muraille – a collectively created production put together the summer before by a group of actors who had spent several weeks investigating the work and lives of farmers in Clinton, Ontario. The piece was called *The Farm Show*, and Smith was excited about the way it captured the lives of ordinary Canadians. He thought that perhaps TWP could do something similar, and he brought with him a book he believed might form the basis for such a production. It was an oral history of the 1930s called *Ten Lost Years*.

The recently published book was a collection of memories of the depression years recorded on tape by the journalist Barry Broadfoot during a fifteen-thousand-mile trip across the country. Broadfoot, himself a child in the thirties, had wanted to discover what survivors of the period felt about that time, and the volume is a record of his findings. In many ways, it is an imperfect mirror of the decade it reflects. Individual speakers are never identified, so their comments cannot be related to a personality or a particular history. Furthermore, the recollections are gathered by theme rather than by region or year and form a kind of disembodied collage of impressions devoid of distinguishing regional or class characteristics. The result is a generalized 'portrait' of a period that is necessarily backward-looking and for that reason coloured by nostalgia and sentimentality. It was a mine of dramatic material, but lacking in many of the essential ingredients of drama.

The company Luscombe assembled to begin work on the new project was a heterogeneous group. Six of the actors, including June and John Faulkner's son Peter, Cedric Smith, François Klanfer, Peter Millard, Ross Skene, and Iris Paabo, had worked with Luscombe in the past; Diane Douglass, Jackie Burroughs, and Richard Payne were newcomers. As they began to improvise scenes, it became evident that there was no consensus as to how the work should be organized or what material most deserved to be included. For Luscombe, the period was powerfully evocative. As a child, he had watched young men ride the boxcars through the Don Valley close to his home and seen migrant workers try to sleep in the warm ovens at the Todmorden brick works. He remembered neighbours out of work, and a constant fear among his elders of being 'fired,' a fate he didn't understand but imagined as being completely encircled with flames. The members of the company, by contrast, were products of the fifties and sixties who regarded the depression as ancient history.

To give the actors a sense of the period, Luscombe lectured on the social and economic conditions of the time (which many of the performers found boring) and described the 'given circumstances' of particular scenes. These latter demonstrations were particularly vivid. 'We would feel the heat and hear the swinging screen doors,' recalled one of the actors. 'There was a parade (George would mime the marching of the band), but what was important, he would say, was the little dog who wanders in among the marchers' feet. And as he spoke, George's chunky body would suddenly move like the dog.'[3]

In the early days of rehearsal, the actors picked stories to be tried out in improvisation. Sometimes, they would devise routines to accompany lines spoken by a single individual; at other times, they would dramatize a passage from the book and present it as a 'realistic' sketch or as part of a simulated radio broadcast. The basic configuration of the stage grew out of a series of improvisations around a camp-fire in a hobo jungle. Since there were rarely any women in the hobo camps, the actresses got squeezed to the periphery, where they established different 'homes.' Meanwhile, the actors playing the restless and migrating workers began miming riding the rods. Peter Faulkner pretended to jump on a boxcar, and the company spent hours developing what was to become one of the most theatrical sequences of the production.

At the outset, Cedric Smith served as dramaturge as well as music director and composer. But differences between him and Luscombe soon gave rise to serious disagreements. Smith was a committed Marxist, but he was also a folk-singer with a folk-singer's attraction to the emotionally melodramatic. Although skilful in turning out tuneful burlesques such as a song of the Bennett Buggy or a 'Depressed' square dance, Smith was also drawn to the 'hurtin' vein, as in such lyrics as 'Mama needed help, she didn't feel too strong, / And all the children's sadness it just seemed so wrong.'

Luscombe, however, wanted the performers to exercise emotional restraint in their playing. He was convinced that too much emotion on stage made the audience 'run from it,' and so, like Brecht and Littlewood, he sought to avoid sentimentality in the theatre. His aim was to create a truer and deeper emotion through contrast or anticlimax. An example of the kind of moment he cherished occurs near the beginning of *Ten Lost Years*, where the Quiet Woman (Jackie Burroughs) recounts how, as a result of the failure of their generator, much of the farm work had to be done without electricity. Her mother attempts to console her by assuring her, 'It'll all work out in the end. You'll be a better woman for it.' Instead of concluding with the expected comment that her mother was right, the Quiet Woman remarks acidly, 'God, I was never closer to killing a person in my life.' The laugh the line got on opening night, brought on by the audience's surprised recognition of the truth of the response, convinced Luscombe they had a hit on their hands.

He also recognized that the material had a certain alienation already built in. The monologues were the recollections of tough survivors who were recounting the events of some forty years earlier. In re-creating their reminiscences, it was important to find a style which would convey both the impression of dramatic immediacy and the effect of emotional distance. For example, the character remembering her discovery of a neighbour who had committed suicide would not go through the original emotions again, because she had already dealt with them. The actress had to remember that she was playing not the girl who made the discovery but the woman who remembered it.

To bridge the two times and to create a more complex theatrical effect, Luscombe tried to work on two levels. In that way, the detachment of the remembered past could by made more vivid by the intensity of the mimed 'present.' The speaker's impassive account of the crucifixion of a railway policeman was juxtaposed with a silent search through an imagined railway-yard and the horrifying discovery of the imaginary body.

Even more important than capturing the emotional truth of individual scenes was establishing an appropriate tonal dynamic. One of the most important means to that end was the juxtaposition of contrasting elements. Sometimes, opposing views would be alternated, as in favourable and unfavourable recollections of the trek to Ottawa. Sometimes, the music would provide an ironic comment on the lyrics, as in the square dance melody, in which jaunty rhythms accompany a description of natural catastrophe: 'Got no money in the till, / If the dust don't get you the hoppers will.' Sometimes, a scene of violence would be juxtaposed with a sentimental ballad: at the end of the first part of the play, an account of the murder of a hobo is interspersed with the song 'Do not think about tomorrow, / Let tomorrow come and go, / Tonight you're in a nice warm boxcar, / Safe from all the wind and snow.' In other cases, the mimed sequence would jar with the spoken words, as when a scene exposing the pitiful wages paid to dressmakers is juxtaposed with a silent fashion show.

Perhaps the most complex problem in dealing with the diverse material of the Broadfoot book, however, was that of devising an overall shape. Part way through rehearsals, Luscombe invited Jack Winter to help him give the production intellectual and emotional coherence. Paul Thompson and his actors at the Theatre Passe Muraille had created *The Farm Show* as a kind of three-dimensional photo-album of the Clinton community. Alan Filewod describes how these dramatic 'snapshots' constituted a subjective report of the actors' encounters over several weeks with the farmers of the area.[4] As visitors and guests, the performers could hardly be critical or unflattering. Their purpose was to 'authenticate' the experience of that first audience and, by transforming it into art, enable them to see value and significance in their lives that they might not otherwise have discerned.[5] There was no attempt on the part of the actors (all of whom were outsiders) to evaluate those lives or to place them in a larger social, economic, or political context.

Winter and Luscombe were interested in doing something quite different. They were not content simply to reproduce experience; they wanted to bring out the hidden laws governing that experience. As Marxists, they were convinced that the depression was not a unique or isolated phenomenon but something that was going to happen again. They wanted the audience to understand how Canadians' attitudes had worked against them in the past and how nostalgia for a sentimentalized 1930s – as in the American TV series *The Waltons* – was anti-revolutionary and marked a return to colonialism. In this respect, Winter and Luscombe found themselves at odds with some of the performers, including Cedric Smith, who wanted to eulogize the people's suffering. Winter and Luscombe wanted to attack the system which they felt had caused that suffering.

One method by which they did so was to use agitprop techniques. A sequence entitled 'The Poker Game' shows how men (and women) with capital play with human lives the way gamblers play with cards. Another method was to focus more strongly than Broadfoot had done on the political rebels of the period. To do so, Winter and Luscombe supplemented the material in *Ten Lost Years* with excerpts from another recently published book, Michael Horn's *The Dirty Thirties*. There they found accounts of the exploitation of garment workers by the T. Eaton Company, and several revealing quotations of R.B. Bennett.

While a left-wing political interpretation informed the play, the tone of the social criticism was less strident than usual in TWP productions. It was also better integrated with the other elements in the work. Indeed, the political message was so muted that some critics felt the play was an endorsement of the very blindness Luscombe thought he was attacking.

When it finally opened on 5 February 1974, *Ten Lost Years* was an instant success. Following a couple of lacklustre seasons, some critics had begun to feel that TWP was more interested in American than Canadian politics and that Luscombe's methods of training and style of direction were no longer relevant in the radically altered Toronto theatre scene. All such reservations disappeared in the wake of the almost unanimous praise for the new production. Urjo Kareda, who had been devastating in his dismissal of *Thieves' Carnival*, acknowledged the brilliance of Luscombe's style, which he called 'a kind of musical theatre [which is] funny, insinuating, [and] touching.' Like most of the critics, Kareda was deeply moved by the 'spellbinding human document' and the experiences it revealed, 'aching, immediate and heartbreaking.' But he was also full of admiration for the way in which the documentary material had been handled.[6]

Other critics shared his enthusiasm for the company as not only versatile but disciplined. Audrey Ashley of the *Ottawa Citizen* was struck by the actors' ability to create a world out of simple materials – 'a piano, a chair, a box or two, and a few ramps.'[7] Some praised their skill in mime and their ability to evoke a rich scene on an empty stage; others, their skill in creating an environment that enabled the audience to feel the atmosphere of familiar surroundings.

Ten Lost Years re-established Luscombe and his company as a powerfully creative force in Toronto theatre. It seemed to vindicate his emphasis on actor training and group work, since the distinctive qualities of the production were a result of his efforts over the past fourteen years. His selection of versatile performers and his work in movement and improvisation were largely responsible for the effects achieved. But the production also set him apart from the new alternative theatres. As one critic remarked, 'One of Luscombe's major achievements is his ability to make each piece [of the production] fit together smoothly ... so that the play flows along, never seeming jagged or uneven, unlike much documentary theatre ... that seems to chuck all its cards into the air helter skelter.'[8]

The production continued to attract enthusiastic audiences throughout the spring, so it was decided to cancel the rest of the season and run *Ten Lost Years* for as long as possible. Finally, in late May, the heat in the un-air-conditioned theatre became unbearable, and the play closed after seventeen weeks. By that time, plans were already under way for a national tour which would take the company from Ottawa to Vancouver and back. In mid-September, the company set out, to give seventy-seven performances in forty-three centres, with an average attendance of over 80 per cent.

Everywhere, the actors were praised for their versatility and for their ability to make the period come alive. But most moving to audiences across the country was that the play dealt with actual human beings, the people of Canada who struggled through a painful decade. Although *Chicago '70* had also treated documentary material and reproduced the words of living people, the events of the Chicago trial had seemed remote to most spectators, and the wild, carnival style in which they had been presented had alienated audiences still further. What impressed Lynne van Luven of the *Lethbridge Herald* about *Ten Lost Years* was the experience of seeing something on stage which touched her directly – 'Canadian history, Canadian culture and Canadian thought ... not Ibsen's Norway or Shaw's Britain.'[9]

17

The Indignant Muse

The triumph of *Ten Lost Years* represented a vindication of Luscombe's methods at TWP. For while the immediate inspiration for the work had been Paul Thompson's collectively created *Farm Show*, the nature of the final production grew out of more than a decade of experimentation in the forms of documentary theatre on the part of Luscombe, Winter, and the actors of TWP. During the early sixties, that experimentation had encouraged the company to explore and challenge the conventions of traditional narrative. Whether deconstructing an already existing script (as in *The Death of Woyzeck*) or building their own works on the fragmentary foundation of others (as in *The Mechanic* and *The Golem of Venice*), Luscombe and Winter had tried to move away from 'Aristotelian' or narrative-based structures towards more open forms.

When the company moved to 12 Alexander Street and inaugurated subscription seasons, however, Luscombe found it difficult to find the rehearsal time necessary to develop the kind of collaborative creations he and Winter had worked on at Fraser Avenue. *Chicago '70* had been something of an anomaly, since the collection of the documentary evidence required little research and the actors had a strong response to the material. Luscombe realized that the creation of dramas out of documentary material would normaly require time-consuming research, and in 1971 he invited Jack Winter to rejoin the company.

During the four years since he had left TWP, Winter had pursued a writing career, with mixed results. His original disagreement with Luscombe had been over the direction in which the company was moving in 1967, and Winter left thinking that he could carry out his ideas better on his own. Efforts to sell his work to the CBC and to Theatre Toronto in 1968 came to nothing, but the following year he set up his own production company and wrote and directed a show to open the Studio Theatre at the National Arts Centre in Ottawa. *Party Day* was poorly received, and for the next two years Winter was a regular contributor to the Bruno Gerussi show *Gerussi!* on CBC radio. In 1971, he completed a documentary film set in Prince Edward Island. When Luscombe rang him in November of that year, he was ready to re-establish his contact with the legitimate theatre.

Their first collaboration was a dramatization of Dickens's *Pickwick Papers* entitled *Mr Pickwick*, undertaken at short notice when negotiations between TWP and Carol Bolt broke down and Luscombe was left without a play for the Christmas season. The work was a huge success. It was followed by a production based on Mark Twain's posthumously published *Letters from the Earth*, a series of radically sceptical comments on Christianity which appealed to Luscombe's and Winter's anticlericalism. *Letters from the Earth* was a novel and imaginative stage piece which attracted considerable favourable comment in the press not only in Toronto but in Ottawa, where it appeared at the National Arts Centre.

It was the success of *Ten Lost Years*, however, which consolidated the Luscombe-Winter partnership. Pleased by the widespread popularity of the play, Luscombe and Winter remained unshaken in their conviction that drama must do more than promote a comfortable nostalgia. They wanted their theatre to startle the audiences, to shake them out of complacent attitudes and make them realize that Canada played a role in a larger world and had important international responsibilities. This fact was brought home to the two men in a particularly vivid way in April 1974. At a party organized for several Chilean refugees, they were electrified by stories of Canada's response to the overthrow of the democratically elected government of Salvador Allende. Not only had Canada recognized with unseemly haste the newly established military government under General Augusto Pinochet, but it had acted with uncharacteristic indifference to the plight of Chileans seeking asylum in the country. Canada had gained an international reputation for its hospitality to the fugitives from communist regimes – it had opened its doors to 30,000 Hungarians in the fifties, 11,000 Czechs in the sixties, and some 60,000 'boat people' in the recent past – but refugee claimants from Chile were subjected to detailed security screenings and health investigations which in the end kept their number below 2,000.[1] To Luscombe and Winter, here was further evidence of Canada's subservience to American interests, and a vivid illustration of the double standard in its refugee policy, which favoured victims of leftist persecution over people fleeing from regimes on the right. In September, it was revealed that between 1970 and 1973 the CIA had funnelled some $8 million into Chile in an effort to prevent Allende's election and then to weaken his government.[2] They decided to dramatize these issues in their opening production of the 1974–5 season.

Within a short time, Winter had compiled an impressive dossier of research material and started to work it into a script, which he sardonically entitled *You Can't Get Here from There*. To convey the idea of cleanliness, which Luscombe thought epitomized Canadians in the minds of people in the Third World, Astrid Janson, who had replaced Nancy Jowsey as TWP's designer, devised an ingenious set consisting of a large cube (a floor and two walls covered with white shag rug and two walls of transparent lucite) which could be opened to admit outsiders or closed to act as a barrier. The effect was of a room which shone like a huge display case or store window into which the Chilean refugees could peer, but only rarely penetrate.

Rehearsals went so smoothly that the night before the opening Luscombe let his cast go home early. A couple of members of the technical crew remained behind to paint the stage floor one last time, but they too were able to leave the theatre by about two o'clock in the morning. Luscombe went to bed confident that the production would be a success, and slept so soundly that he did not hear the phone ringing shortly after three. About half an hour later, he was awakened by the sound of someone banging on his front door. He staggered out of bed, wrapped himself in his dressing-gown, and descended the stairs, to find Calvin Butler in a state of high excitement. 'George,' he almost shouted, 'the theatre's on fire.'

After dressing hastily, Luscombe, his wife, Mona, and Butler drove headlong through the silent, snowy streets, to find Alexander Street a scene of noise and confusion. The police had closed off Yonge and Alexander streets, and the still burning building was surrounded by some seventeen fire department vehicles and a crowd of curious and concerned onlookers.[3] Making their way through the crowd, Butler and Luscombe located June Faulkner, who had been the first company member the fire department had been able to reach after the blaze had been discovered. Together, they watched in horrified disbelief as smoke poured in sickening profusion from the building. It seemed that only a miracle could prevent the fire from engulfing the entire theatre. Gradually, however, the fire-fighters succeeded in containing the blaze, and finally, as dawn began to break, they brought it under control.

The fire had started at the back of the theatre and had completely destroyed the dressing-rooms, the costume workshop, the stage, the lighting equipment, and all the costumes and scenery for *Mr Pickwick* as well as *You Can't Get Here* stored in the area. The heat had melted the covers of the seats in the auditorium and severely damaged the equipment in the lighting and sound booths.[4] It had also affected the roof. The shell of the building, however, appeared to be sound, and it was just possible that the theatre could be restored without having to build from the foundation up.

What was still unknown was the cost. Insurance would pay for some of the damage, but the pre-production expenses of *You Can't Get Here*, estimated at about $23,000, were irrecoverable, and the show would have to be entirely remounted. In addition, the Christmas show was now in jeopardy: unless an alternative performing space could be found, it would be necessary to cancel *Mr Pickwick* as well. While everyone agreed that Toronto Workshop Productions must not be allowed to die, it was unclear on the morning of 5 November just how its death could be prevented.

During the next hectic week, Faulkner got estimates on the cost of rebuilding the stage and auditorium and replacing lost equipment. Luscombe consulted the actors to see if they would be willing to remain on rehearsal pay until the show could open, and he investigated alternative staging possibilities for *Mr Pickwick*. Meanwhile, support for Luscombe and the theatre flowed in from all parts of the theatre community. Leon Major of the St Lawrence Centre scheduled a benefit performance of Sheridan's *The Rivals*; the performers in *Clap Hands* staged an extra performance of the revue in a local supper club; the National Ballet offered workshop space; Robin Phillips of the Stratford Festival organized a campaign for contributions within his company and promised the receipts from preview performances of *Two Gentlemen of Verona* and *The Comedy of Errors*; Toronto Dance Theatre gave a benefit concert with several guest stars; and the Shaw Festival, the Firehall Theatre, and Toronto Free Theatre all offered facilities. Overwhelmed by this spontaneous generosity, June Faulkner reported to Herbert Whittaker, 'Every single theatre has come forward with offers of assistance – except for the Royal Alexandra and O'Keefe.'[5]

Luscombe seemed in his element during the crisis. Never happier than when confronting adversity, he oversaw the return to Toronto of *Ten Lost Years*, which opened at the Bayview Playhouse on 12 December for a three-week run; he cast and rehearsed *Mr Pickwick*, which opened five days later in the St Lawrence Centre's Town Hall for fifteen performances;

and he re-rehearsed *You Can't Get Here*, which opened on 31 December, the anniversary of the first performance in the Alexander Street theatre. It was a display of energy and resourcefulness which made those who could remember them hark back to the early days of TWP at Fraser Avenue, and it prompted Herbert Whittaker to remark that Luscombe and his company of actors were 'as much a Toronto treasure as the Moore collection.'[6]

The general feeling of the critics who attended the opening of *You Can't Get Here from There* was that once again Winter and Luscombe had been betrayed by their indignation into an oversimplified theatrical presentation of the issues. The central stage image of the gleaming white cube inhabited by actors in antiseptic white costumes was so arresting that it distracted from the meaning of the play. Slides of tanks in the streets or of political opponents being rounded up in the soccer stadium did not adequately convey the horror outside the sterile showcase. The problem was compounded by the doubling of the roles of the Canadians and Chileans, which muted the impact of the reported atrocities.

A related problem was the totally unsympathetic portrayal of the villains of the piece, Ambassador Ross and his wife. Here, the critics were divided between those who felt the issues involved were made clearer by the melodramatic characterization and those, like Urjo Kareda, who were tempted to 'cease trusting even the given information' when confronted with character portrayal so simplistic.[7] Winter denied that there was an element of caricature in the play. 'I see her as a complete characterization of an incomplete personality,' he remarked of the portrayal of Mrs Ross. In the same interview, however, the dramatist revealed a surprising attitude towards his public. 'I'm less interested in a specific audience,' he said, 'than in getting a general audience to account for themselves.'[8]

A number of critics, especially those not sharing Winter's political convictions, resented being lectured at and thought he had failed to find suitable artistic expression for his ideas. Even the normally sympathetic Urjo Kareda was cool in calling the play 'a thick file-folder of research that [Winter] hasn't yet resolved into a dramatically viable form. There are too many snippets of incident that never build a narrative momentum, and since the only continuing character of any interest at all is almost entirely repellent ... the play's political arguments seem lopsided.'[9]

After the qualified success of *You Can't Get Here from There*, Luscombe and Winter turned to another project they had been contemplating for some time – an investigation of the relationship between idealism and commerce in the Olympic Games. It seemed to them that the Olympics were a perfect paradigm of the way in which the achievements of individuals were appropriated and subverted by commercial and political interests. The humbug and hypocrisy which had marked the development of the events, especially in the twentieth century, were blatant in the hype surrounding the preparations for the 1976 Montreal Games, in which there was already evidence of kickbacks, non-tendered contracts, and horrendous cost overruns. The persistence of the organizers and supporters in maintaining that they were above politics and that the Games were instrumental in eradicating the differences between peoples and nations represented exactly the kind of self-delusion that the two collaborators delighted in puncturing.

As usual, it was Winter's job to dig up the facts. He soon discovered that the Olympics had never been the unalloyed celebration of *mens sana in corpore sano* that its supporters had idealistically maintained. Greek athletes, it turned out, had been hardly less mercenary and self-indulgent than Roman gladiators. Indeed, the spirit of the Games seemed to Winter to be summed up perfectly in the mythical account of the first chariot race at Olympia, between Pelops and Oenomaus for the hand of Hippodamia. Pelops won that contest not by any superior skill but by sabotaging his opponent's chariot so that it crashed during the race, killing its driver.

Luscombe had retained the core of the *Ten Lost Years* company, including Iris Paabo, Ross Skene, Peter Millard, Grant Roll, Diane Douglass, and Rich Payne. These actors had been playing together now for six months and had developed their ensemble skills to a high degree. As the work proceeded, some of the actors felt that Winter's material was insufficiently dramatic and began doing research of their own. They discovered William O. Johnson's 1972 history of the Olympics, *All That Glitters Is Not Gold.* The book provided them with a solid historical framework by means of which they could give the play some shape. They also watched films of the 1972 Munich Olympics and listened to comments by the former Olympic athletes Bruce Kidd and Abby Hoffman, who had been brought in to make suggestions.[10]

Astrid Janson designed a brilliant setting reminiscent of the proposed Montreal Olympic stadium. It consisted of a broad white track of white canvas which seemed to recede into the distance towards the back of the stage, where it swept up into the air and arched forward over the heads of the actors. On either side of this track, on the red floor of the stage, were a few musical instruments.[11] The actors performed in athletic outfits (running shoes supplied by Adidas), with just three props – a bamboo pole and two lengths of coloured nylon rope.

As usual, the play developed out of the creative tension between the bitterly ironic and often prolix rhetoric of Winter and the exuberant and playful mummery of the performers – all moderated by Luscombe's uncanny feeling for sound and movement. It was not always easy to maintain a balance. The actors had become masters of witty pantomime. For example, in one routine, Ross Skene portrayed a weightlifter, with Grant Roll and Rich Payne acting as the weights. After Skene's humiliating failure to lift the bar, Diane Douglass walked out, glared at the two 'weights,' picked up the bar, and threw it into the audience. In another sequence, one of the actors began running in slow motion, gradually increased his speed, and ended up skipping with the rope that marked the finishing line. These improvisations combined both a genuine respect for the skill of the athletes and a deft irreverence, like circus clowns' duplication of the feats of acrobats.

Not all the hilarity at that time was caused by on-stage activities. The design for the promotional poster turned out to be one of Theo Dimson's masterpieces. Dimson, a Toronto graphic designer who had created brilliantly original posters for the company for several years, had a genius for capturing the spirit of the productions. When told that the new play was to be an attack on the commercial exploitation of the Olympics, he produced a design featuring a huge Coca-Cola bottle with a tiny muscle-bound athlete emerging from its mouth. On the bottle was the five-circle Olympic symbol instead of the Coca-Cola trade mark. The company's delight with the poster was redoubled when they received a letter from Coca-Cola (Canada)'s general solicitor insisting that the design represented an 'unauthorized reproduction of the trade mark bottle' which would tend 'to distort and dilute the distinctiveness of such a trade mark.' All offending posters, he insisted, must be 'removed and destroyed forthwith.'[12] Luscombe greeted this information with huge guffaws and immediately ordered wider distribution.

Summer '76 opened on 22 April 1975, to mixed reviews. Urjo Kareda, Joseph Erdelyi of the *Ottawa Citizen*, and Herbert Whittaker all had serious reservations about the script. They called it, respectively, 'a confusing jumble of Greek legend and history, incomprehensible anecdotes about early Olympians';[13] 'a poorly written semi-documentary';[14] and 'a narrow-eyed, disapproving look at the Olympics [which] ... bogs down in its righteous indignation.'[15] All objected to the almost total absence of references to the Montreal Olympics but praised the company and director for their skill and imagination.

The play ran for four weeks, attracting 1,647 spectators to twenty-four performances for an average attendance of 23 per cent. While not a disaster, the piece had clearly not been the hit Luscombe and Winter had hoped for. That was especially disappointing in view of their plan to include the work in a nine-week tour of Europe scheduled for the summer of 1976. Tentative plans called for the mounting of three Winter-Luscombe collaborations, but in the end the European program had to be reduced to just two productions, *Ten Lost Years* and *Summer '76*.

The company's destination in London was the Young Vic Theatre, where it opened on 3 May 1976 with a performance of *Ten Lost Years*. Audiences were small, and the reception of the play muted. The response to *Summer '76*, which opened the following week, was more positive, and audiences began to grow. Jeremy Kingston of the *Financial Times* compared the company favourably to Littlewood's Theatre Workshop, saying that TWP had kept in mind what its predecessor forgot, 'a feel for construction': 'Inventive, intelligent and carefully paced, the show is from first to last an arresting entertainment.' Ben Duncan of the BBC was equally positive; 'I think that the company has a technique which I've never actually seen before,' he reported, 'a way of weaving together the dialogue and the songs and the dancing [which] produces a peculiar texture which is ... quite unique ... Over the two evenings, the cumulative effect was very very strong, indeed.'[16]

Following the final performance, Winter and Luscombe emerged from the theatre and stood on the street contemplating the marquee. Winter had been dissatisfied with his travel allowance and was not going on the rest of the tour. Behind them lay some fourteen years of intermittent and often stormy collaboration, a period of shared triumph and narrowly avoided disaster. At the beginning, Winter, who was ten years Luscombe's junior, had been very much the apprentice. But from the outset their imaginations and talents had been so complementary that both seemed to work better in collaboration than alone. In the end, Luscombe, who is grudging of his praise, recognized Winter's contribution: speaking of *The Golem* in 1989, he said, 'All of a sudden, [part way through the rehearsals,] it dawned on me what he wanted ... what he was writing for, and I became a fan of his vision. Most of the time I was bringing him into my vision of the play, but on this occasion he was bringing something that was much better than where I thought we were going.' That evening, however, he said nothing. Many years later he remembered the moment spatially: 'He was standing there with his wife just down there, and I was standing here

(I think Mona was back there). And he said, "I'm going." I said, "Yeah." We'd just run out of things to say. We'd said it all. There was nothing, nothing left to say. I stood there and looked at him; he looked at me, and we turned around and walked away from each other. Didn't shake hands. Just turned around. Gone.' It was the end of a chapter.

18

A Vintage Season

Luscombe returned to Toronto from England in the summer of 1976 to a troubled theatre scene. The first wave of creative energy which had produced the alternative theatre movement in the early 1970s seemed to have spent itself. Factory Theatre, Theatre Passe Muraille, Tarragon, and Toronto Free Theatre, the theatres primarily responsible for creating an interest in new Canadian plays, were being challenged by a group of more recent arrivals such as New Theatre (1971), Open Circle Theatre (1973), and the Phoenix Theatre (1975). This development increased competition and was beginning to force all the theatres to re-examine and modify their mandates. Artistically, they began to retreat from a policy of producing only new plays or collective creations and to rely more heavily on scripts from the international repertoire. The change of direction was due to a new conservatism on the part of the more successful companies, who found themselves confronting higher productions costs and dwindling financial resources. The LIP grants, which had contributed so substantially to the early success of the alternative theatres, were discontinued in 1975, and the Canada Council announced new budget restraints.[1]

Not only the economic climate but also the critical atmosphere had changed dramatically by 1977. Herbert Whittaker had retired from the *Globe* in 1975, and in the same year Urjo Kareda had left the *Star* to become literary adviser to Robin Phillips at the Stratford Festival. The new critics did not share their predecessors' committed enthusiasm for the new Canadian theatre, and in the case of Gina Mallet, Kareda's replacement at the *Star*, they harboured a preference for the kind of slick commercial productions that were beyond the resources of the alternative theatres. As a result of these changes, Toronto theatres approached the 1980s with a sense of disorientation and uneasiness.

As Luscombe considered the development of TWP over this same period, he realized he was little closer to his dream of a permanent company than he had been in 1959. Determined to try once more to realize that ambition, he submitted a request to the various funding agencies for what he called a 'fallow year' – a period during which he could devote his full time to training a new company. The idea was not without precedent – the Canada Council had supported Tarragon Theatre in 1975–6 during Bill Glassco's absence on a sabbatical – but the notion of asking for government subsidy for training as opposed to production was novel. He estimated that his plan would cost some $75,000.

David Peacock, theatre officer at the Canada Council, prepared TWP's request for submission to the September 1976 meeting but had considerable difficulty in deciding what he should recommend. His own staff felt the scheme was ill advised. In a memo to Peacock, the finance officer, Thomas Bohdanetsky, pointed out that TWP had an accumulated deficit of $33,000 and that without a line of credit at the bank, the prospect of box-office revenues, or a board of directors willing to raise the necessary funds, the company would face a serious cash problem. 'To plan on a Fallow Year and, at the same time, add a high cost, non-revenue-generating program,' he wrote, 'does not seem reasonable the way it is currently planned.'[2]

Peacock had his own reservations. He felt that giving the company a total of $75,000 for a non-producing season (really 'half a training programme and half an extended rehearsal period') would lead the theatre community to 'revolt' and other companies to ask for similar treatment. He agreed, however, that Luscombe needed to take time off to revitalize himself. Suggesting that the training period might be reduced in scope, he recommended the company be granted $45,000.[3] In his letter to the theatre in October, Peacock cited financial restraint and said he hoped that 'with budgetary adjustments you would be able to achieve the objective of developing a new ensemble company.'

Shocked and disappointed by what he considered the Council's misunderstanding of his project, Luscombe determined to find additional financing elsewhere. But he had reckoned without the quickening pace of Toronto's economic development. While he had been focusing on the growth inside the theatre, others were more interested in the neighbourhood surrounding it. Located as it was a few steps from one of Toronto's principal shopping streets, 12 Alexander Street had become a very valuable piece of real estate. If the fact had escaped Luscombe's attention, it had not gone unnoticed elsewhere.

One individual who had been watching the site was an engineer from the Philippines by the name of Domingo Penaloza. Penaloza, a relatively small player in the Toronto development game, had recently attracted attention by constructing the fanciful Dragon Mall in the city's Chinatown area, well away from the theatre district.[4] In the fall of 1976, however, he had taken out an option to purchase two parcels of land on Alexander and Maitland streets, and on 8 November he had applied to the City of Toronto Committee of Adjustment for a minor variance to allow him to put up thirty-four town houses on the site. Notice of such applications is automatically sent to residents in the area affected, so one morning Luscombe learned to his stupefaction that his theatre was slated for demolition.

Contacting his alderman, Allan Sparrow, Luscombe demanded to know if there was any way he could save the building. As it happened, the Penaloza development also conflicted with a project dear to Alderman Sparrow's heart – the provision of adequate parkland in his ward. By a remarkable stroke of good fortune, the Alexander Street property had been considered as parkland as long ago as 1973, and the Official Plan for the City still designated the site as a potential parkette. With support from Aldermen Dan Heap and William Kilbourn, Allan Sparrow drafted a request to the Committee of Adjustment that the Penaloza application for variance be deferred.[5] This argument won the day and put off, at least temporarily, the threat to TWP.

Realizing that their reprieve was only temporary, however, Luscombe and June Faulkner decided they would have to fight. As luck would have it, the city councillors were facing an election, and TWP resolved to make its survival an issue in that contest. They surveyed all candidates, asking them whether or not they would support the acquisition of the land by the City and promising to make the results of their survey available to the media. The election returned most of the aldermen who were sympathetic to the theatre, but on 21 December Luscombe received a registered letter from Fobasco Limited, the owners of the building, notifying him that they were exercising their right to terminate his lease on 29 June 1977.[6]

Meanwhile, as a result of his rebuff by the Committee of Adjustment, Penaloza had withdrawn his application and submitted a reduced plan for twenty-six town houses which conformed to the existing by-laws and therefore did not require a variance. The Planning Board informed Penaloza that, in view of the concern expressed by ward aldermen and members of the community at large, it was incumbent on them to 'investigate all possible opportunities to continue the location of the theatre in the Core.' One way to achieve this, they suggested, was for the developer to retain the theatre on its present site and submit a revised residential proposal for the remaining area utilizing the maximum density allowed. They hinted that any necessary amendments to the zoning by-law or the Official Plan could be considered.[7]

When the civil servants at City Hall began discussions with Penaloza, they discovered that the solution to the problem would not be simple. The Parks Committee had a budget of $1 million for land acquisition in 1977, of which approximately one-quarter had been earmarked. Penaloza's asking price for the property – $2 million, later reduced to $1.6 million – was well beyond the City's resources. Alderman John Bosley, whose family was in the real estate business, finally saw a way out of the impasse. He pointed out to the developer that the by-laws governing the acquisition of parkland made provision for the exchange of property for density rights. That meant that if Penaloza was willing to build on half the lot, leaving the theatre intact and leasing or giving the land to the City, then he would be allowed to add the air rights from the leased property to those permitted on the remaining land. That way, Bosley argued, everybody would win.[8]

As the negotiations proceeded behind closed doors, Luscombe and Faulkner watched the eviction date get nearer and nearer. In a letter to the Executive Committee of City Council on 2 May 1977, they stated that they had already committed themselves to a 1977–8 season and were afraid the arts councils would not process their applications unless assured that the company would have a theatre in which to perform. By the middle of June, Luscombe and Faulkner had learned that, in exchange for extra density on half the site, Penaloza had agreed to lease the theatre to TWP for a dollar a year, and the land beside the theatre to the City for the same amount. To protect his investment, however, Penaloza proposed that until all planning obstacles were removed and a building permit issued, TWP would assume responsibility for all carrying costs on the theatre and pay $6,000 a month in rent. While ecstatic about the long-term prospect, Luscombe and Faulkner did not see how they would be able to afford the increased costs in the interim. They sent a telegram to City Council stating that they would be agreeable to leasing the theatre, or even purchasing it at a reasonable price, but that any interim rise in their rent should reflect only an inflationary increase and not the more than 300 per cent rise being proposed. Finally, on 22 June, Penaloza agreed to extend the theatre's lease to June 1978 at $2,100 a month.[9]

The season that Luscombe and Faulkner had planned confident in the belief that they would still have a theatre in which to present it was intended as a celebration of the company's first twenty years. Promoted as the 'Champagne Season,' it reflected many of June Faulkner's programming ideas as well as a perception that the theatre was at a crossroads. Representing the past were a number of productions embodying the company's traditional aesthetic aims and socialist orientation: *Les Canadiens* by Rick Salutin, *The Komagata Maru Incident* by Sharon Pollock, *Nothing to Lose* by David Fennario, and *Westmount Blues* by Rick Davidson were all original Canadian plays dealing with political themes, set in Montreal or Vancouver. *The Island* by Athol Fugard was a powerful drama about apartheid in South Africa. But *The Club*, a musical by Eve Merriam, and two productions by the Lindsay Kemp Company, *Flowers* and *Salome*, were altogether novel for the company and suggestive of new directions the theatre might follow in the future. Above all, the season was designed to re-establish TWP's position in the Toronto alternative theatre scene after a year's absence.

The Champagne Season opened on 20 October 1977 and proved to be one of the most successful in the theatre's history. The first production, *Les Canadiens*, traced the history of the well-known Montreal hockey team and set it in the context of the evolving sense of nationalism in the province of Quebec. Salutin had originally written the piece on the suggestion of the Canadian director Guy Sprung, and it had played to enthusiastic audiences at the Centaur Theatre in Montreal. Salutin had been disappointed with the Montreal production, however, and was anxious to have it done in Toronto. Luscombe was attracted both by the premise of the script – that hockey in Quebec had been a kind of 'opiate' helping the spectators forget the humiliations of their defeat on the Plains of Abraham – and by the opportunities it provided for imaginative staging.

Astrid Janson designed a miniature rink which jutted out into the theatre, necessitating the removal of several seats. The rink was surrounded by ramps and bleachers that allowed the audience to spread right around the action. In the higher stands at the back, she arranged a number of life-sized puppet hockey fans including a likeness of Rick Salutin. She spent long hours experimenting to get a plastic surface rough enough not to endanger the skating actors but smooth enough to look like ice. The final result was a softly shining white surface surrounded by colourfully dressed patrons which exactly captured the feeling of the Montreal Forum.

The actors soon gained confidence on their roller-skates, but finding the proper shape for the play was more difficult. Serious disagreement developed between Luscombe and Salutin over the ending. An underlying theme was the idea that, with the election of the Parti Québécois, politics had replaced hockey as the major preoccupation of the people. This notion had been suggested by the Canadiens goaltender Ken Dryden's description of the atmosphere in the Montreal Forum on the night of 15 November 1976, the night of the PQ victory, when the fans had gone wild as the election results were posted on the scoreboard. Salutin wanted to suggest that hockey had served as a source of vicarious national pride, but that when it was no longer needed for that purpose after the election of the PQ, it reverted to what it truly was – just a game. He thought he conveyed this idea by having the play end with a group of young boys practising on a neighbourhood rink. The image is ambiguous, however, and in Montreal it had suggested to Maureen Peterson of the *Ottawa Journal* that, after a successful bid for political power, sports victories seem like 'kids' stuff.'[10] Luscombe felt that the ending was sentimental and left the focus on the game rather than on the political context.

These differences grew to a head on the morning before the opening. Salutin arrived at the theatre to discover that Luscombe had made several changes without his approval. Enraged by what he felt had been unwarranted interference, Salutin stormed out of the rehearsal and into the theatre office, where he said he wanted to call his lawyer to request an injunction. Hearing what he was up to, June Faulkner rushed out of her office exclaiming, 'If you get an injunction the theatre will close forever.' Using her considerable diplomatic skill, Faulkner managed to get the two men together and have them agree on what changes should be made. That evening, just before the performance, Salutin greeted Luscombe in the lobby. 'Surely,' he said wearily, 'it isn't necessary to go through this sort of thing every time in order to produce a decent product.' Luscombe eyed him quizzically and replied, 'I'm not sure I can agree with that.'[11]

For Salutin, the continual exploration and revision of the script was soul-destroying agony; for Luscombe, it was a necessary part of the creative process. Salutin attributes the difference to Luscombe's instinctual mode of directing: 'He rarely knows what he wants and has to discover it as he goes along. Only gradually does he realize where he's going or what he should be doing.'[12]

Opening night of *Les Canadiens* proved to be more exciting than anyone could have anticipated. The former Canadiens hero Maurice Richard had come from Montreal to attend the performance. When he walked into the theatre he saw Conn Smythe, the former owner of the Toronto

Maple Leafs, in the audience. As the spectators gawked, the two former hockey rivals greeted one another like old friends.[13] The performance on stage was hardly less dramatic, calling forth rarely used superlatives from the Toronto critics. Gina Mallet applauded 'the liveliest acting in Toronto,'[14] and McKenzie Porter of the *Toronto Sun* called the play 'the best theatrical work ever written in English about Canada's endemic illness.'[15] Bryan Johnson, replacing John Fraser at the *Globe*, later said it was 'arguably the best production of the most Canadian play ever written ... far and away the most exuberant, exciting home grown product to hit Toronto this season.'[16]

Pam Brighton's production of Eve Merriam's *The Club*, a satirical attack on the male chauvinism of a New York men's club with an all-female cast, proved so successful that Faulkner transferred the theatre's third production to another theatre to make room for an extension of the run. That meant she could hold over *The Club* at Alexander Street and run the Centaur Theatre production of David Fennario's *Nothing to Lose* at Toronto Free Theatre. Athol Fugard's *The Island* had been planned as a studio production. In view of the success of *The Club*, which ran until mid-February, however, *The Island* could be presented in the Alexander Street theatre before the arrival of the Lindsay Kemp Company, scheduled for early March. Directed by Calvin Butler, *The Island* too proved to be successful. Gina Mallet called it a 'production that gleams with integrity from start to finish,'[17] and Robert Wallace of *Toronto Theatre Review* saw in it evidence that 'art and politics do mix – not only in agit-prop satire and epic remove, but in intensely human interchange.'[18]

Meanwhile, information was beginning to arrive about the staging and other requirements of the Lindsay Kemp Company. Staff members were confronted by requests for such items as dead rats, a live pigeon, four kilos of confetti, a dozen bottles of white body paint, and seemingly endless quantities of glitter. Kemp, who claimed to be descended from the Elizabethan clown Will Kemp, had trained as a painter and designer in his native Bradford, England, before he studied dance and mime. He had worked in film, theatre, ballet, musicals, variety, cabaret, strip bars, and even the circus before founding his own company in 1962.

Kemp's reputation had preceded him, and on the opening night of *Flowers* there was an atmosphere of curiosity and anticipation in the theatre. The audience consisted partly of TWP regulars and partly of an entirely new group drawn from the dance and homosexual communities. Not surprisingly, many of the theatre's regular patrons were more than mildly astonished by what they saw taking place on the stage. Several were deeply offended. One of them was Dick Beddoes, the sports columnist for the *Globe and Mail*. 'Call the Lord's Day Alliance and the Toronto Blue Laws Brigade,' he wrote, 'and tell 'em to knock off campaigning against Sunday sport and confront a real threat to our collective morals! Wake up Roy McMurtry in the provincial Attorney-General's lair! He thinks hockey is dirty, f'r hevvin's sake! Dirty – pronounced *dirt-tee* –is the word for *Flowers*, a pantomine [*sic*] that has been playing right under Censor Sims' blue nose up there in Toronto Workshop Productions.'[19] Oscar Ryan, a longtime TWP supporter, felt almost betrayed: 'I felt like a captive in the theatre of cruelty, assailed by an orgy of blinding psychedelic fury, rolling clouds of smoke, pounding rock music and raucous organ chords .... *Flowers* is quite out of character for TWP, a theatre long dedicated to plays of social concern. Kemp in a recent interview said, "What I really want to do is give people magic ... a breath of decadence, and hope their consciousness will be expanded." But *Flowers* inspires no cleansing of the soul, offers no hope at all – only decadence and death ... Are we back in the Berlin of the Twenties, grubbing in Doomsday culture? Who needs this kind of morality? Who needs that type of aesthetic? Especially now.'[20] Most critics, however, were overwhelmed by the sheer theatricality of the evening, which Kaspars Dzeguze of the *Sun* described as 'nothing less than magic. Black magic, yes. Kinky magic, and magic that upsets, revolts, scandalizes and intrigues, but magic unlike any this reviewer can recall on the Toronto stage ever.'[21]

Nor were the critics alone intrigued. The Toronto theatrical community turned out in force. Bill Glassco went to eight performances; the dancer Robert Desrosiers performed in the second show, *Salome*; and Peter Faulkner, who had built the set and was acting as technical director, was so impressed that he considered joining the company for their South American tour. 'The technical effects were just a minor part of it,' he said later. 'Kemp is like a composer who puts together a series of notes that makes you weep. You don't know why the hell you are weeping; there is no explanation. My response was similar to the first time I saw George Luscombe's work.'[22] Faulkner was not the only one who made the connection between Luscombe and Kemp. Diane Douglass also thought that *Flowers* was 'quintessentially George.'[23]

The second Kemp production, *Salome*, stirred the same kind of controversy. The conservative critics were even more raucously indignant. Dick Beddoes thought the pigeon the best thing in the show. McKenzie Porter, who dismissed the production as a 'sideshow for the titillation of sexual perverts,' considered the presence of the English ballet dancer Anton

Dolin in such a troupe a 'great show business tragedy.'[24] Three days after making that statement, the experience still rankling, he returned to the subject of homosexuality on the stage, which he deplored as a 'reflection of the decadence of western society ... and [responsible for the] widespread loss of respect for the martial arts.'[25]

While not everyone perceived Kemp's influence in the city to be quite so baleful, there was no question that the company's visit had energized the Toronto arts community. Kemp revealed new possibilities for the theatrical imagination and challenged actors and dancers to explore realms which had been largely ignored by the 'revolution' in Canadian drama. The visit also affected TWP, but in ways that were difficult to recognize at the time. As Luscombe and June Faulkner at last were able to catch their breath, they looked back on what had been the most successful season in the theatre's history. Almost everything they had touched had turned to gold. Luscombe's production of *Les Canadiens* had won a Floyd S. Chalmers Canadian Play Award; all three main-stage attractions had played to sell-out houses and been held over; the theatre had set several records, including for number of performances (214 main-stage and 44 studio, for an average 82 per cent attendance) and total box-office revenue ($267,000, or 40 per cent of their budget). TWP's success would leave them with an accumulated surplus of some $20,000. The future looked brighter than it had in years.

19

Looking Backward

The year and a half following the triumph of the Champagne Season was a period of disappointment and frustration. Like other Toronto arts organizations in the inflationary 1980s, TWP faced financial problems brought on by rapidly escalating costs and shrinking subsidies. In the spring of 1978, the government had cut the budgets of the CBC, the national museums, and the National Film Board and had put a virtual freeze on Canada Council funding.[1] Those difficulties were compounded by internal problems at Toronto Workshop Productions. The theatre fire, the European tour, and the fight with the developer all had taken their toll. Although he would not admit it even to himself, Luscombe was beginning to feel the effects of the long struggle for survival. Furthermore, the larger battle to which he had committed his life – the battle against fascism – seemed no longer the crusade it once had been. The civil rights movement, the war in Vietnam, and other issues that had kept alive a passion for social justice and racial equality during the 1970s were being replaced in young people's consciousness by stories of corporate mergers and real estate development. The New Left ideals of participatory democracy and personal fulfilment seemed to leave no room for the Old Left principles of discipline and collective responsibility. The crying voice of TWP had gradually been surrounded by a wilderness.

At the end of 1979, June Faulkner left the company to take up the position of administrative manager of the Shaw Festival. Faulkner's abilities had always complemented Luscombe's almost perfectly, and over the years the two had established an extremely well integrated style of management. Basically, Luscombe had assumed responsibility for the artistic side of the theatre, while Faulkner had taken care of administration, publicity, fund-raising, and most aspects of public relations. During her fifteen-year association with Luscombe, Faulkner had become the company's eyes and ears. She had built up an astonishingly wide network of contacts, not only among theatre personnel but also with civic and provincial politicians. Her loss was to prove irreparable.

Faulkner's departure left Luscombe even more isolated than he had been in the past. Although he liked to remark that he could accomplish everything he wanted to by himself, and frequently sought to convey an impression of total self-sufficiency, in fact Luscombe had relied heavily on those around him, especially the small core of trusted colleagues that included Tony Ferry, Jack Winter, Nancy Jowsey, and John and June Faulkner. It was these colleagues who frequently alerted Luscombe to international developments in the theatre and suggested ways in which TWP might branch out. Now on his own, he found himself drawn back to the subjects that had interested him as a young man. One of these was the conflict in Spain in the mid-1930s.

The story of the Mackenzie-Papineau Battalion of the International Brigade and the experiences of the men who fought with it in Spain in 1936–9 had intrigued Luscombe for years. He had first learned of the Spanish civil war from Joan Littlewood, but it was only during rehearsals for *Ten Lost Years* that he began to track down references to Canadian participation in the conflict. About that time, he discovered that the CBC producer Mac Reynolds had compiled an oral history of the period by recording interviews with some sixty Mac-Pap veterans, and that the tapes of those interviews were lying forgotten in the CBC archives.[2] With Reynolds's help, Luscombe began transcribing the material, and he used it as the basis of improvisations during a workshop with actors in June 1979.

One of the things that attracted Luscombe to the story was the discovery of a personal connection to the material. A barber on Pape Avenue to whom he had been taken as a child had been part of a recruiting ring for the Mackenzie-Papineau Battalion. Because the King government had passed a law making volunteers liable to imprisonment and a $2,000 fine, Canadians wishing to fight in Spain had to be screened and helped out of the country by an underground network. Luscombe discovered that one of his neighbours on Humewood Avenue had been a doctor responsible for examining prospective recruits.[3]

As he worked on the material with Larry Cox, a TWP actor and writer, it seemed to Luscombe as moving as the personal recollections out of which *Ten Lost Years* had been fashioned. He began to envisage an equivalent success, possibly with another tour and even movie rights. The problem, of course, was devising a framework to give the scattered and discon-

nected accounts some kind of coherence. He decided to use a recruit-
ment meeting as the linking device. Astrid Janson designed a simple
setting of a table and four chairs in front of a backdrop constructed out of
stretched rubber bands on which photos of the civil war and of Picasso's
Guernica could be projected. The elasticity of the material allowed performers to enter and exit through the pictures. The action could thus
move freely back and forth from the meeting hall to the battle front with
the four actors doubling as recruiters and as the participants in the
improvised scenes. Iris Paabo, who had contributed so much to *Ten Lost
Years* and many subsequent TWP productions, devised a musical score
from songs of the period.

The première of *The Mac Paps* took place on a freezing cold 31 January
1980. Twenty-eight veterans of the battalion were in the opening-night
audience, and the performance raised $1,400 to assist them in their peti-
tion to Ottawa to repeal Mackenzie King's 1937 Foreign Enlistment Act,
under which they were still labelled as criminals. During the run, some
thousand patrons added their signatures to the appeal. If the play did
much to elicit sympathy for the men who had fought against fascism more
than forty years previously, however, it was less successful in winning over
the Toronto critics. Gina Mallet, somewhat uncharacteristically, hardly
mentioned the details of the performance at all and devoted most of her
review to an attack on what she considered to be one-sided propaganda.[4]
Rick Groen in the *Globe* agreed with Mallet's contention that the work was
more like a 'solemn pageant' than a drama. While he found the acting
'first-rate' and the staging 'consistently imaginative,' he felt the separate
stories never really cohered or developed any dramatic momentum.[5] As
usual, several critics admired Luscombe's distinctive and imaginative style
(tables and chairs that become a sinking ship torpedoed by a U-boat or
the mountains across which the Canadians are smuggled into Spain) but
felt unengaged by the story. 'Since the actors play so many roles,' wrote
Anton Wagner in the *Varsity*, 'it is difficult to identify with any single character or to empathize with his suffering.'[6]

Gordon Vogt, an occasional critic on CBC, responded to accusations
that the production was naïvely one-sided by pointing out the irony in the
performance. Far from presenting a blinkered view of the war, Vogt
thought, the production 'seriously questioned political idealism no matter what flag it operated under' and called into question 'the efficacy – or
even the possibility – of heroism in the modern world.'[7] He cited the
example of the juxtaposition of two scenes, one in which the fascists
round up a group of villagers and shoot them without trial and another in

which the Mac-Paps, after a prolonged battle against enemy snipers, execute their prisoners, also without trial. The singing of the 'Internationale' following this episode, which might easily have been taken as a sort of mindless flag-waving, Vogt took as an ironic comment, reinforced by the off-stage echoing of the song in a minor key.

Luscombe had pinned great hopes on the production, but after opening night, houses dropped off and attendance hovered between 60 and 70 during the week and climbed to about 150 on Saturday. Privately (and not so privately), people were beginning to say that Luscombe and TWP were repeating themselves, that the old formulas were boring, and that there was a need for change and revitalization. Many felt that Luscombe was stuck in the past, unable to grow. Unless he could find help to generate new artistic input, those critics feared, there was a real danger that he would kill the theatre himself.

The central problem, as most observers recognized, was Luscombe's complex personality. Charming yet suspicious, sensitive and overbearing, dogmatic and insecure, idealistic and ruthless, a genius incapable of great flexibility, Luscombe had forged the theatre in his own image. During the late sixties, TWP's beaded and long-haired actors seemed to be part of the vibrant youth culture of the time and to speak directly to that culture in productions such as *Che, Mr Bones*, and *Chicago '70*. In the mid-seventies, however, things began to change, and the creative energies of the company seemed more and more frequently to have been directed towards a rather sentimental exploration of the past. The new and changing face of Toronto – whether reflecting the subculture of drugs and sex or the establishment culture of real estate and conspicuous extravagance – was no longer mirrored in productions at the Alexander Street theatre.

In the autumn of 1982, Luscombe tried once again to forge a collaborative work of art out of the material of the past. The piece, to be called *The Wobbly*, was a celebration of the creation and brief life of the Industrial Workers of the World, the 'One Big Union.' The IWW had evolved in the early part of the century as a result of the growing exploitation of unskilled labour and the reluctance of the labour movement at that time to unionize non-skilled workers. It was formed in 1905 and lasted only about fifteen years before it collapsed as a consequence of the Red scare following the First World War.

The stories, songs, and heroes of this grass-roots wing of the labour movement had appealed to Luscombe for years. The educational methods of the 'Wobblies' – music and street-corner theatrics – were the ones Luscombe himself had learned in the Co-operative Commonwealth Youth

Movement, and the Wobblies' ideals of equality, their utopianism, and their celebration of the disadvantaged and downtrodden had always moved him and provided an outlet for his passion and frustration. The 'mythology' of the early labour movement was the motherlode of his imagination, and the values it endorsed were the ones that formed the foundation of his work.

The actual writing of *The Wobbly* had taken several years. Luscombe had got the idea during a visit to an anarchist bookshop in Vancouver and had asked Ron Weihs, a former TWP actor then living and writing in Vancouver, to undertake the project.[8] By 1982, after several delays, the play was ready to go into production. During rehearsals, Luscombe used the written text as a thread to connect improvised scenes of work and confrontation. When the play opened in January 1983, critical response, as usual, was split between admiration for the ingenuity of the stage images and impatience with what many regarded as a simplistic or naïve view of the world. Ray Conlogue of the *Globe* wrote, 'When the workers organize themselves into complex, but powerful physical tableaux, dramatically backlit and sidelit; or when a group of them fetchingly underline a speech by rhythmic choreography behind a piano; or when a line of women steadily march toward an invisible line of bayonets and collapse convulsively without the sound of a shot being heard; then Luscombe's gift for animating the stage and choreographing history is vindicated.'[9] Particularly admired was a sequence in the textile mill which, in the words of Karen Sprenger of the *Ryersonian*, 'revealed the terror of a young girl forced to learn how to operate dangerous machinery. She joins the other four women in a tightly choreographed mechanical motion. Their hand movements, their zombie-like chanting, and Allen Booth's pounding music combine with eerie back lighting to create a violently frightening yet passionately beautiful vignette.'[10]

But a number of critics, including even those sympathetic to the left-wing bias of the theatre, were beginning to question whether Luscombe's directorial style was not distracting from the political message of the work. According to Brian Burch of the *Toronto Clarion*, Luscombe and Weihs wanted 'the audience [to] take home the joy and hope that is behind the IWW and find a way to confront the world in a similar manner.' Instead, Burch reported, the spectators seemed 'more concerned with the theatrical techniques involved than in the solution to the social problems being portrayed in front of them.'[11] Moira Farr of the *Newspaper* also expressed uneasiness about the wedding of a social message and vaudeville. She found the effect similar to that of a Pete Seeger concert, 'a little too jolly and earnest.' In her opinion, *The Wobbly* needed 'more fire and less show-biz razzle dazzle.'[12]

What impressed many commentators was the contrast between the world of the play and that of the streets outside the theatre. Audience members, encouraged to sing along with members of the cast, could not help but be struck by the irony of the lyrics:

> In our hands is placed a power greater than their hoarded gold;
> Greater than the might of armies, magnified a thousand-fold.
> We can bring to birth the new world from the ashes of the old,
> For the Union makes us strong.

As Conlogue remarked, *The Wobbly* was 'an evocation of a golden moment when people really did think like children.' But it was a complex experience, one that 'summons up not only the hopes and idealism of our grandparents' day, but also (and inadvertently) the lassitude and despair of [our own].'[13]

The Wobbly played to 62 per cent attendance for three weeks, after which it had to be withdrawn because the theatre had been rented to Factory Theatre for its production of George F. Walker's *The Art of War*. While not a success on the order of *Ten Lost Years*, *The Wobbly* did seem to demonstrate that the audience for Luscombe's kind of theatre had not disappeared altogether. What was needed, in Luscombe's opinion, was for the theatre to remain true to its original mandate.

A little less than a year after production of *The Wobbly*, Luscombe returned to another subject that had been a part of his youth – government persecution of the left. The event that had rekindled his interest was the publication of Victor Navasky's *Naming Names*, a history of the activities of Senator Joseph McCarthy and the House Committee on Un-American Activities in the early 1950s, during their investigation of the loyalty of various American theatrical and film personalities. While it was true that certain aspects of the story seemed quintessentially American (can we imagine a Committee on Un-Canadian Activities?), Luscombe felt, the plight of artists in the United States raised issues of interest beyond that country's borders, and he asked Larry Cox to work on a script.

To Cox, who was too young to remember the events, a matter of fascination in Navasky's account was the way in which people could be destroyed without anyone's laying a hand on them. Instead of thumb-screws, dripping taps, sleep deprivation, or other instruments and methods of torture, the Committee was able to use forces in American society (as well as in the victims themselves) to lead those being questioned to betray themselves or their friends.[14] For 'witnesses' at the committee hearings were not charged with any crime, nor were they threatened with imprisonment. So powerful was public opinion that to refuse to cooperate with the Committee was to risk social ostracism and loss of livelihood. Larry Parks, the star of *The Jolson Story*, after being described as an 'unfriendly' witness was 'blacklisted' by Hollywood producers and was hired for only three supporting roles between 1951 and his death in 1975. While the evils of 'McCarthyism' had often been dealt with dramatically, notably in Arthur Miller's play *The Crucible*, it seemed important to Cox that that history not be forgotten.

Luscombe too was interested in the politics of the story, but as always he was equally excited by theatrical metaphors. In *Names*, which opened in October 1983, he became fascinated by images of disguise and reflection. What unity the show had was provided by the figure of Larry Parks, the man who is slowly broken by the pressure of the investigation. Parks was best known at the time for his impersonation of Al Jolson, a Jewish entertainer who performed in black face. Rick McKenna, the actor playing Parks, was on stage throughout, sometimes answering questions from the senators, sometimes putting on make-up or donning a black mask to lip-sync Jolson's vaudeville songs. The members of the Committee sat with their backs to the audience, their faces visible only on two TV monitors, which recorded their questions to the witnesses. The actors (as usual) played many roles, often doubling as inquisitor and witness and thus making a visual comment about the interrelationship between judge and victim.

One of the entertainers who appeared before the Committee was the black basso Paul Robeson. Instead of getting a black actor to impersonate the singer, Luscombe had Tom Butler play the role without any attempt to disguise the colour of his skin. It seemed to Luscombe that the contrast between the powerful impact of Robeson's words spoken by a white actor and the travesty of the black spirit and music in the Al Jolson impersonation constituted a wonderfully theatrical juxtaposition.

The majority of the reviewers, however, failed to see much beyond the politics and could be lined up according to their own political persuasions. Gina Mallet dismissed the show as 'particularly malignant lib think' and judged it would have been more interesting if it had told the story from the congressmen's side of the committee table. Returning to her oft-expressed preference for commercial theatre, she concluded, 'There's more food for thought in a single speech in *Equus* than there is in two hours of *Names*.'[15]

Bob Pennington of the *Sun* would have preferred his politics straight, without the distraction of incongruous theatrical images. 'What could have been fascinating sequences with Ayn Rand and Paul Robeson are senselessly interrupted by Parks, mouthing Jolson numbers, romping around the audience and dancing with a dummy.'[16] Stewart Brown, who had been reviewing TWP productions for the *Hamilton Spectator* for almost twenty years, found this latest production deeply moving. 'Despite some moments of lighter relief, *Names* remains a nightmare,' he wrote, 'abetted by Luscombe's almost surrealistic use of mime, including McKenna in blackface or mask, mouthing Jolson songs. It is a harsh, bleak and unnerving piece of theatre – strong medicine – and as such, not something you "enjoy".'[17] Ray Conlogue was one of the few critics to display much interest in the formal characteristics of the production. He described *Names* as a 'vaudeville' and admired Luscombe's weaving together of the testimony of various witnesses. 'About once every two years lately,' he wrote, 'the original talent bursts through.'[18]

Audiences seemed generally receptive, and they grew steadily until the theatre was doing 40 per cent business, enough to justify holding the production over for a week. In announcing the extension to 12 November, the staff took great delight in digging out a derogatory comment from Gina Mallet's review – 'Bully for Mr. Cox' – and using it out of context as a plug.

20

New Blood

In the early 1980s, the two major funding agencies began to receive increasingly negative comments about the work of George Luscombe and TWP. The majority of these comments were incorporated in the reports prepared by the theatre panels whose responsibility it was to assess the company's annual grant applications. They reflected a growing sense of disappointment and frustration on the part of the panel members with what they perceived to be a decline in standards and a failure of vision. While acknowledging the significant contribution Luscombe and his theatre had made in the 1960s and 1970s, the assessors began to ask whether the time had not come for him to make way for new and younger talent.

It was undoubtedly true that between 1980 and 1985 TWP began to lose its distinctiveness and to look more and more like all the other Toronto theatres. Because of financial constraints, the exhaustion of much of the staff, and a rapid turnover of administrators, the theatre had had to abandon many of its original ideals. It could no longer rely entirely on actors trained in Luscombe's methods, and work on original, collaboratively created productions had to be carried out in unseemly haste. As a consequence, of the 34 productions presented in those years, only 11 were original works, and 4 of those were revivals. Furthermore, only 3 (*The Wobbly, Names,* and *The Medicine Show,* a play about a travelling patent medicine salesman) had been created out of documentary material; the remainder had been adapted from previously written plays. The company's efforts to find worthwhile Canadian scripts also had been disappointing. Half the scripted shows produced during the period were Canadian, but critical response to all of them had been cool or hostile. As the company found itself squeezed between dwindling revenue and rising costs, it had been forced to find ways to reduce its production expenses. Nearly half the productions mounted during those five seasons were co-productions or rentals. That meant that the company could no longer stamp its identity on each season, as it increasingly lost control over what appeared on its stage.

At first, the criticism of Luscombe and the theatre was prefaced by expressions of genuine respect and admiration. 'Since I began working in theatre George Luscombe has been a hero and leading-light for me,' wrote one assessor. Another called him 'the most accomplished and exciting director in the city,' and yet another spoke of him as a 'living national treasure.' Many referred to the 'distinguished service' of the company, to its long history or 'oddball status,' but felt that it could not go on living on the glories of the past.

The question mark in most assessors' minds was whether Luscombe was merely in a fallow period or whether he had spent his creative force and was now simply repeating himself. On this point the assessors were divided. Those who felt he was still in a creative mode said that some TWP productions provided more creativity 'per square inch' than the productions of almost any other company in the city. Some assessors, however, recognized that the problem went deeper than Luscombe's abilities as a director. They commented on the poor quality of the scripts produced in recent years and the inability of the company to find new playwrights. Others mentioned the crisis with the developer, which had interfered with the regular operations of the theatre. Since, as one assessor observed, 'the history of TWP is the autobiography of George Luscombe, the waning of the central figure is of central concern.' Luscombe's isolation as the single animating spirit of the theatre had been intensified after the departure of June Faulkner, and many assessors felt that the company was paying a price.[1]

As the councils began to get conflicting advice about the theatre, they were faced with increasingly difficult decisions. In theory, they disclaimed any wish to influence the artistic policies of the organizations they financed. And yet it was impossible to disentangle questions of financial responsibility (such as a realistic debt reduction plan) from the larger considerations of repertoire and attendance. Reluctant to appear intrusive, the councils at first tried to ignore the warnings.

In preparing his report for the July 1982 meeting, William Lord, theatre officer for the Ontario Arts Council, found a new note creeping into the comments of his advisers – a sense of impatience or even outright hostility. 'There is no energy or profile at the theatre,' wrote one assessor. 'George has not changed or grown – his work is passé. Something must be done to shake him up.' Another confessed: 'I do not respect what is happening at TWP – Luscombe is not challenging himself or others with whom he is working. There is no growth or revitalization in the theatre. The old formulas are boring.' One consultant thought it was 'essential that George realize he needs help and, especially, new artistic input.'[2]

As the liaison between the advisers and the Arts Council, Lord was in a particularly delicate position. He knew that his recommendation carried considerable weight with busy members who relied primarily on the memoranda he prepared in deciding how they would vote. Since it would be impossible to circulate the complete consultants' reports, Lord included a larger than usual number of excerpts from those documents for the Council's guidance. In his memo for the July meeting, he omitted most of the negative comments, and the few he did include he buried in the middle of much more supportive remarks. His own recommendation, a modest increase from $81,000 to $85,000, was accepted by the Council with the proviso that Lord convey to the theatre the Council's concern and arrange for a meeting to discuss that concern with Luscombe and members of his board.

The requested meeting took place in September 1982, and while the atmosphere was congenial, it soon became evident that the two sides were talking at cross purposes. Lord and Walter Pitman, the executive director of the Arts Council, were quite properly concerned that the taxpayers' money with which they had been entrusted be spent to best advantage. That meant guarding against giving money to organizations which were poorly or irresponsibly managed. The TWP business manager and members of the TWP board, for their part, were all too conscious of the paradox that it takes money to make money. In response to Council suggestions that they hire a person to engage in audience development, TWP could say only that they were in the process of looking for one but that they had no provision in their budget for an adequate salary. The reason they could not afford experienced help in this area, they explained, was that they had been told by the funding organizations to cut back on a budget which they felt was already pared to the bone. To meet the request that they submit revised spending estimates, they had cut the number of productions and juggled the figures of projected revenue. But both sides recognized the futility of the exercise.

The meeting between the Arts Council representatives and their TWP 'clients' broke up with expressions of confidence and renewed resolve. But in spite of the great mutual respect they had for one another, neither

Walter Pitman nor George Luscombe was free to do exactly as he pleased. Both were caught up in larger movements which were to bring the two men into collision.

Similar problems were beginning to develop between TWP and the Canada Council in Ottawa. The new head of the Theatre Section, Robert Spickler, seemed less responsive than his predecessors to Luscombe's enthusiastic descriptions of work accomplished and optimistic projections of future success. In announcing a grant of $125,000 for the 1983–4 season (the same amount TWP had received for the last two years), Spickler referred to the clarity of Luscombe's personal vision and his determination to establish a Canadian theatre. But he also commented on the 'serious challenges' facing TWP. 'Over the next season,' he went on, 'members of the Canada Council will require evidence that Toronto Workshop Productions' place is being restored with the public and in the artistic community.'[3]

During the following two years, the tension between TWP and the councils continued unabated. The advisers of both funding agencies regarded the theatre as moribund. For most of them, the problem had become one of artistic renewal. 'Like many Artistic Directors in Toronto (and, presumably elsewhere),' wrote one, 'George is not much interested in other people's work and doesn't have a knack for sharing power. And yet that's exactly what must happen if a strong company is to develop and the theatre is to grow. Not only does this mean injecting new blood into the performing core – "the young company" which George says is now being prepared – but there must be a willingness to share power at the top. George must develop an ongoing creative association with a team of *peers*: veteran actors, yes, but *especially* writers and directors.'[4]

By the spring of 1985, Luscombe could see that it would be impossible to resist the pressures on him much longer. He had himself come to the conclusion that he would soon have to step down, and had reported as much in his latest application to the Canada Council. But since his contemplated retirement would involve handing over what was literally his life's work, he was understandably anxious to ensure that it went to the right person.

On 4 June 1985, he asked his board of directors to create a new position on the theatre staff to facilitate the anticipated transferral of power from himself to a successor. It was his suggestion that a resident director be hired for a period of one year, after which, if things worked out satisfactorily, the individual named should be given full authority as artistic director. The candidate he proposed was Robert Rooney, a young English-born director who had produced successful shows at TWP in the previous two seasons.

Although board members were familiar with Rooney's work and respected Luscombe's opinion, several of them were surprised by his choice of an 'heir apparent.' They were not alone. Many members of the Toronto theatre community also found it more than mildly surprising that, having spent a lifetime railing against colonialism in the Canadian theatre, Luscombe should bring in a virtual outsider and an Englishman to carry on the traditions of the theatre he had created. It was not as though there were no alternatives. Over the years, a surprising number of TWP actors, including Ray Whelan, Diane Grant, Geoffrey Read, Peter McConnell, Peter Faulkner, Jeff Braunstein, Phil Savath, Barry Wasman, Michael Ayoub, Steven Bush, Rick McKenna, and Maja Ardal, had blossomed under Luscombe's guidance only to depart to found companies of their own. It seemed, on the face of it, that almost any one of these actors might have been a more logical successor than a man whose only connection with the company had been as a visiting director.

If Luscombe's selection of Rooney seemed sudden, even quixotic, it was in fact a decision that had been some two years in the making. The two men had first met in the autumn of 1983, when, along with R.H. Thompson, Rooney had dropped into the Alexander Street theatre with a joint proposal. The two had spent the summer in the acting company at Stratford, where Rooney had introduced Thompson to a play about racism in South Africa called *The Jail Diary of Albie Sachs*. When the three men met in Luscombe's office, they found they shared many enthusiasms. Thompson and Luscombe had worked together on *The Mac Paps* and greatly respected one another. Rooney at first was overshadowed by the rangy and ebullient Thompson. Soft-spoken and diffident in manner, the Englishman presented a rather bland exterior, but in conversation he revealed a passionate concern for social justice, to which Luscombe naturally responded. Luscombe was also delighted to find that, like himself, Rooney had been trained in the Laban method and that he had even taught for a time with Lisa Ullmann, the woman responsible for getting Laban out of Nazi Germany.[5]

Rooney's sense of social outrage had been nourished by the experience of working for a wire service monitoring news stories coming out of Africa. He had been appalled by the injustices occurring in former British colonies and especially incensed by the atrocities of the South African policy of apartheid. By the mid-1970s, he had found the growing conservatism of Britain increasingly uncongenial, and in 1975 he fled the country to launch a career as actor and freelance director in Canada. So far, that career had taken him to the Banff Playwrights' Colony as a visiting director, to Brock University, where he had spent four years as resident director, and to a stint as actor at the Stratford Festival, where he had met R.H. Thompson.

Luscombe was not in the habit of spelling out his reasons for making the decisions he did, but in choosing Robert Rooney to succeed him he was undoubtedly motivated by two conflicting concerns. On the one hand, he was determined that TWP should continue its left-wing, socially committed stance. He had watched as one after another of the alternative Toronto theatres, launched in the early seventies with much social idealism and revolutionary rhetoric, had abandoned its early political commitment to drift into safer ideological waters. It was important not only for the continuity of TWP but for the health of the Toronto theatre scene, he felt, that there be at least one troupe in the city to act as a gadfly in the complacent 1980s. Rooney shared that conviction.

On the other hand, he had to think of his own position. He was in no mood to retire altogether, so he would have to find a way to retain a toehold in the theatre he had founded. At thirty-five, Rooney was Luscombe's junior by a quarter of a century. It is possible Luscombe felt more comfortable dealing with a younger person than with someone closer to his own age. For most of his career, he had dominated those around him rather like a proletarian King Lear, and it may be that he shared with Lear a reluctance to give up all vestiges of authority with his crown. By choosing a successor whom he might be able to influence, who was politically committed but uninterested in actor training, he might ensure a division of labour which would free him from some of the tiresome aspects of theatre administration and allow him to do what he enjoyed and did best – work with actors in the development of original scripts.

21

Board Games

The designation of Robert Rooney as resident director marked the culmination of a struggle between Luscombe and his board of directors that had been going on for a number of years. Through the 1960s and 1970s, Luscombe had successfully resisted all suggestions that he enlarge the theatre's token board or grant it any real power. In 1980, however, the theatre's financial position had become so precarious that the Ontario Arts Council grew alarmed. Studying the theatre's mid-season report in that year, William Lord, the Council's theatre officer, learned that box-office revenue was well below projections (amounting to just over $25,000, including subscription sales), that fund-raising was down, and that receipts from rentals were practically non-existent. The theatre's total earned revenue for the period was less than 24 per cent of expenses, and the most optimistic forecast indicated that, by the end of the 1980–1 season, TWP would be facing a $48,000 shortfall on top of an already accumulated deficit of $86,000.[1]

Not surprisingly, Lord contemplated these figures with some dismay. Council policy specified that grant money could not be used to pay off company debts, and since TWP had allowed itself to fall so far into the red, it was imperative that it now devise a strategy for recovery. In a meeting with Luscombe and his new business manager, Jack Merigold, Lord emphasized that it was important for TWP to put in place a reasonable deficit reduction plan duly authorized and approved by a properly constituted board of directors.

For his part, Luscombe had every reason to be suspicious of boards. Nevertheless, it was becoming evident TWP would not be allowed to continue as it had in the past. So with considerable apprehension Luscombe invited a number of friends of the company to attend a meeting in the theatre. After some discussion of the financial problems facing TWP, those gathered agreed to form a new board of directors. It included Derrick Kershaw of the original TWP advisory board, Tom Patterson, the founder of the Stratford Festival, Richard Ballantine, a Toronto businessman, Jerry White, an accountant with Thorne Riddell, Karl Jaffary, a lawyer and former city alderman, George and Mona Luscombe, and Jack Merigold. In the following weeks, they recruited Karl Stevens, an architect, and Sherrill Cheda, the executive director of the Canadian Periodical Publishers' Association, to join them and elected Karl Jaffary as chairman.

This new board approached the challenges facing the theatre with enthusiasm but for the most part with little understanding of what would be required of them. The task ahead was daunting. The new auditors, appointed by Jerry White as treasurer, determined that the theatre's deficit in September 1981 was $97,000 'give or take a thousand,' which did not include a bank loan of $111,000 and a number of unpaid bills.[2] In analysing their rather precarious position, Jaffary and the board decided that it had three major tasks, each of which would require substantial funding. The most immediate was to devise a deficit reduction plan that would satisfy the arts councils; the second was to obtain the deed for the theatre; and the third was to address the problem of the theatre's dwindling popularity.

Several of the board members were convinced that a major obstacle to developing audiences was the theatre itself. The Alexander Street building was gloomy, decorated in the dark red and black colours of the Communist party, and its orange-covered bleachers hard and uncomfortable. The backstage facilities were cramped, and the auditorium was unusable during the hot summer months. The era of warehouse theatres and their attendant discomfort was ending. It was typical of the time that the St Lawrence Centre for the Arts, built in the sixties as a 'people place,' had embarked on an extensive renovation of its two theatres to bring them more into line with contemporary standards of comfort and elegance.

Another problem troubling the board was the size of the theatre. While it was true that the company had conducted the successful Champagne Season in its three-hundred-seat space and that for two years they had come nowhere close to filling the seats available, the board felt that a larger, and especially a more comfortable, theatre was essential if they were to produce the extra earned revenue they so badly needed. In the autumn of 1981, therefore, the board submitted a deficit reduction plan to the Ontario Arts Council and, in anticipation of obtaining the deed for the theatre early in 1982, began formulating plans for a $1 million capital fund-raising drive to renovate the building.

Soon, however, the company found itself in a frustrating bind. It could not legitimately embark on a fund-raising campaign to renovate a theatre it did not own. At the same time, however, it was reluctant to compromise such a campaign by approaching the same potential donors for smaller sums. That meant that the theatre's efforts to find operating funds were being hamstrung by plans for an ambitious (but continually delayed) capital campaign. It was becoming increasingly important to settle the ownership question as soon as possible.

Since the apparent resolution of the theatre's conflict with Penaloza in July 1977, several new developments had undermined the sense of security temporarily afforded by that resolution. Following the proposed compromise (whereby Penaloza had agreed to rent half the Alexander Street property to the City in exchange for an increase in the allowable density on the other half), Penaloza had encountered financial problems which prevented him from fulfilling his part of the agreement. When he allowed his option on the property to lapse, 12 Alexander Street reverted once again to its owner, the development company Fobasco. Fobasco determined to proceed with its own development plans. In the spring of 1979, it arranged a meeting with Luscombe and Jaffary, at that time the theatre's lawyer. The landlord wanted vacant possession of the property at a time in the near future which would be convenient for TWP. Instead of being crestfallen (as the agent no doubt expected), Luscombe bridled with righteous indignation. Eyes flashing, he insisted that 12 Alexander Street was not just any building to be traded, vacated, or demolished. Whether the landlord liked it or not, his property housed a theatre, and such a facility was a spiritual resource to be preserved and cherished. Jaffary remembers Luscombe as being at his most passionate and defiant during the meeting,[3] but no amount of eloquence could alter the facts. And the facts were that TWP didn't have a legal leg to stand on.

In the months following, Jaffary tried to persuade Fobasco to settle for development on only half the property and negotiated a purchase price of $100,000 for the theatre and the land beneath it. The success of the proposed compromise depended on Luscombe's being able to raise the needed money from the province and on Fobasco's working out a development plan that would meet with the approval of the City. When this twofold object had not been achieved by July 1980, Fobasco decided it wished to develop the whole site within the existing zoning restrictions and again threatened the company with eviction.[4] His back seemingly up against the wall, Luscombe called an emergency meeting at the theatre. It was attended by about a hundred supporters, who pledged themselves to work for the survival of TWP.

On 20 August 1980, a delegation including Luscombe, Jaffary, and several other prominent supporters of the theatre appeared before the Executive Committee of City Council. Following the meeting, the Council informed the commissioner of planning that 'it [viewed] the retention of the theatre as an overriding planning objective for the site.' Finally, in October, after further negotiations between Jaffary, Fobasco, and the City, the Council approved the construction of a fifteen-storey, 145-apartment building on the north half of the Alexander Street property in exchange for the transfer of the land under the theatre to TWP when all Planning Department approval had been secured.[5] For its part, the theatre agreed to pay a lump sum of $100,000 to cover rent arrears, renovations and repairs to the building, and the deed.

Several years were to pass, however, before the theatre finally acquired the deed for the building. On 14 August 1984, the necessary $100,000 was provided by the newly named Ministry of Citizenship and Culture in the form of a 'repayable grant' on condition that the theatre agree to take out a mortgage in the name of the Ministry. The following day the title to the theatre was officially conveyed to the theatre. It looked at last as though the important fund-raising could proceed.

Instead, the board became increasingly embroiled in details of theatre administration which brought it into conflict with the artistic director. After one acrimonious meeting in Karl Jaffary's home in late 1984, the board decided to set up a long-range planning committee to consider the question of a successor to George Luscombe. At a lunch in January 1985, Gordon Floyd, acting on behalf of the board, offered Luscombe a contract as artistic director emeritus at a gradually diminishing salary that would cease altogether at the end of three years. At that meeting, Floyd restated his opinion that ultimate responsibility for running the theatre (including making the selection of Luscombe's successor) was in the hands of the board. Luscombe found that claim utterly unacceptable. He maintained that the history of TWP was unique and that as founder he should have a different relationship to his board from that of other artistic directors to theirs. In the end, he refused to sign the contract.

It was in an atmosphere of mutual suspicion and hostility, therefore, that Luscombe presented his plans for the 1985–6 season. They called for five previously scripted productions (of which Robert Rooney would direct two) and a new work to be based on the life and music of Jelly Roll

Morton. The proposed productions included *Jack and His Master* by the Czech author Milan Kundera; *Woza Albert*, about apartheid, to be presented by the Market Theatre of Johannesburg; *Traitors* by Stephen Sewell; *The Struggle of the Dogs and the Black*, a second play about apartheid; and a co-production of *Julius Caesar*. In submitting this schedule to the board in March 1985, Luscombe reported that he intended to employ Robert Rooney as 'resident director' until his own resignation took effect 'at the completion of this season.' At that time, he would recommend to the board of directors that they accept Rooney as the new artistic director of TWP.

The proposed program precipitated a confrontation that had been brewing most of the year. The administrative manager, Catherine McKeehan, refused to sign the application on the grounds that she was leaving before the 1985–6 season and could not in good conscience commit herself to it.[6] Gordon Floyd, as acting chairman, also refused to sign the application. He objected to the fact that the decisions had been made without any discussion by the board, and he had little confidence in the proposed budget, which, he felt, though not exactly dishonest was not based on reality. He concluded that the differences between the board and Luscombe had now reached a point where he could no longer serve a useful purpose, and he decided to resign.[7] In a letter to Luscombe, he wrote:

Despite our many meetings and conversations since November, despite our common desire to see TWP continue as a unique and important force in Canadian theatre, we have been unable to agree on some fundamental matters. It seems to me that there is virtually no prospect of resolving our basic differences of opinion. I believe that it is time for a transition at TWP, to bring new energy and new vision to the fulfilment of the theatre's artistic mandate, to build a stronger base of audience support, and to establish more effective administrative, marketing and fundraising operations. I believe that this transition can only be achieved under the leadership of a new Artistic Director who is supported by an experienced and professional General Manager, and an expanded, revitalized Board of Directors.[8]

Floyd did not wish to be part of a board which seemed to be used only 'to legitimize an operation in which they have no voice, where they are seldom consulted, and which is entirely controlled by the founder.' Within a few days, Luscombe received a similar letter of resignation from Karl Jaffary.

When, in mid-April 1985, Luscombe heard from the Canada Council that they would not consider the theatre's application without a signature from the chairman of the board, he sought clarification of his legal position from his old friend Norman Endicott, a long-time theatre supporter and the son of the Communist and peace activist James Endicott. Consulting the information filed with the Companies Branch, Endicott reported that, in his opinion, Luscombe had ample authority to call a meeting of the directors and to fill the existing vacancies.[9] Accordingly, on 1 May Luscombe convened a meeting in the theatre to constitute yet another board of directors. The officers elected at that time included George Luscombe as president and artistic director, Jerry White as chairman, and Mona Luscombe as secretary. The members at large were Tom Patterson, Karl Stevens, and Michael Lyons from the previous board and Norman Endicott, the publisher Caroline Walker, the theatre critic Gordon Vogt, and the actor Douglas Campbell as new appointments. An important item of business was the introduction and approval of a new by-law providing for the general management of the corporation. Under its terms, all management decisions were to be made by the president, except in the case when the artistic director was a person other than the president, when artistic matters would be left in the hands of the artistic director.[10] As in the past, Luscombe prudently secured signed letters of resignation from all new members, thereby re-establishing the lines of authority as he wanted them.

Among the first actions of this new board were the approval of Robert Rooney as resident director and the submission of a new application to the Canada Council. At the end of June 1985, the company heard that their grant would be reduced by $30,000 from the previous year's level. This bombshell was accompanied by a letter from Anna Stratton, the Council's theatre officer, warning that the Council's decision to cut back its support reflected its very serious concerns regarding the artistic and organizational vitality of the company. She reported that assessments of the work of TWP had been increasingly critical in recent years, and that the Council had concluded 'that the previous level of support awarded to Toronto Workshop Productions was not commensurate with the returns.'[11]

The news from the Ontario Arts Council in July 1985 was not much better. Although the communication from the chairman, Donald McGibbon, was somewhat friendlier in tone, its underlying message was the same: 'The reduction in the 1985/86 grant [by $6,000] and the conditions attached reflect the concerns expressed by Council's advisors.'[12] Feeling a little like the victims of anonymous informers, Luscombe and Rooney were doubly confounded. Not only would they need to rethink their original plans in an attempt to cut more than $36,000 from their budget, but they would have to come up with a season to please the face-less judges on the councils' theatre panels in whose hands their very future now lay.

They decided to open their 1985–6 season with a new play from the Soviet Union which Luscombe had brought back from a recent visit there. The work, by Edward Radzinsky, was entitled *Theatre in the Time of Nero and Seneca,* and it would, they felt sure, make a significant splash in the rather quiet waters of Toronto theatre. They overestimated their pub-lic. Reviews were lukewarm and audiences apathetic, and the play had to be taken off two weeks early.

If their opening show had not caused the stir they had hoped for, their second more than made up for it. *Ghetto* by the Israeli playwright Joshua Sobol dealt with Jewish collaboration in the Nazi-occupied ghetto of Vilna during the Second World War. It had been brought to the company's attention by Marion Andre, the artistic director of Theatre Plus, who had received it from the Montreal director Alexandre Hausvater. Rooney and Luscombe had been immediately struck by the play, although they real-ized they would run substantial risks in producing it. Quite apart from the challenging nature of the subject matter, there were serious administra-tive difficulties to be overcome.

The first was finding a suitable director. Both Luscombe and Rooney felt it was essential that the play be staged by someone fully familiar with the nuances of Jewish life. Fortunately, Hausvater, himself a Jew, was avail-able and willing to direct the production. There was no denying that Sobol's subject was unsettling and his treatment of it provocative. Set in the Vilna ghetto in 1942 just ten days before the massacre of all but about six hundred of the inhabitants, the play examines the relationship between a young SS officer, a Jewish chief of police responsible for law and order in the ghetto, and a group of performers. The Nazi officer pro-fesses admiration for Jewish culture, including the forbidden music from Broadway shows, which he persuades the Jewish musicians to play for him. In the context of the bleak moral choices forced on the Jews by their Nazi persecutors, songs such as 'I Want to Be Happy' and 'Swanee' provide a grotesque musical comment. Hoping to ameliorate the fate of some of his compatriots, the Jewish police chief collaborates in the selection of vic-tims to be executed by the Nazis. A Jewish profiteer points to the 'produc-tive' jobs he has created by helping the German war effort. The performers themselves must choose defiance and death or accommoda-tion and survival.

Sobol was a journalist for a left-wing Israeli newspaper and a graduate in philosophy from the Sorbonne. As a schoolboy in Israel, he had boycotted history classes that dealt with the holocaust because of his outrage that there had been so few acts of resistance. Later, in Germany, however, he came to realize that the question of collaboration was not so simple. How would he have behaved, he wondered, if he had had the misfortune to be caught up in the Nazi tyranny? He came to believe that, far from being an act of cowardice, survival is the ultimate form of human resistance.

The play he wrote to explore these ideas is deeply disturbing, raising painful questions about the nature of community and culture and the price paid in the struggle to stay alive. Intending his work primarily for an Israeli audience, Sobol wanted to point out the evil effects of Zionism, which he thought were inconsistent with Judaism as he understood it. Believing that 'what the Germans have done to us explains what has happened to us as Israelis,' he suggested that the victims might be played by Palestinian actors and the Nazis by Israelis. In spite of its provocative nature, the original Haifa production had played to receptive audiences and complimentary reviews. Most critics recognized that the play was a tribute to the spirit of resistance and survival in the face of annihilation.

Understandably, perhaps, Toronto audiences, being less intimately involved with the issues, responded to the play somewhat differently. Several commentators seemed reluctant to accept its disturbing view of human nature. Salem Alaton of the *Globe* thought the work 'bruised the memory of recent events in German-occupied Europe, not least by explaining itself too carefully' and thereby making the proceedings dull.[13] Marianne Ackerman, a visiting Montreal critic, however, called the play 'one of the few Holocaust-based dramas which goes beyond indicting the guilty and complacent, and actually draws the entire public into the story. *Ghetto* addresses a universal moral question. It is not exclusive. Hausvater has changed Sobol's ending, keeping Gens [the police chief] alive to mourn the dead, his lone praying image one of the production's most powerful. It is a superb, engrossing evening of theatre.'[14] In many ways, *Ghetto* was a perfect example of the kind of politically concerned, artistically daring theatre that Luscombe had been trying to establish in Toronto for almost three decades. Ironically, it was to mark the beginning of the end of his company.

22

Catastrophe Averted

At first, the looming clouds went unnoticed. Indeed, prospects looked bright as attendance at *Ghetto* hovered around 51 per cent, a significant improvement over recent productions. Part way through the run of the play, however, as unforeseen bills continued to come in, it became apparent that the theatre was in serious financial trouble. With some $50,000 in accounts payable, the company was informed that it had come to the end of its $200,000 line of credit at the bank. Lacking any other reserves, the management was unable to meet its payroll and was forced to lay off half of the theatre's ten employees. To make matters worse, since the company was some six months behind in its bookkeeping and therefore could not prepare financial statements, the money still due in payments from the federal and provincial arts councils might not be forthcoming. As the true nature of the situation began to dawn on him, Luscombe put his pride in his pocket and appealed to the director of the Ontario Arts Council for advice and assistance.

Walter Pitman, formerly the president of Ryerson Polytechnical Institute and before that a New Democratic member of the provincial legislature, had been a long-time supporter of TWP on both aesthetic and ideological grounds. He listened sympathetically to Luscombe's litany of misfortunes and responded with three very practical initiatives. He arranged to release the second instalment of the Council grant to cover the bank overdraft; he proposed that the Council hire a firm to write up the company's books; and he took it upon himself to arrange a meeting with the other funding agencies to consider how they might collectively assist TWP to turn around its current position.[1]

At a hastily called meeting of the board of directors in early January 1986, Luscombe reported his conversation with Pitman and announced that a meeting with the funding agencies had been set up for later that month. He stressed that it was important for the board to prepare a strong position paper for that meeting to avoid being put on the defensive by the Council officers. He offered to work with the theatre staff to draft a proposal and to bring that proposal to a board meeting before the end of the month.[2]

Following his meeting with the board, Luscombe approached Gerry Eldred, a theatre consultant, for advice on how the company might overcome its problems. He stressed that he had no intention of altering TWP's artistic policy or moving from their current location and expressed his conviction that the main reason for dwindling audience support was the size of the theatre. Eldred proposed conducting a six-week study to determine the feasibility of raising $2 million to retire the theatre's debt and to renovate and enlarge 12 Alexander Street. He anticipated that three-quarters of that sum would come from federal, provincial, and Metropolitan Toronto agencies and that the remaining $500,000 could be raised through a public campaign. Eldred would not himself be involved in any direct fund-raising, but he would propose an administrative structure to work closely with Luscombe, the board of directors, and an unspecified fund-raising team and other interested parties.

The proposals were brought to a meeting of the TWP board on 21 January, where, after some discussion of the need for such a study, they were approved. Luscombe said that an even more desirable solution to their problems would be the construction of a six-hundred-seat theatre at a cost of $3 million, and it was agreed that this possibility would be raised at the meeting.

Meanwhile, the Ontario Arts Council had decided to conduct a study of its own and had engaged the arts consultant Graeme Page to carry it out. On 23 January 1986, the day before the scheduled meeting with the theatre, Page delivered his assessment of the situation. He emphasized that TWP's most serious challenge was to generate some cash flow. Just to continue its present level of productions and to pay the carrying costs of the growing debt (without contributing to the deficit or the mortgage), he warned, the company would need revenues of close to $600,000. Furthermore, the company's position would not be substantially improved even if the Ministry of Citizenship and Culture were to forgive the mortgage, since such a move would contribute nothing to current income. Page predicted that unless there was an improvement in the situation, the bank would 'pull the plug,' possibly insisting on the sale of the building. To this sorry state of affairs, Page saw only three possible solutions: the company could sell the building to a financially sound theatre with a provision that TWP share the space over a three-to-five-year period; it could undertake a massive fund-raising effort; or it could sell the building outright.[3] Glancing over these sombre conclusions, Pitman foresaw a difficult session with the theatre the following day.

On the afternoon of 24 January, nearly twenty concerned individuals gathered in the comfortable boardroom at the Ontario Arts Council's offices on Bloor Street. Although the tone was cordial and Chairman Walter Pitman reassured the TWP representatives that everyone present really cared about the theatre's situation, the atmosphere was one of mutual suspicion. For his part, Luscombe knew that the bank was threatening to call in its loan, a move that would force him into bankruptcy and destroy the theatre he had devoted his life to. He was not prepared to let that happen without a fight. For their part, the representatives from the funding agencies shared a certain scepticism. While admiring Luscombe's pioneering achievements, tenacity, and undoubted talent, they were beginning to question his ability to deal realistically with the financial crisis now facing him. Nevertheless, they had come to the meeting with open minds, ready to have their doubts allayed.

Luscombe began the company's formal presentation by reading from a prepared statement. He attributed what he called 'the most serious financial crisis in the theatre's history' to three factors: the refusal of the bank to extend further credit without collateral security, chronic underfunding from the arts councils, and a decline in audience support. This last, he argued, was a consequence less of programming than of the condition of the building. The uncomfortable benches and black-painted walls conveyed the impression of a theatre still living in the 1960s rather than one that had moved with the times. In fact, Luscombe argued, TWP could still play an important role in the Toronto theatre scene and provide a focus for like-minded men and women whose concerns for humanity's plight had led them to seek solutions in the theatre. The prerequisite for the kind of renaissance he envisaged, Luscombe was convinced, was the construction of a new, six-hundred-seat theatre more congenial to audiences in the prosperous nineties.[4]

He found it ironic that the very thing the company had fought so long to achieve – ownership of their own theatre – was now their main problem. Not only was the building deteriorating faster than they could afford to repair it, but the very by-law which the City had passed to ensure its continued use as a theatre limited its commercial value. Although the theatre's auditor had assessed the property at $1.2 million, the bank considered the building as worthless and the land as worth no more than $500,000. That meant that the bank was unwilling to increase the theatre's line of credit without some kind of security, preferably in the form of a mortgage on the property. Luscombe was unwilling to provide such security for fear that the theatre might some day fall into the hands of the bank and be lost to the theatre community.

Luscombe's intention, he informed the Council, as he prepared to relinquish the artistic leadership of the company, was to see it properly settled in its home. To that end, he asked the councils to support the theatre through a reduced 1986–7 season, plans for which would be submitted by April. He also asked that they support the proposed feasibility study by Gerry Eldred and make a special arrangement so that the theatre would be allowed to remain open for the balance of the current season.

The representatives of the funding agencies listened politely but with mixed feelings of amazement and incredulity. It seemed to many that, in his preoccupation with the building, Luscombe had lost sight of the real issues at stake. In his presentation, he had made no mention of just how the present theatre board (which had so far shown no ability in that direction) would be able to raise their share of the cost of a new theatre. Nor did he address the question of cash flow posed by Graeme Page. There was no mention of what steps might be taken to strengthen the administration of the company, nor was the matter of the transfer of power discussed. Luscombe referred indirectly to his eventual replacement but gave no indication of when such a change of direction might take place or how it would be carried out.

In the ensuing discussion, several of these issues were raised. Pitman noted his concern about linking discussion of the management of the building with discussion of the operation of the theatre. He wondered whether sorting out the problems of one would necessarily resolve the problems of the other and suggested that decline in audience support might not be related to the condition of the theatre. Other representatives wondered if the company had considered alternative solutions, such as selling the building or renting it to others. The TWP representatives were adamant that selling the theatre would simply aggravate their situation since it would deprive them of their capital. In response to a proposal that top priority should be the employment of a competent general manager, TWP replied that they had no money to hire one.

Pitman and others expressed concern about the structure of the board and its relationship to the administration. They hoped the urgently required fund-raising could be done by an ad hoc body, from which several new board members might be chosen after the campaign had been successful. Asked when he would step aside, Luscombe refused to give a definite answer. Rooney explained that his appointment as resident director was for a year only, to see if he would get along with the current artistic director. Luscombe suggested that he would retire as artistic director 'this year' but added that he didn't make the decisions. The meeting finally broke up with universal expressions of goodwill but with unspoken fears and suspicions on both sides.

In private discussions following the departure of the TWP delegation, the representatives of the funding agencies were more forthright. It was evident to those present that whatever he might say, Luscombe was in effective control of the theatre and that the board was virtually inoperative. After discussing several options, they agreed that a joint response should be drafted and conveyed to the theatre the following week.

The attempt to arrive at the wording of such a response in the days following revealed profound disagreement among the representatives about the continuing relevance of TWP's kind of theatre. An opening paragraph stating that 'all levels of government continue to believe in the artistic mandate promoted by TWP ... are convinced of the value of what TWP wants to accomplish artistically, support the socially relevant theatre TWP wishes to produce, and believe there is a large audience for TWP productions in Toronto and Canada' was debated and finally rejected. It was replaced in the final document by a much more qualified endorsement: 'All levels of government recognize the importance of the artistic mandate promoted by TWP and the contribution of George Luscombe and TWP to the development of Canadian theatre.'

The document then went on to list a number of concerns and requirements. It underlined that the funding cuts suffered by the theatre reflected a perception that TWP had deteriorated in its ability to fulfil its own mandate – a deterioration demonstrated by a diminishing audience and an absence of ongoing community support. The cause of the deterioration, it suggested, was, first, the failure of the company to evolve adequate board, management, and administrative structures, and second, the diversion of resources and attention away from artistic objectives towards the management and development of the theatre property. It further stressed that the recent discussions had failed to demonstrate that TWP had addressed any of these problems.

To assist the theatre in working out realistic solutions, the Ontario Arts Council offered to pay for a ten-week study by a consultancy team which would analyse the situation and recommend alternative courses of action for the theatre to consider. As an incentive, the Council specified that the release of any further funds to TWP would be dependent on the findings and recommendations of the consultants. Following the completion of such a study, it was expected that TWP would provide a balanced operating budget for the remainder of the season, a plan to eliminate the deficit in five years, a realistic program for 1986–7, and an administrative structure which would ensure sound fiscal and operational management. The Council also expressed its willingness, subject to the creation of a board/management structure capable of exercising the necessary public stewardship, to recommend that the Ministry of Citizenship and Culture forgive its $100,000 mortgage. Finally, the Council made clear that the various government agencies were unanimous in their opposition to any capital expansion of the theatre, and it refused the request to underwrite a feasibility study of such expansion. The completed document was hand-delivered to Luscombe on 28 January.[5]

The theatre's response was uncharacteristically prompt. At a press conference called that very afternoon, Robert Rooney read from a prepared release announcing the planned appointment of a consultancy team and TWP's commitment to strengthen their board of directors. The following day, Luscombe wrote to Walter Pitman formally requesting the services of the consultants and accepting the terms of the proposal. Two days later, however, at a meeting of the theatre's board, the first item of business was the election, by the five members in attendance, of a new slate of board officers. They consisted of George Luscombe, president, Larry Cox (not previously on the board), vice-president, Norman Endicott, chairman, Tom Patterson, vice-chairman, Caroline Walker, treasurer, and Mona Luscombe, secretary. Following discussion of the Council's response, the board passed three motions. Norman Endicott suggested considering the creation of a holding company with the same executive as TWP which would assume ownership of the theatre and responsibility for its renovation. Caroline Walker proposed that TWP investigate the possibility of a 'proper loan agreement' with a bank or credit union. Larry Cox moved that a committee be struck to recruit additional board members. Susan Puff, the theatre's publicity director, then described plans for a fund-raising drive to collect $10,000 to tide the theatre over the next few months.[6]

Using the slogan 28 Days to Save 28 Years the theatre announced its campaign to the press on 5 February and at the same time sent out letters to supporters with the admonition The Doors at 12 Alexander Street Must Not Be Closed!!! A separate copy was addressed to Walter Pitman at the Ontario Arts Council, with a personal note from Susan Puff suggesting that he might want it for his files. Pitman was furious. Far from demon-strating the theatre's initiative and responsibility, as Puff no doubt intended that it should, the letter simply confirmed Pitman's worst fears that the organization was bound on a course of self-destruction. Instead of addressing the company's long-term problems, the proposed drive, hastily planned without consultation with the Council, would simply jeop-ardize attempts to raise the much larger amounts needed by the company in the immediate future. Furthermore, Pitman had also learned that TWP had entered into direct negotiations with the Canadian Imperial Bank of Commerce concerning an increase in its line of credit and was thereby limiting what the Council could do to obtain more advantageous finan-cial arrangements for the company. He had also heard that Luscombe was already looking for a new general manager, before any decisions had been taken about the most desirable form of administrative structure for the theatre.

For about twenty-four hours, Pitman considered imposing strict limita-tions on TWP to ensure that no further actions affecting the legal or financial status of the company would be taken before the report of the consultants had been received. In the end, however, he relented, feeling that little would be gained by such adversarial tactics. But it was beginning to dawn on him that saving Toronto Workshop Productions was going to be a more frustrating operation than he had originally imagined.

Negotiations between the theatre and Graeme Page were completed fairly rapidly, and Page was able to begin his investigation of the company in mid-February. By the end of the month, he had reported as follows: 'Everyone involved with the company is totally overwhelmed by the crisis and no one is able to see a way out. The fundraising drive toward $10,000 had been fairly successful, but the money has been used to pay salaries without making any headway in the long list of payables. Board and staff relations are strained, and any attempt by directors to take a hard line position has met with considerable resistance. The company has been operating without any financial management or sense of fiscal controls.'[7]

Page also reported that people who had been associated with TWP in the past were very supportive of the organization, but that some of them questioned whether Robert Rooney had the necessary experience to assume the responsibilities of artistic director. The same people felt that the board should exercise some influence in the selection of a new artistic director, but, Page found, the staff and directors could not agree on how they should do so.

The Page report was completed on 30 April 1986, and the TWP board gathered to consider its recommendations. The most far-reaching of these concerned the functions of the board of directors and the creation of a board of trustees. Page concluded that the theatre's financial crisis had developed from 'a lack of understanding by the Board of Directors as to what controls are suitable ... for proper decision-making ... The present Directors have inherited a system whereby the management and decision-making were left to the Artistic Director [with the Board being asked to] approve decisions or to accept budgets and plans which have been drawn up without its participation.'[8] Page also implied that the board was in violation of the law covering the boards of non-profit organizations in that several of the directors were employed by TWP. It was important, he maintained, since public money was involved, that the board should not appear to be self-serving.

Hoping his remarks would provide a guide for future members, Page went on to describe what he considered the appropriate functions of a board. Artistic and management decisions, he recommended, should be left to hired professionals, while the board should act as a senior management team to oversee the progress of the company and accept responsibility for the allocation of public funds. To that end, the board should be involved in discussions of overall policy, planning, budgets, fund-raising, and promotion.

In recommending a radical restructuring of the theatre, Page was dealing with that aspect of the problem which seemed most tractable. Clearly, there had been major weaknesses in the theatre's administration which had contributed to the company's misfortunes. The appointment of a new artistic director and general manager, the renewal of the board of directors, and the establishment of working committees to deal with fund-raising, audience development, finance, and so on would go a long way towards ensuring better fiscal control and responsibility. But such measures could do nothing to address the more profound malaise of the organization. For the unspoken truth was that the spirit had gone out of the theatre. It remained to be seen if administrative changes could revive that spirit.

Members of the Ontario Arts Council meeting in July had to wrestle with their own doubts. Both the consultants and the officers of the Council were inclined to be supportive of a company which had contributed so much to the theatrical life of the province. Nevertheless, several of the council's advisers wondered whether it wasn't too late to save the theatre. 'There is little in this application,' wrote one, '(from the continuing structure of the board, to the choice of plays) to indicate a renewed vision, or a revitalized sense of direction.'[9] Others felt that it was desirable to retain the theatre building at 12 Alexander Street as an invaluable performance space. In the end, the Council decided to award the company a preliminary grant of $20,000 and to defer consideration of the balance of the request until the October meeting, at which time it would have further information on the current status of the board, plans for the implementation of the Page report, the new general manager, the 1986–7 budget, and fund-raising and deficit reduction proposals.[10]

By October, the company could report that they had moved some distance towards satisfying the criticisms of the various funding organizations. The board had been enlarged by the addition of three new members; it had set up a subcommittee to review the theatre's by-laws; and it had approved a drastically reduced but financially manageable season. Furthermore, some progress had already been made on reducing the company's debt. The new plans for 1986–7 involved renting the theatre to the Shaw Festival for two productions (*Breaking the Silence* and *B Movie, the Play* by Tom Wood) in November and January, bringing in a production of the Market Theatre of Johannesburg entitled *Woza Albert* in December, mounting a production of Ken Mitchell's one-man play about Norman Bethune, *Gone the Burning Sun*, in April, and producing George Luscombe's long-delayed *Mr Jelly Roll* in May. In addition, with help from the Department of External Affairs, the company proposed to take the play about Bethune to China.

Those moves won the theatre a reprieve. The Ontario Arts Council granted $85,000, and the Toronto and Metro councils confirmed their support. As 1986 drew to a close, it seemed that the worst of the crisis was past.

23

Harlequin in Hogtown

The emergency meeting with the Ontario Arts Council had dramatically underlined the importance of revitalizing the artistic direction of TWP. By March 1986, therefore, the company had worked out an arrangement whereby Robert Rooney would take over as artistic director in July, at which time Luscombe would become the theatre's artistic director emeritus at a slightly reduced salary. The plan called for the two men to share administrative duties, with Rooney taking responsibility for the choice of repertoire and the formulation of artistic policy and Luscombe concentrating on teaching and directing the occasional production. Luscombe would retain his position as president of the board.

The board hoped to forestall public discussion of the changes until they took effect. When Robert Crew learned of the plans and reported them in the *Star*, however, the directors reluctantly called a press conference to confirm that Luscombe had at last agreed to relinquish his hold on the reins of power at TWP. Understandably, perhaps, the press showed less interest in the new incumbent than in the long-embattled Luscombe, whose tenure at last appeared to be coming to an end. Describing his action as 'moving aside' rather than retiring, Luscombe told reporters that he would continue to direct as well as fund-raise and organize the theatre's archives. 'I'm not sure I know how to retire from the theatre,' he said. 'Someone would have to teach me.'[1]

Like so many of Luscombe's pronouncements, the words had an ambiguous ring to them. Observers critical of TWP predicted that the moves were merely cosmetic and that the new artistic director would prove to be nothing but a puppet in the lap of the master ventriloquist. Luscombe had evaded past efforts to replace him, and there was little in his comments to suggest that he had lost any of his proprietary attitudes and autocratic ways. If the theatre was to be saved, such critics argued, it would require a completely new artistic vision. It remained to be seen if Rooney had such a vision, and if he did, whether it would be allowed to prevail.

Away from the public spotlight, the transfer of authority proceeded more smoothly than might have been predicted. Luscombe installed a second desk in the cramped upstairs office, and the two men crowded into the tiny space to grapple with their new duties. Freed for the first time in more than twenty-five years from the burden of administration, Luscombe began to devote most of his attention to the creation of the much delayed *Mr Jelly Roll*, now scheduled for production in the spring of 1987.

Luscombe's interest in the Creole pianist 'Jelly Roll' Morton was part of his long-standing fascination with what might be described as the radical fringe of the entertainment world. Inspired by the Marxist aesthetics of Littlewood and MacColl and the experiments of Meyerhold and Vakhtangov, Luscombe was drawn to the cultural 'outsiders,' the artistically disestablished, the wandering performers and minstrels who live in a precarious world of their own somewhere between privilege and disgrace. For Luscombe, there was something almost mythic about these 'licensed jesters' – clowns, musicians, or professional athletes – whom he celebrated in play after play. They constituted for him a kind of archetype, the embodiment of an undying human quality. It was this quality that he and Nancy Jowsey had tried to capture in the theatre's logo – the half-clown, half-harlequin figure that served for more than twenty years as the signature of Toronto Workshop Productions. In its association with the circus and commedia dell'arte, the logo recalls the tradition of slapstick and pantomime so important to the aesthetic of TWP. The disconnected head with the conical cap, falling off or being lifted into place, suggests a repudiation of reason and language – associated with the mind – in favour of impulses rooted in the body. Or it may intend a sense of incompletion – the clown in the act of putting himself together. Whatever its symbolic connotation, the design was a reminder of the non-political dimensions of the company.

The inspiration for the logo, of course, had been the company's first hit, *Hey Rube!*, in which so many of Luscombe's ideas had come to fruition. Indeed, that play, revived in 1966, in 1972, and again in 1984, had become something of a touchstone for the theatre. It was useful as a means of taking Luscombe and his actors back to their roots, but it also served as a kind of litmus test of Toronto's current attitude to its resident

radical clowns. The first revival of the play had been held at 47 Fraser Avenue in November 1966, after performances in Stratford in the Theatre-in-
the-Park. There, it had been introduced into the repertoire by a new
group of actors, most of whom were unfamiliar with the original production. The process of revival proved to be very different from that involved
in the original creation.

For this second company, *Hey Rube!* was not an expression of immediate
personal experience but simply another script to be learned. Instead of
treating it that way, however, Luscombe encouraged his new actors to
develop new characters and business. But he seemed satisfied only with
what had been done before.[2] Not surprisingly, his attitude resulted in
unhappiness on both sides. The actors felt they were being restricted,
while Luscombe grew impatient with the slow pace of the work.[3]

Nathan Cohen thought the revival less successful than the original production since the lines improvised by different actors were inappropriate
in the mouths of new performers. He was also more conscious of the inad-
equacies of the script, which 'had not seemed so crucial [in the original
production] because of the sheer primal force and animation of the proceedings and ... because the show seemed to be the inception of something genuinely progressive in our theatre.'[4]

When the company came to do the play again in 1972, their circumstances, and those of the Toronto theatre in general, had changed drastically. Productions such as *Dionysus in 69* at the Studio Lab, David French's
Leaving Home at Tarragon, and *The Farm Show* at Theatre Passe Muraille
had created a new theatrical climate in the city. The reappearance of *Hey
Rube!* marked the beginning of a new relationship between TWP and Toronto audiences.

Herbert Whittaker, who had championed Luscombe in the early sixties,
thought the show 'bigger, flashier and more appealing than ever.'[5]
Joseph Erdelyi, the critic for the *Peterborough Examiner*, who had also seen
the first production in 1961, thought it 'just as exhilarating as it was when
it was first presented.'[6] Both critics enjoyed the exuberant mixture of circus turns and backstage scenes and felt that plot was as unnecessary as in a
real circus.

But there were new voices beginning to be heard among the theatrical
reviewers. Don Rubin, a recent arrival from the United States and soon to
become editor of the *Canadian Theatre Review*, had not seen the earlier
production but was able to pronounce that TWP had travelled only a
small distance in the years since 1961. While admitting that Luscombe was
an imaginative director and that his company was getting stronger each

season, he found 'the sameness of Luscombe's work ... rather depressing.' He noted that the 1972–3 TWP season would include other revivals (both *Pickwick* and *Schweik* had been announced) and implied that this backward-looking stance was at odds with that of other theatres across the country, who were looking ahead.[7] Like Feste, TWP was beginning to find its antics out of favour.

It was more than a decade before the old retainer was brought back into service once more, in 1984. At that time, the theatre was struggling with a growing deficit and fighting to attract audiences to its shows. Rehearsals ran through October and November and were a vivid reminder of how much things had changed. The cast itself was a mélange of old and new. Peter McConnell and Douglas Livingston returned to re-create roles they had first played in the 1966 revival. Jeff Braunstein, Peter Millard, and Ross Skene, all veterans of the 1972 production, had been recruited to play the three clowns, Moss, Charlie, and Pandro. The newer members of the company, however, had no personal knowledge of the production's history, and one of the youngest of them, Luscombe's daughter Nadine, had not even been born when the play had its first success.

The different generations also came to the rehearsals with very different preconceptions. Braunstein, Millard, and Skene had become so attuned to Luscombe's way of working that they could modulate their performances in rhythm or adjust them in space almost instinctively. McConnell and Livingston remembered the days of struggle at 47 Fraser Avenue and understood how closely the experiences of the beleaguered Wagnerian circus troupe corresponded to Luscombe's own story. But the younger actors had none of that experience to draw on. Their models were films and television, and the older actors felt they never learned to invest the admittedly stereotypical roles with any emotional truth. The result was a mechanical alternation of soap opera and circus acts rather than the more subtle juxtaposition that had been achieved in earlier productions.

There were also ways in which the content of the play seemed jarring to the younger actors. In the original production, Joan Maroney as Josie had given expression to the performers' feeling of desperation and frustration in a song that began 'Rape me and ravish me.' But what had seemed innocent enough in the early 1960s was intolerable to the more aware actresses of the 1980s. Mary Durkan refused to sing the song, and Luscombe recognized that she was right to object to a latent anti-feminism which he had not seen in the work before.

The play opened on 29 November 1984, and the response of the younger critics now writing for the Toronto dailies was mixed. Matthew Fraser of the *Globe* felt that it had lost none of its magic, and called it a 'wonderful orchestration of all the chaotic elements that make circuses so strangely fascinating.'[8] But Henry Mietkiewicz of the *Star* was more temperate in his enthusiasm. 'A kindly old grandfather of a play,' he called it, which we allow 'to babble away because of our feelings of affection and gratitude for what it accomplished as a pioneer.' While acknowledging that the work contained half a dozen hilarious and breathtaking acts, he felt that, without the diverting circus acts, 'the story collapses into pure melodrama.'[9] Something of the same ambivalence was reflected in the attendance figures, which reached only 35 per cent.

If *Hey Rube!* had run like a leitmotif through the company's history, it was also the grandfather of a number of other TWP productions celebrating the marginal life of talented rogues and vagabonds. *Summer '76* explored the world of Olympic athletes; *The Medicine Show* dug into the tradition of the travelling patent medicine salesman; *Les Canadiens* dealt with professional hockey. But one group Luscombe kept returning to was the doubly disadvantaged population of black entertainers. In *Mr Bones*, he had paid tribute to the minstrels. In 1980, he discovered an entirely new area of dramatic interest in the activities of itinerant black baseball teams.

In the autumn of 1979, Luscombe chanced to hear an interview on Don Harron's CBC morning radio show. The guest was a Canadian writer by the name of John Craig who described his remarkable experiences during a summer in the 1940s when he had disguised himself in order to travel with a black baseball team called the Colored All-Stars. He had recently turned those experiences into a book, *Chappie and Me*, and Luscombe thought the material might be adapted for the stage. What attracted him to the story was the way in which the black athletes had developed a critical perspective on the white society which condemned them to life on the margins. Clearly superior to the teams they encountered in the small towns of western Canada and the United States, they nevertheless had to disguise their ability with humour to avoid giving offence to their employer-opponents. They did so through a series of comic turns called 'reams.' In one of these, the first-base player, pretending to be watching something in the sky, would stand on the base with his back to the pitcher, apparently ignoring the game. The pitcher would then throw inside to force the batter to ground to third. At the count of seven, the first baseman would put his hand behind his back, and the third baseman would throw out the runner by hitting the open mitt. This routine seemed to Luscombe to sum up exactly the mixture of apparent insouciance and wariness that characterized the blacks, and he decided to call the stage version of the story *Ain't Lookin'* after that particular 'ream.'

As he had done with other adaptations of novels, Luscombe got his actors to improvise various scenes – the conversations on the bus, the disagreement with the gas station attendant, the white boy's encounter with a racist white girl. To these plot incidents, he added music of the period – an imitation of the Inkspots – and a number of pantomime scenes of warming up and playing ball. He invited John Craig to attend rehearsals and give suggestions as to how the players should move and wear their uniforms. Terry Gunvordahl designed a simple setting consisting of a few baseball posters, an electric piano, and a set of drums. Much of the action took place in the 'bus,' a number of suitcases on which the players sat and mimed the joggling, monotonous journey. The sounds of the bus as well as the sudden prairie storms were suggested by the on-stage musicians.

The production opened on 29 May 1980, when the critics from the major papers were in Niagara-on-the-Lake reviewing the Shaw Festival. Caught short-handed, the *Globe* and the *Star* assigned their sports writers to cover the show. Both Victor Paddy and Kevin Boland were entranced. Paddy found the work 'innovative and moving,'[10] and Boland called the play 'a little gem about the black diamond.'[11] Critics from the smaller papers were even more enthusiastic. Gordon Vogt gave the fullest and most thoughtful account of the production. 'Except for Luscombe's two previous productions [*Refugees* and *The Mac Paps*],' he reported, 'there has been nothing within hailing distance of it for imagination, intelligence, warmth and a shrewd sense of what the stage can render up to an artist who approaches it with an open eye ... It is closer to film than any stage show I've ever seen.'[12] Elsewhere, he described the climactic chase, in which 'the team in their (imagined) bus is pursued by a group of (imagined) louts in their (imagined) car around imagined curves, over imagined hills and across imagined fields.' The dénouement of the scene 'in which the team draws together in a dark field, tensely awaiting an attack, and silently passes out baseball bats, brought audiences to peaks of excitement and fear ... that would be an achievement in any medium.'[13]

While he was working on *Ain't Lookin'*, Luscombe became attracted to the idea of doing a show to celebrate one of the early black jazz musicians. At first he had considered the career of Fats Waller, but after the appearance in Toronto of the musical production *Ain't Misbehavin'* he turned his attention to the lesser-known Ferdinand 'Jelly Roll' Morton. As the financial crisis of the theatre deepened, however, Luscombe became side-tracked, and only in 1987 was he able to settle down to develop the production.

This time the material he worked from was less dramatic. It consisted primarily of an anecdotal biography, *Mister Jelly Roll*, compiled by the noted historian of American music Alan Lomax from hours of recollections recorded in the music auditorium of the Library of Congress. Rich as this source material was, however, Luscombe soon found it did not lend itself easily to adaptation. The published interviews capture the flamboyance of the raconteur and something of his penchant for self-aggrandizement. But there is little of the inner life of the man behind the public figure, the Creole Ferdinand La Menthe, who was driven out of his home by his grandmother when she discovered that he had been playing piano in the New Orleans 'tenderloin' district and who changed his name to Morton so that he wouldn't be identified as a 'Frenchy.'

Nor is there a strong narrative line in the life of this wandering minstrel/composer who travelled the 'barrellhouse' circuit in the southern United States. In developing his vision of Jelly Roll as a musical innovator, therefore, Luscombe found it difficult to reconcile the talented and original genius with the more mundane Ferdinand Morton. Away from the piano stool, Jelly Roll was unexceptional – a small-time pimp, con man, and pool shark, who lived his life on the borderline of the law without much concern for the rights or feelings of others. He was a hard man to admire, but when he sat down to the piano, he seemed to give voice to all the joy and yearnings of the dispossessed.

Another difficulty Luscombe faced in working on the show was the casting. He managed to gather together a talented group of black performers, but most of them were more familiar with musical productions than with the legitimate theatre. They had little experience in movement or improvisation and found it difficult to bring to the work the kind of imaginative creativity and invention which Luscombe depended on. Forced to capitalize on his cast's strengths, he and Larry Cox, whom he had brought in to assist with the script, put more and more emphasis on the music at the expense of the dramatic story. In the end, the show was little more than a series of Jelly Roll's songs, with minimal dramatization of the events that lay behind the composition of those songs.

As rehearsals progressed, it became evident that the show was not working. In the days before the opening, Luscombe was uncharacteristically upset.[14] Sensing the atmosphere of apprehension and feeling that this might be Luscombe's last show with TWP, the staff members did their best to make the production succeed. Sensed, but unexpressed, was the awareness that if *Mr Jelly Roll* failed, it would not only jeopardize the current season but seriously undermine the argument that there was still an audience for the kind of work Luscombe had pioneered and developed.

The production opened Thursday, 30 April 1987, and played to a near-capacity house in which 246 tickets were complimentary. The reviews were lukewarm. Ray Conlogue felt that Luscombe was still without equal 'when it comes to a fond funky staging idea,' but that the script lacked a point of view or any special passion.[15] Subsequent performances were poorly attended, with box-office figures sinking to 14 per cent of capacity, the lowest of the season.

It seemed indeed that the old magic no longer worked. Toronto had changed and with it the expectations of the audiences. No longer Toronto the Good or Hogtown, the city was eager to establish itself as 'world class.' Perhaps the TWP aesthetic seemed too naïve; certainly, its idealistic socialism was out of fashion. Whatever the reason, by the criteria that now held sway *Mr Jelly Roll* was a failure. It was a bitter disappointment to Luscombe and to all those who, like him, had hoped that the company might still recapture something of its past glory.

24

Final Act

By the end of the 1986–7 season, the situation seemed marginally less desperate. Although *Mr Jelly Roll* had failed to attract the audience they had hoped for, the company's overall financial position had improved. With the help of a stabilization grant of $109,489 from the Ontario government, TWP had managed to reduce its deficit (not including the $100,000 mortgage to the Ministry of Citizenship and Culture) from $235,000 to $85,000. But their own fund-raising efforts had been disappointing. Of the $38,000 targeted from corporations, foundations, individuals, and special projects, the board had managed to collect less than $6,000. Attempts to find corporate sponsorships for future productions had proved futile, and a planned fund-raising concert by the pianist Anton Kuerti had had to be cancelled. In spite of the income showing in their books, the harsh reality was that the company could not meet its payroll. In an effort to keep the theatre afloat, the recently appointed business manager, Pam Rogers, approached the bank for $10,000, only to be told that any loan would have to be guaranteed by members of the board and repaid in three weeks.

To wrestle with these problems, the board voted to restructure itself along the lines suggested by Graeme Page. Chairman Norman Endicott stepped down, and Pamela Hampson was elected to replace him for the summer. A nominating committee consisting of the education administrator Florence Silver, Robert Rooney, and Pamela Hampson set out to find new board members with the requisite political and financial connections. At a stormy annual general meeting on 15 September 1987, this nominating committee informed the Luscombes and Larry Cox that they were not being put forward for re-election.

On 5 February 1988, the new board met to discuss a worsening situation. Revenues from the two opening productions of the 1987–8 season, Ralph Burdman's *Tête à Tête* and the musical *Rap Master Ronnie*, had failed to reach their budgeted projections, and TWP was facing imminent bankruptcy unless revenue could be increased and costs drastically curtailed. They agreed to cancel the last production of the season. That settled, the discussion turned to the question of Luscombe's position as artistic director emeritus. There was general agreement that the theatre could not afford to pay salaries to two artistic directors. While it was true that Luscombe had founded the company and contributed enormously to its success, it was also true that his present position was without precedent in the country. Directors with similar close connections to the theatres they had run such as Bill Glassco, Paul Thompson, Martin Kinch, and Ken Gass had not been given retainers at the end of their tenure. It was unreasonable, the members argued, for Luscombe to expect to be pensioned off by an organization that was itself virtually bankrupt. After lengthy discussion, the board members decided to discontinue Luscombe's salary. They agreed to arrange a meeting with him to deliver a letter of dismissal to take effect in eight weeks.[1]

Meanwhile, Robert Rooney was in the midst of rehearsals for his second production of the season and at the same time drawing up his preliminary proposals for a 1988–9 program. In these plans, he forecast earned revenue of $320,000 (significantly higher than the company had ever collected), government grants of $210,000 (including Canada Council support at previous levels), and private sector fund-raising of $81,000. Even at these optimistic levels of subsidy, Rooney predicted a deficit of more than $55,000. When the board looked at the figures, they were appalled by what seemed to them irresponsible planning, and asked Rooney to submit a new proposal reflecting a more realistic budget to be considered at a subsequent meeting.

By the end of February, the financial situation had deteriorated to the point where the board was forced to approach the bank for further operating funds. This time they agreed to supply collateral, and the chairman and treasurer drew up a sealed undertaking to provide the bank with a second mortgage for $250,000, to be executed and registered as soon as reasonably possible but no later than 30 April 1988. By mid-April, however, the operating deficit for the season was almost five times the anticipated $32,000 shortfall, and little or no money was being raised privately.

Oppressed by their inability to pry funds out of the private sector, the board came increasingly to believe that the company's problems could be solved only by selling the TWP property to a developer in exchange for a promise to include a theatre in any building erected on the site. While such a scheme seemed attractive in the short run in that it would enable the board to pay off its existing debts and make a fresh start in new quarters, it failed to address the long-term structural difficulties. It was beginning to appear unlikely that the company would ever obtain the private support necessary for its continued survival unless it changed its artistic direction. Accordingly, the board decided to ask for Rooney's resignation, citing the 'financial situation of the theatre,' and at the same meeting authorized Tom Patterson to negotiate with the celebrated Canadian actress Frances Hyland in the hopes that she might be persuaded to take his place.

With the closing of the last scheduled production of the season, the Market Theatre of Johannesburg's *Bopha*, on 26 June 1988, the board was forced to shut the theatre and lay off all staff. Without either artistic or administrative personnel, the directors now faced two alternatives. Either they could wind up the company and dispose of any assets remaining after paying their debts, or they could attempt to carry on the business themselves. Although few of the board members had been associated with TWP for more than a couple of years, most had developed a sense of loyalty to the organization and felt they should do their best to keep it alive.

To achieve their objective, they hoped to appoint an artistic director whose ability and vision would persuade the funding agencies to support the organization at previous levels, and to parlay their rapidly decaying physical asset into a larger and more attractive performing space. To that end, they authorized a subcommittee to study a development plan for the 12 Alexander Street site which they had received from the George and Helen Vari Foundation. The scheme called for an immediate contribution of $300,000 to the theatre, which would enable it to pay off its debts and leave a little to spare. The builder, George Vari, would then negotiate a rezoning of the property with City Hall to allow the construction of a condominium and theatre development. If successful, Vari would turn the new auditorium over to TWP, and the $300,000 would be considered the purchase price of the property; if not, the developer would write off the initial payment to TWP as a charitable donation. In their enthusiasm for the project, its sponsors estimated that it could be completed by January 1990 and that TWP would be able to mount its 1990–1 season in new quarters.

On 29 June, Florence Silver, acting as pro-tem chairman of the TWP board, called a press conference to announce the deal, for which she said an agreement in principle had been signed that morning. She made it

clear to reporters that there might be some changes in the theatre's political orientation, which she acknowledged might have been too leftist in
the past. Pam Rogers agreed that TWP had become a 'political forum
rather than a theatre company' but told Robert Pennington of the *Sun*
they intended to stay on the 'cutting edge' in social relevance.[2]

In the twenty-four hours following the press conference, however, it
emerged that George Vari, who had not been at the meeting, had a
slightly different interpretation of the proposed agreement. He stressed
that while he hoped the deal would go through, 'neither myself nor the
theatre company has signed anything yet.' Furthermore, he differed
slightly in his vision of the theatre's future.

Vari had been born in Hungary and had emigrated to Canada in 1956,
after the Hungarian uprising. Now chairman of the Paris-based Sefri Construction International, one of the largest hotel builders and owners in
the world, he had established the George and Helen Vari Foundation to
endow projects related to improving the quality of life. He confirmed that
the theatre auditorium in the new building would be named after his wife
and that the Foundation would appoint eight of the fifteen members of
the newly formed theatre board. In response to queries by Robert Crew of
the *Star*, he stressed that he and his wife were 'out of all politics' and that
their main interest was in using the new theatre to contribute to cultural
exchange between Canada and France by mounting plays in both English
and French.[3] Stung by this public disagreement and by the outrage
expressed by many in the theatre community that control of TWP was
being turned over to a developer, the board broke off negotiations with
Vari and resolved in future to be more circumspect about announcing its
plans.

If the attempt to secure an adequate performing space had run into a
snag, efforts to recruit a new artistic director were more fruitful. On 21
July 1988, the board announced the appointment of Leon Pownall, a veteran mainstream actor who had appeared at all the major festivals (the
Stratford, the Shaw, and the Charlottetown) and had founded the Shakespeare Festival in Nanaimo, British Columbia. In making the announce-
ment, the board expressed confidence that the appointment would mark
the beginning of a new life for the theatre. Pownall himself prudently
admitted that he needed time to talk to people and assess the situation
before commenting extensively. Nevertheless, he told Robert Crew that
he accepted TWP's mandate with the realization that he was 'inheriting
one of Canada's great theatrical traditions.'[4]

Pownall's introduction to his new job was to prove something of a baptism by fire. Incensed by the prospect that 12 Alexander Street might fall into the hands of a developer, supporters of TWP who had participated in the long, eight-year struggle to save the building were galvanized into action. Under the leadership of Ken Gass, a group of Luscombe associates formed the 'Committee of Concern,' which included the actor Tom Butler, the playwright Rick Salutin, Walter Pitman, Herbert Whittaker, and a number of long-time TWP actors and friends. This group felt that some effort should be made to prevent the board of directors from betraying a twenty-eight-year history of anti-establishment theatre. They proposed a mid-July meeting with the board, trustees, and newly appointed artistic director to secure a firmer commitment that the theatre's original mandate would be respected. When the board refused to deal with what it considered little more than a pressure group intent on reinstating the former artistic director, the Committee resorted to direct action.

On a humid evening in late July, a small group of TWP supporters gathered outside 12 Alexander Street in the hope of confronting members of the board with their questions and getting the reassurance they hoped for. When they learned that the board not only refused to meet with them but denied them access to the theatre, the group resolved to conduct their protest on the theatre steps. After speeches by Pitman, Luscombe, Salutin, and others deploring the high-handed behaviour of the board and trustees, the assembled protesters voted to empower a small executive committee to proceed as it saw fit to pressure the current management of the theatre not to abandon its traditional mandate.

Finding himself in the middle of a controversy he barely understood and under pressure to come up with a program that would satisfy as many of the interested parties as possible, Pownall suggested four works – Edward Albee's *Who's Afraid of Virginia Woolf?*, *Peace on Earth*, *Stand Up Shakespeare*, and a 30th Anniversary Gala to consist of excerpts from some of the more successful TWP plays of the past. The first agency to consider his proposal was the Toronto Arts Council, who in late August rejected the application and cancelled the grant they had tentatively approved for the 1988–9 Robert Rooney season.[5]

Meanwhile, Luscombe and his supporters were making their own plans. After due notification of the 134 individuals who had bought memberships in TWP in the previous season, the Committee of Concern called an annual general meeting at the Metropolitan Toronto Reference Library. There they elected their own board of directors, consisting of Larry Cox as president, George Luscombe as vice-president, the actress Sandi Ross as secretary-treasurer, and Tom Butler, Mona Luscombe, the dancer and choreographer Danny Grossman, Ken Gass, and the theatre administrator Robin Breon. Wasting no time in asserting its authority, this rival board wrote to Lily Munro, the minister of culture, with copies to officers of the recently renamed Ministry of Culture and Communications and the Ontario Arts Council, requesting a meeting to discuss their plans to reopen the theatre.[6]

In a more daring assertion of their newly proclaimed prerogatives, the group made a dawn raid on 12 Alexander Street, where they changed the locks and laid claim to the building. Arriving for work later that morning, Leon Pownall was forced to summon the police to gain access to his office. To his chagrin, the police officers refused to arbitrate between the two sides and left the new artistic director shut out of his theatre. Later that afternoon, however, the trustees were able to demonstrate their legal responsibility for the property and were allowed to change the locks once again, thereby barring all contending parties and taking control of the building.

In these chaotic conditions, without either salary or office space, Leon Pownall and Pam Rogers attempted to reformulate an approach to the Ontario Arts Council. Pownall described the previous ninety days as 'the most tangled and disquieting theatrical scene I have ever experienced. A scene that includes a mandate that drew 30% attendance last season, the misguided concerns of an ad hoc committee fueled by bitterness and hysteria, the opportunism of eager developers, and a fiscal cancer that has all but consumed TWP's morale, its artistic vision and its very raison d'être.' Possibly reflecting Pownall's reaction to the events of the past three months, the new proposal took a more critical attitude to the theatre's past. 'Let us realize,' it asserted, 'TWP's left-wing mandate as practised in the past has lost its appeal in the marketplace and box-office revenue decreased to a debilitating level.'[7]

The submission went on to maintain that TWP's programming had become 'insular and exclusive to the point of elitism,' had lost contact with the community at large, and seemed to be informed by no policy beyond that of simply 'putting on plays.' Asking the Council to dissociate him and the new management from the 'old concept of TWP,' Pownall requested that they consider a new and broader concept of the company's activities. Pownall promised a modification of what he thought was generally perceived as the 'hysterical left-wing mandate' of the theatre. 'Times have changed,' he asserted, and the expectations of audiences 'have been raised above dusty political cabals whose mere elitism make them attractive.' The new TWP mandate, he promised, would interpret rather than preach.

Pownall's interpretive season consisted of three plays which he felt confident would 'breathe new life into our mandate and at the same time have specific appeal in the market place.' The works he proposed included *Conquest of the South Pole* by Manfred Farge, a study of unemployed youth in Britain, to be directed by Derek Goldby; *The Day They Shot John Lennon* by James Mclure; and *A Warm Wind in China*, a study of homosexual love devastated by AIDS which he felt would be marketable because of TWP's location in the heart of Toronto's gay community. He also planned to host political meetings and neighbourhood seminars in the theatre in order to regenerate its presence in the area.

By the time the Ontario Arts Council met to consider this latest application from TWP in January 1989, the new theatre officer, Timothy Leary, had heard much disquieting news. Both the Canada Council and the Toronto Arts Council had rejected the theatre's applications, and Metro's action was conditional on the decision of the Ontario Arts Council. But the most disturbing information was that communicated by a panel of consultants Leary had assembled to advise him on the situation. This group of thirteen theatre professionals had gathered in the Council offices on 23 January to assess the TWP proposal.

Many of the consultants felt that TWP had been a pioneering and energizing force in the city and resented the present management's rather cavalier dismissal of that history. Even those who felt less strongly about the traditions of the company agreed that the present application showed no distinctive vision and seemed, on the contrary, to have been thrown together without understanding or sympathy for what TWP had stood for. The conclusion of the discussion was a recommendation that the theatre's request for funding be denied.[8]

News of the Council's decision fell like a thunderbolt on the beleaguered board. It seemed to most of the members that they had exhausted their options. The theatre's debts were growing at an alarming rate, having been increased by some $226,000 in the previous year alone. While the directors were not personally liable for these debts, the majority felt a commitment to do what they could to wind up the affairs of the company in as dignified and responsible a fashion as possible. If they had failed in their efforts to negotiate a new theatre for themselves, then at least they could guarantee that the price they received for the 12 Alexander Street property would cover their outstanding bills.

By early May, however, having failed to persuade the Ministry of Culture and Communications to underwrite them, the board was faced with imminent catastrophe. Several of the theatre's creditors had served collection notices; George Luscombe had launched a $200,000 lawsuit, claiming wrongful dismissal; and the Bank of Commerce had given notice that it intended to sue to recover its loan. At an emergency meeting on 10 May in the offices of the Ministry attended by several of the funding agencies, Florence Silver outlined the scope of the theatre's problems. She estimated that the current liabilities of the company amounted to some $470,000 and stated that the board was seeking a way to ensure that the building would be used for non-profit, socially responsible theatre without leaving any of the directors liable. It was agreed that every effort would be made to persuade the City to pay the company's debts and acquire the building with assistance from the Ministry and Metro. A meeting was scheduled for 30 May to discuss how that could be accomplished and how the building might best be operated.

As representatives of the Toronto Arts Council attempted to persuade the City of the importance of acquiring the 12 Alexander Street site to provide badly needed performing space for the many alternative theatres operating in Toronto, the TWP board suddenly received offers from two individuals interested in purchasing the building as a commercial theatre. The first of these offers, from Ozona Realty, stipulated that the purchaser would 'if possible after Closing ... co-operate on a reasonable efforts basis to make the Building available to non-profit companies if this is in accordance with its operations of the Building.'[9] The second, from William Scoular of Prominent Features Inc., was a letter of intent only, in which the writer declared his intention 'to make the theatre available for rental or lease to the Toronto Theatre Community and to have the facility in use for the production of live professional theatre.'[10]

When these windfall bids were discussed at a hastily called meeting on 23 May, members of the board were in favour of accepting the offer from Ozona. However, the two trustees present, Simon Waegemaekers and Anna Stratton (replacing Patrick Shepherd), pointed out that the offer's commitment to providing space for the non-profit theatre companies in the city was so loosely worded as to be totally ineffective, and argued that it would be preferable to wait to consider what the City might offer. Norman Endicott replied somewhat caustically that the sum mentioned at the 10 May meeting had been only $250,000, and that a further sum of $30,000 from Metro, promised for running expenses, had not been forthcoming. He insisted that no commitment had been made at that meeting and that accordingly TWP should be free to accept the best offer to come along. When the vote was taken, the board members approved the sale of the building, but they were opposed by Waegemaekers and Stratton.

Since the trust agreement specified that the building could not be sold without the unanimous consent of the trustees, the meeting adjourned in a stalemate.[11]

In the following months, the board attempted unsuccessfully to have the trust agreement set aside, and when this strategy failed, they capitalized on the rival interest of the two developers to initiate a bidding war, which resulted in the offer to purchase being raised by Scoular to $650,000. By this time, feelings were running high on all sides. The trustees and representatives of the theatre community felt very strongly that because of its history and because it had been virtually given to the company by two levels of government, the theatre should be considered a public trust to be operated for the benefit of the community at large. The theatre board had no such notion. Judging from their behaviour and pronouncements, it appeared to outsiders that the directors considered the theatre their property to dispose of as they wished. Not only did they refuse to acknowledge any moral obligation to the City or the Ministry, but they insisted that $650,000 represented the fair market-value of the building.

Thwarted by the court ruling disallowing them to vary the trust agreement, Endicott wrote to the trustees demanding that they consent to the sale of the building to William Scoular or face a lawsuit for breach of fiduciary trust. Finally, in an atmosphere of considerable rancour, the board and trustees gathered to consider the competing offers – $500,000 from the City and $650,000 from William Scoular. After some discussion, during which it was pointed out that TWP could sign back the City's offer at a higher figure, the board members voted to accept the Scoular bid but were again opposed by the trustees.

Speaking to Ray Conlogue the next day, Norman Endicott maintained the board's right to 'accept the best offer for the property to which it holds the title.' The City's offer, he declared, 'wasn't sufficiently high to pay the debts – and the Board would be compelled to declare bankruptcy.' He stated in the same interview that the Scoular offer would leave a surplus of about $100,000 and that the board had felt a duty to 'get money to put on more plays if we could.'[12] While it was true that the actual liabilities of the theatre were difficult to determine because of a number of outstanding lawsuits, it appeared to many outsiders that the board had ceased to regard itself as a guardian of the tradition and spirit of Toronto Workshop Productions and had started to act like any other commercial producer.

In the impasse caused by the disagreement between the board and the trustees, Endicott decided to appeal directly to the mayor. He set out the history of the board's negotiations and a breakdown of the financial situation, arguing that TWP would be unable to settle with Luscombe unless it received more than $500,000 for the building. He even suggested that members of the board would be more than happy to resign in favour of directors appointed by the City if the City wished to assume responsibility for the theatre. The mayor promised to try to find additional funds. A few weeks later, the City and Metro together made an offer of $655,000, which, under pressure from the trustees, the board finally accepted.

In the end, the sale of the building was something of an anticlimax. Perhaps the process had gone on too long. Efforts to cure the invalid during its protracted final illness had often been unseemly, marred first by disagreements about the remedy and then by quarrels over the will. Even now, those who mourned the death of TWP did so with mixed feelings. Like an old soldier, the theatre had survived forgotten battles only to be rewarded by neglect and derision. Now it was the turn of a younger generation to take up the challenges of the future, inspired but unfettered by the past.

25

Curtain-Call

With the collapse of TWP and the sale of the Alexander Street theatre, George Luscombe contemplated the wreckage of nearly thirty years of struggle and effort. He made a reasonable financial settlement with the board over his dismissal and took up a teaching position in the drama department at the University of Guelph, but his active life in the theatre effectively came to an end. From the beginning, he had committed himself wholeheartedly to a particular vision. Now, without company or working space, he felt that further pursuit of that vision was impossible. After a lifetime in the most ephemeral of the arts, Luscombe might well have wondered what he had left behind.

The question is not easy to answer. When Luscombe returned to Toronto in 1956, it was to a city still Edwardian in many of its tastes. Theatres catered to, and were supported by, the university-educated middle class, and their repertoire reflected the interests and prejudices of that audience. Canadian directors drew their inspiration from English rather than European sources and thought of Toronto as a distant satellite of London's West End. Luscombe hoped to challenge those attitudes, and from his basement theatre at 47 Fraser Avenue he launched the most thoroughgoing theatrical revolution ever conducted in the city.

During the first decade – 1959 to 1969 – Luscombe began by attacking the two cornerstones of current theatrical practice – text-based performance and proscenium staging. To start with, he experimented with ways of developing plays from actors' improvisations. Drawing on his own working-class background and passionate commitment to socialism, he stimulated his actors to take a more radical perspective on social questions. At the same time, he introduced a movement-based method of training in an effort to promote an acting style distinct from the drawing-room realism then prevailing on Toronto stages. The result was a series of revolutionary productions which demonstrated that drama could provide a forum for vigorous political debate.

During this decade, he also broke out of the traditional proscenium arch. Starting with *Hey Rube!*, he attempted to bring the audience into closer proximity to the actors in an effort to shatter the social barriers implicit in proscenium theatres. Both at 47 Fraser Avenue and, later, at 12 Alexander Street, he pushed the performers forward onto an open stage, where they would be more intimately involved with the spectators. By 1969, with radically inventive productions such as *Chicago '70* and *Mr Bones*, Luscombe had established TWP as the most innovative and successful theatre company in the city.

That position of pre-eminence was to be challenged during the next ten years – 1969 to 1979 – as a steadily growing number of younger directors with similar radical ideas established their own theatre companies in Toronto. In many respects, these new small theatres had much in common with TWP. Most saw themselves as opposed to the values of the dominant class and dedicated to the subversion or transformation of society. They all drew their inspiration from a common source, the rich vein of theatrical ideas originating in revolutionary Russia and Germany in the early part of the century. But they mined those ideas in very different ways. Luscombe felt he was part of a continuous tradition stretching back through Joan Littlewood to Brecht, Vakhtangov, Meyerhold, and ultimately Stanislavski. It was a tradition rooted in Marxist ideology and dedicated to revolutionary social change. His younger contemporaries, by contrast, identified more closely with theorists such as Antonin Artaud or directors such as Jerzy Grotowski, Peter Brook, or Richard Schechner. These men tended to adapt or modify the ideas they inherited and to place more emphasis on the individual than on society. Their productions sought to involve and transform the spectator as a necessary precondition of any social revolution.

During the second decade of its existence, therefore, TWP faced several challenges. Foremost among these was the need to mount a program that could compete with the new Canadian plays being discovered and presented by the other alternative theatres. Pressured to mount a regular season in their new quarters, Luscombe and his actors could not devote as much time as in the past to the creation of new works and were forced to fall back on the established repertoire. Instead of programming contemporary plays from Britain's exciting Royal Court Theatre or the vital off-off-Broadway scene in New York, however, Luscombe turned to the lesser-known plays of continental Europe such as *The Captain of Köpenick*, Günter Grass's *Flood*, and *The Good Soldier Schweik*. This comparatively exotic repertoire proved less alluring to young Toronto audiences than the unashamedly nationalistic plays of TWP's rivals.

When TWP did create original plays such as *Ten Lost Years* or *Summer '76*, their methods differed from those of other companies who employed a process that came to be known as 'collective creation.' Productions such as Paul Thompson's *The Farm Show* or *1837: The Farmers' Revolt* sought to engage the spectators emotionally in the personal lives of the characters portrayed. Luscombe favoured a more extravagantly theatrical approach. Instead of 'mythologizing' individuals, Luscombe's actors looked for the general significance of historical events and then tried to communicate that significance in arresting theatrical images. 'Our job,' Luscombe told his actors, is 'to draw the raw material of the theatre from the community, interpreting it in our own way and giving it back to the community, not as real life but like an image in a purposely distorted mirror.' To that end, he focused on the social rather than the personal, emphasized general laws rather than individual psychology, and tried to prevent the spectators from becoming emotionally involved in the dramatic situation to the point where they could no longer see it dispassionately. In many cases, these techniques proved puzzling or distracting to audiences, who seemed to prefer more conventional stage realism.

Another challenge was that whereas Luscombe in the 1960s had been virtually alone in his pioneer work, he now found himself jostling for room in an increasingly crowded theatrical environment. Luscombe felt somewhat uncomfortable between the old and the new, not altogether easy with either. While TWP could certainly not be called an establishment theatre, neither was it part of the brash new wave. It continued to maintain a high profile with successful productions such as *Ten Lost Years* and *Les Canadiens*, but as the decade drew to a close there was a growing sense that the company was beginning to show its age.

This perception intensified during the theatre's third decade, from 1979 to 1989. Those were years of growing financial and administrative problems which drained more and more of Luscombe's energy away from the creative side of the theatre. The period was also one of increasingly ostentatious entertainment, which was to culminate at the end of the 1980s in a passion for extravagantly renovated theatres and lavish megamusicals. In this new era of conspicuous consumption, the ideology of TWP seemed increasingly out of date. And unlike some of his competitors, Luscombe seemed unwilling or unable to compromise his ideals.

Instead of moving with the times and adapting its message to new circumstances, TWP seemed to adopt a siege mentality and to confront its opponents with a stony inflexibility. The result was a gradual decline of quality
and influence as theatrical tastes in the city moved on to other political
issues – such as race and gender – or to more glitzy promotion and pack-
aging. By the time the theatre finally closed in 1989, it seemed to have lost
almost all its original relevance.

The problem with attempting to sum up the importance of TWP is that
what started as a clear and distinct movement became inextricably entan-
gled with subsequent developments in the city. The question of identify-
ing 'influences' in such a public art as theatre is notoriously difficult since
theatrical ideas are literally 'in the air,' where actors, designers, playwrights, and directors inhale them as they breathe. Such ideas are not
confined to a single country but flow freely across international borders
with the movement of news, pictures, and theatre practitioners. The
period of TWP's existence – 1959 to 1989 – was one of almost indiscriminate experimentation, with directors and writers borrowing magpie-like
from whatever bright sources attracted their notice. Attempting to analyse
this confusing ferment of ideas and practices is rather like trying to
describe the effect of a single colour on the design of an Easter egg
dipped into a mixture of pigments floating on water.

The paradox at the heart of the TWP story is that while Luscombe was
admired as a director, revered as a teacher, and listened to as a kind of
fire-eyed prophet, he was not imitated. His productions were praised, but
he was not asked to direct at other theatres. Luscombe's mode of combining text, movement, music, and lighting – closer in some ways to opera or
musical theatre than to drama – was at odds with the styles being developed by the new theatres. And unlike those new theatres, which were
actively promoting the publication of new plays, Luscombe continued to
keep his works out of the public realm. Because of this, and because the
performances themselves were not passed on to other directors and performers (as ballets are transmitted from company to company), the
pieces disappeared and the performance tradition was lost.

At one level, then, the TWP legacy is minimal, consisting of a few published plays, a collection of yellowing newspaper reviews, and the fast-fad-
ing memories of the original spectators. At a deeper level, however,
Luscombe's contribution has been immense. Not only did his achievements at 47 Fraser Avenue in the 1960s break trail for all those who came
after, but his burning idealism and indomitable determination have been
a source of inspiration for a whole generation of actors and artistic direc-

tors. Luscombe was one of the first and most articulate defenders of the need for an indigenous drama, and works such as *Hey Rube!*, *Before Compiègne*, and *Mr Bones* (to name only the most successful Canadian works produced by TWP in the 1960s) provided concrete evidence of the viability of such drama. In more direct ways, his teaching has influenced numerous actors, writers, and directors who continue to work in theatre in Canada and abroad.

In the autumn of 1989, however, it was the physical legacy of Toronto Workshop Productions – the strategically located theatre on Alexander Street – that most concerned individuals 'in the business.' The building represented a much-needed new venue for Toronto's many homeless theatre companies, and there was concern in the theatre community that it be retained for use by the non-profit sector. To assist it in running its new acquisition, City Hall decided to look for an independent, non-profit operator. It approached the Toronto Arts Council and the Toronto Theatre Alliance, who recommended the establishment of a selection committee made up of a cross-section of politicians, arts administrators, and artists. City administrators welcomed the suggestion, but until a manager could be found, they faced a difficult decision. Should they invest the money necessary to bring the theatre up to acceptable building code standards so that it could be rented to performing groups in the interim? Or should they limit an already substantial investment and authorize only those repairs essential to prevent further deterioration of the premises? Several employees of the City's Real Estate Department visited the theatre to assess the situation.

They found the building little more than a derelict shell. Plaster was loose in several areas, and large patches of the office ceiling had collapsed. Floor coverings had been ruined by water from a leaky roof – carpets were sodden, tiles detached and heaving – and everywhere was a smell of damp and encroaching mould. Old costumes hung in no apparent order in the basement; theatrical equipment and discarded pieces of scenery cluttered the stage; filing cabinets filled with administrative documents, photographs, and promotional material sat abandoned in the office; mail had been pushed through the front door and lay scattered and uncollected. On the north wall of the lobby, mounted behind a curved arch which looked like a proscenium but was actually the entrance to the auditorium, was a huge photographic collage of early TWP productions. In almost life-sized reproduction, fantastically arrayed clowns, musicians, and entertainers gazed out at departed audiences. Their faces seemed a curious mixture of love and contempt; their eyes were intense, their bodies frozen in gestures of mute supplication or command, their mouths grotesquely shaped in unheard speech or song. In the dim light, they looked like spirits waiting for some spell to release them into the lobby and the darkening city beyond.

The City inspectors concluded that major renovations would be impractical, and they decided to do the minimum to protect the City's investment from weather and vandals. Over the course of several days, City workmen repaired the worst of the damage to the exterior, fixed the roof, sealed cracks in the walls, and secured the building against trespassers and vagrants. One of their last acts was to board up the huge plate-glass windows facing onto Alexander Street, thereby plunging the lobby into darkness. That done, they gathered up their tools, locked the front door, and departed, leaving the theatre to its ghosts.

Epilogue

Those ghosts were to remain undisturbed for almost four years. During the months following the sale of 12 Alexander Street, the selection committee solicited proposals from individuals and organizations interested in restoring and running the theatre. Responses trickled in during the winter, and in the late summer of 1990 the committee sat down to consider the options. It finally narrowed its choice to two radically different candidates. The first was a consortium of thirteen alternative Toronto theatres calling itself The Edge and including, among others, Buddies in Bad Times and Native Earth Performing Arts. The second was a producers group called simply the Alexander Street Theatre Project and made up of the theatre manager Catherine McKeehan, the technical director Fred Mendelson, the designer Bill Fleming, the impresario Mark Hammond, and the former head of the Ontario Arts Council Christopher Wootten.

Several members of the committee thought the first group's submission was by far the more adventurous. If the purpose of the search committee was to find an organization able to carry on the ground-breaking tradition of George Luscombe, then a group calling itself The Edge – to indicate its position on the artistic spectrum – seemed the logical choice. Other members argued that some of the groups associated with The Edge were too controversial, certain elements of the Toronto public having already demonstrated their hostility to the gay orientation of Buddies in Bad Times. The nomination of The Edge, they maintained, might be seen as unnecessarily provocative and be difficult to sell to City Council.

Not surprisingly, the selection committee was split almost evenly between those who favoured turning the theatre over to the group of young artistic directors and those who felt it should be entrusted to the more experienced administrators. In the end, they voted by a narrow margin to support the less risky choice, and on 1 October 1990 they recommended that the Alexander Street Theatre Project be named as the operating agent. The City not only accepted the recommendation but set aside a sum of just over $1 million for the new operators, with the hope that their contribution would be matched by an equal sum from the provincial and federal governments.

Funding from the province, however, was not approved until December 1991, by which time four of the five members of the Alexander Street Theatre Project had left Toronto. The selection committee then notified Christopher Wootten that his organization would have to reconstitute itself or lose its funding. Accordingly, a new group was formed, consisting of Christopher Wootten and Fred Mendelson of the original project, Sky Gilbert and Tim Jones from Buddies in Bad Times, and three representatives of the Toronto theatre community, Anne Marie MacDonald, Jane Marsland, and Paul Thompson. This group submitted a new proposal, which was approved by the selection committee in November 1992, and which incorporated most of the objectives of the original submission by The Edge. It called for the Alexander Street Theatre Project to supervise the renovation of the building, after which Buddies in Bad Times would assume complete responsibility for the running of the theatre. This proposal was approved by City Council in February 1993.

Plans calling for the complete transformation of the former TWP premises were drawn up by the Alexander Street Theatre Project and the architect Martin Liefhebber, and construction began early in 1994. The existing stage and seating were removed, the interior gutted, and a large area beneath the auditorium excavated to make room for dressing-rooms, offices, and washrooms. The space on the main level was divided to make room for two performing areas – a cabaret-style space at the front and a larger studio theatre for regular productions behind it. The entrance was relocated from the front of the building to provide access from the side through the adjoining city parkette. In October 1994, the first audience passed through that entrance. A new chapter had begun.

Chronology

1959–60

Tony Ferry founds Theatre Centre and organizes a summer school with the help of George Luscombe, Powys Thomas, and Carlo Mazzone. In September, several students persuade Luscombe to start evening classes in acting at 47 Fraser Avenue. The group, now called Workshop Productions, stages a double bill of García Lorca's *The Love of Don Perlimplin and Belisa in the Garden* and Chekhov's *The Boor* from 14 to 19 December. The new company enlarges its basement theatre to seat sixty and produces a second evening of one-act plays consisting of Chekhov's *The Marriage Proposal* and Len Peterson's *Burlap Bags*, from 6 to 21 May.

1960–1

During the summer, Luscombe conducts classes at 47 Fraser Avenue, and he and Ferry organize a two-week training session in Haliburton, Ontario. Back in Toronto the group receives notification that it must vacate the Fraser Avenue premises by 20 November. They begin improvisations on circus themes, which culminate in the production of *Hey Rube!* (6 February to 17 March). Ferry leaves the company. In June, Workshop Productions merges with the Arts Theatre Club, and Luscombe becomes artistic director.

1961–2

At a second two-week summer session in Haliburton, Luscombe and Jack Winter start work on an adaptation of Aristophanes' *Lysistrata*. Work continues on the production through the autumn, and it is finally presented under the title *And They'll Make Peace* (28 December to 3 February). The amalgamation with the Arts Theatre Club dissolves. Winter and Luscombe submit plans for a drama program to York University.

1962–3

Luscombe and a group of his actors form Theatre 35 to tour Haliburton during the summer with productions of Chekhov's *The Boor* and *The Marriage Proposal* and an adaptation of a Pirandello play by Winter called *The Evil Eye*. Toronto Workshop Productions is incorporated under letters patent on 10 August. The three one-act plays are presented at 47 Fraser Avenue from 13 September to 6 October. Luscombe receives a personal award of $4,000 from the Canada Council. Ibsen's *When We Dead Awaken* opens on 8 November for three weeks. *Woyzeck* opens on 29 March and runs until 30 May. Luscombe and Winter submit designs for the Burton Auditorium to York University. Luscombe conducts a workshop in Atikokan, Ontario.

1963–4

In September, the company receives a $3,600 grant from the Canada Council, and Luscombe launches his first professional company. Their first production is Winter's *Before Compiègne* (13 December to 12 January). The company receives its first grant from the Ontario Arts Council. The City of Toronto Committee on Parks and Recreation turns down a request by the company to perform in the parks during the summer. *Before Compiègne* opens at the Colonnade Theatre (3 to 30 April).

1964–5

The company performs *Before Compiègne* and *The Mechanic* at the University of Waterloo and in Stratford (27 July to 3 August). In mid-August, they receive $10,000 from the Canada Council, and Luscombe puts his company on year-long contracts. They receive their first grant from Metro Toronto. The group rehearse John Herbert's adaptation of *Woyzeck* but decide to abandon it for their own version of the play, which they present as *The Death of Woyzeck* (9 January to 11 April).

1965–6

The first Theatre-in-the-Park season at Stratford runs from 27 July to 8 August with outdoor performances of *Before Compiègne* and *The Mechanic*. On 14 October, the company opens its Toronto season with *The Mechanic*, which runs until 28 February. CBC radio broadcasts a performance of *Before Compiègne* on 1 December. Negotiations for a New York run of *The Mechanic* begun in the summer finally fall through. Most of the members of the company leave to find work elsewhere.

1966–7

At its second Stratford season, the company presents *Hey Rube!*, *Before*

Compiègne, The Mechanic, and *The New Show* (15 July to 14 August). In August, they give two performances in Nathan Phillips Square. The Canada Council informs the company that future support will depend on their reaching a wider audience, and they begin to search for larger premises. They enter into negotiations with East York to become the resident company at a proposed Todmorden theatre. They mount a revival of *Hey Rube!* (22 November to 22 January) at 47 Fraser Avenue. In March, the company tours to Queen's University and the University of Western Ontario. *The Golem of Venice* opens on 17 March and runs to 23 April. The company plays at Expo 67 for a week (28 April to 4 May), after which Brooky Robins and Jack Winter leave the company. Luscombe hires June Faulkner as business manager.

1967–8

The company's six-week Stratford season (1 July to 13 August) includes *Hey Rube!, The Mechanic,* and Luscombe's adaptation of Zuckmayer's *The Captain of Köpenick.* In August, Luscombe announces plans to move to larger premises downtown. Tony Ferry rejoins the company. *The Captain of Köpenick* opens on 8 November for a six-week run, to 23 December. On New Year's Eve, the company presents a preview of *Gentlemen Be Seated* in its new theatre at 12 Alexander Street. The official opening is delayed until 10 January, after which the show runs until 11 February. The company begins a regular repertory season with productions of Ben Jonson's *The Alchemist* (15 February to 3 March), Ewan MacColl's *The Travellers* (1 to 11 May), and Norman Kline's *Faces* (28 May to 27 July).

1968–9

In August, the company appears at the International Theatre Festival at Brandeis University in Boston. Their fall season begins with Günter Grass's *Flood* (5 November to 7 December) and continues with Mario Fratti's *Che Guevara* (17 December to 18 January), Michael John Nimchuk's adaptation of Jaroslav Hašek's *The Good Soldier Schweik* (25 February to 12 April), and the collectively created *Mr Bones* (22 April to 9 June). The theatre then closes for the summer.

1969–70

Luscombe directs *Faces* in New York, which plays one performance, on 16 September. The company presents *Che* and *Mr Bones* at the Venice Biennale (25 to 28 September). After a tour to the University of Western Ontario and Brock University, the company opens Shakespeare's *The Tempest* (25 November to 14 December). It is followed by Carol Bolt's *Daganawida* (13 to 31 January) and by *Chicago '70* (10 March to 9 May).

The company then takes *Chicago '70* to New York (15 May to 14 June), after which the play returns to Toronto, to the St Lawrence Centre for the Arts for a week beginning 22 June.

1970–1
Following appearances at the International Festival of Theatre Arts in Wolfville, Nova Scotia, the company returns to Toronto. Their season includes Nancy Jowsey's *The Piper* (24 November to 13 December), Brendan Behan's *The Hostage*, directed by Geoffrey Read (19 January to 2 February), Ann Jellicoe's *Shelley, the Idealist* (9 March to 4 April), and Dürrenmatt's *The Visit of an Old Lady* (20 April to 9 May).

1971-2
During the summer, John Faulkner dies in a drowning accident in the Caribbean. The season opens with Brecht's *Arturo Ui* (9 November to 4 December). Jack Winter returns to help with a collaborative adaptation of Dickens's *Pickwick Papers*. The production opens as *Mr Pickwick* on 23 December and runs until 23 January. It is followed by Rick Salutin's *Fanshen* (15 February to 5 March) and a revival of *Mr Bones* (30 March to 23 April). In April, the company signs a new five-year lease for their theatre at double the rent. The final production of the season is Len Peterson's *The Workingman* (25 May to 25 June). The theatre closes for eight weeks during the summer.

1972-3
An almost entirely new acting company opens TWP's season with a revival of *Hey Rube!* (7 December to 14 January). Gogol's *The Inspector General* runs from 25 January to 18 February and is followed by Arthur Kopit's *Indians*, directed by Barry Wasman (15 to 31 March), and a collaborative adaptation of Mark Twain's *Letters from the Earth* by Winter and the company (3 to 19 May). The final show of the season is a revival of *The Good Soldier Schweik* (12 to 30 June).

1973-4
After performances of *Hey Rube!* in Wolfville, Nova Scotia (8 to 15 July), Luscombe conducts workshops in Prince Edward Island. Back in Toronto, he creates two companies that will perform simultaneously in Toronto and Ottawa. The first presents an adaptation of Shakespeare's *Richard III* by Steven Bush and Rick McKenna called *Richard Thirdtime* (23 October to 10 November) at 12 Alexander Street and then performs

Letters from the Earth at the National Arts Centre in Ottawa (13 November to 2 December). Meanwhile, the second, a young company under Peter Faulkner, stages Jean Anouilh's *Thieves' Carnival* (22 November to 9 December) in Toronto. The production is designed by Astrid Janson, who replaces Nancy Jowsey as the company's designer. After a performance of *Letters from the Earth* at Queen's University, the first company returns to Alexander Street, where it remounts *Richard Thirdtime* (18 December to 12 January). Rehearsals for Milton Acorn's *Road to Charlotte-town* are abandoned, and the company begins work on an adaptation of *Ten Lost Years* by Barry Broadfoot. The new collaborative production opens on 5 February and runs until 28 May.

1974–5

On 16 September, the western Canadian tour of *Ten Lost Years* gets under way with a performance in Hamilton, Ontario. The tour, which takes the company to Vancouver and back, lasts until 30 November. The Toronto season opens with *From the Boyne to Batoche* by Steven Bush and Rick McKenna, directed by Steven Bush (17 September to 6 October). On 5 November, fire destroys much of the interior of the theatre at 12 Alexander Street. Many of the theatres in Toronto contribute to a rebuilding fund. In mid-December, the touring company returns and performs *Ten Lost Years* at the Bayview Playhouse (12 December to 4 January). The regular company mounts a revival of *Mr Pickwick* at the Town Hall, St Lawrence Centre (17 to 28 December). On the last day of the year, 12 Alexander Street reopens with a production of Winter's *You Can't Get Here from There* (31 December to 25 January). The CBC presents a television version of *Ten Lost Years* (2 February). To conclude the season the company mounts a revival of *The Captain of Köpenick* (25 February to 22 March) and a work written by Winter and the company entitled *Summer '76* (22 April to 17 May). In June, Faulkner and Luscombe go to England to make arrangements for a European tour.

1975–6

In the summer, the company gives performances of *Ten Lost Years* at the St Lawrence Centre (21 August to 6 September) prior to embarking on an eastern Canadian tour, which takes it to thirty-nine cities and lasts until 18 November. In October, the theatre plays host to an Open Circle Theatre production of Rod Langley's *Grey Owl*, directed by Ray Whelan (30 October to 15 November). It is followed by Len Peterson's *Women in the Attic*, directed by Frank Norris (20 November to 6 December). A seasonal

production of Dickens's *A Christmas Carol* adapted and directed by
François Klanfer plays from 26 December to 4 January. The final produc-
tion of the season is a revival of *The Golem of Venice* (10 to 21 February).
During the spring, the group undertakes a European tour of *Ten Lost
Years* and *Summer '76* (3 May to 3 July), during which Winter leaves the
company.

1976–7

On its return to Toronto, TWP gives several performances of *Summer '76*
at the St Lawrence Centre (2 to 7 August). Luscombe applies to the Canada Council for support for a 'sabbatical' year to train a new company.
On 21 December, the theatre receives notification that it must vacate the
premises by 29 June. Faulkner and Luscombe organize political and press
opposition to the plan to develop the Alexander Street site. Without productions of its own, TWP rents its facilities to a number of outside companies. Visiting attractions include Centaur Theatre of Montreal's
production of David Fennario's *On the Job* (20 September to 2 October),
the five-week Toronto Dance Festival beginning on 16 November, a
remounting of Tarragon Theatre's production of Michel Tremblay's
Hosanna (13 January to 20 February), a revival of David Freeman's *Creeps*
(6 March to 2 April), and two Theatre Compact bills, *Easter*, by August
Strindberg (11 to 30 April), and *Orators*, a triple bill of *Hands* by Yuli
Daniel, *Swan Song* by Chekhov, and *Rounders* by Michael Brodribb (9 to 20
May). In June, a compromise worked out between the developer and the
City of Toronto Planning Department ensures the survival of the theatre.
George Luscombe wins the Toronto Drama Bench Award for Distin-
guished Contribution to Canadian Theatre.

1977–8

The 'Champagne Season' opens with Rick Salutin's *Les Canadiens* (20
October to 19 November). It is followed by a studio production of Sharon
Pollock's *The Komagata Maru Incident*, directed by Alex Dmitriev, at Fac-
tory Lab (22 to 30 October) and Eve Merriam's *The Club*, directed by Pam
Brighton, at the Alexander Street theatre (1 December to 14 February).
The company sponsors the visit of the Centaur Theatre production of
David Fennario's *Nothing to Lose* at Toronto Free Theatre from 17 January
to 5 February. Calvin Butler directs a production of Athol Fugard's *The
Island* at 12 Alexander Street (28 February to 18 March). Two Lindsay
Kemp productions, *Flowers* (28 March to 15 April) and *Salome* (19 April to
7 May), prove so successful that the company extends the run of *Flowers*

(12 May to 10 June). A studio production of Rick Davidson's *Westmount Blues*, directed by Milo Ringham, is staged at Toronto Free Theatre (25 April to 7 May).

1978–9

On 2 December, Luscombe receives an honorary degree from York University. Shortly thereafter, he opens his first production in more than a year – *Esmeralda*, an adaptation by Andrew Piotrowski of Victor Hugo's *The Hunchback of Notre Dame*, which runs from 14 December to 6 January. It is followed by Brecht's *St Joan of the Stockyards*, directed by Pam Brighton (14 February to 3 March). In April, Tarragon Theatre rents space at Alexander Street to remount its successful production of David French's *Jitters* (28 April to 2 June). Luscombe begins work on *The Mac Paps*.

1979–80

In September, the theatre is rented out to Ann Mortifee for her production of *Journey to Kairos* (19 to 30 September), following which TWP, in a co-production with Co-opera, presents Raymond and Beverly Pannell's *Refugees*, directed by Luscombe (18 October to 3 November). A second rental production, Théâtre sans Fil's *Tales from the Smokehouse*, fills the theatre from 13 to 17 November, after which TWP stages Michael Hastings's *Carnival War a Go Hot*, directed by Pam Brighton (1 to 29 December). June Faulkner leaves the company to join the Shaw Festival. Eric Donkin's one-man show *Sarah Binks* plays from 15 to 19 January, after which Luscombe's production of *The Mac Paps*, with a script by Luscombe and Larry Cox from Mac Reynolds's interviews, runs from 31 January to 15 March. The Video Cabaret production of Michael Hollingsworth's adaptation of George Orwell's *1984* plays from 27 March to 26 April. The final production of the season is *Ain't Lookin'*, Luscombe's adaptation of John Craig's novel *Chappie and Me*, which runs from 1 May to 19 July.

1980–1

During the summer, the owners of the theatre inform TWP that they will have to vacate 12 Alexander Street. On 12 August, about a hundred supporters meet at the theatre and pledge to work for the survival of the company. A delegation of prominent theatre supporters appears before the Executive Committee of City Council. In October, Council approves the construction of a fifteen-storey apartment building in exchange for the transfer of land to TWP. The theatre agrees to pay $100,000 in rent arrears and renovations.

The new rent is set at $1,800 a month. In September, TWP brings in the Centaur Theatre production of Athol Fugard's *Lesson from Aloes* (4 September to 4 October) and follows it up with a revival of *Ain't Lookin'* (7 October to 1 November). Susan Cox's one-woman show *Valentine Browne* (12 November to 13 December) closes early, forcing TWP to stage the hastily mounted *Holiday Show* for eleven performances in December. A production of Luscombe's adaptation of Walter Hasenclever's *Christopher Columbus* (8 January to 4 February) draws poorly, as does a visiting production of Eduardo Manet's *Madame Strass* (5 February to 7 March). The Ontario Arts Council requests that the theatre prepare a debt reduction plan approved by a properly constituted board of directors. On 9 March, *Mac Paps* and *Ain't Lookin'* win Chalmers Awards, and on 16 March Luscombe wins the City of Toronto Award of Merit. In April, the company revives *Ten Lost Years* (2 April to 12 June) as its contribution to the Toronto Theatre Festival (11 to 31 May).

1981–2

On 19 August, the company establishes a new board of directors with Karl Jaffary as chairman. They draw up deficit reduction and fund-raising plans. The season opens with Walter Bruno's *Shouting for Joy*, directed by Luscombe (15 October to 1 November), and it is followed by a revival of *Mr Pickwick* (26 November to 3 January). A production of *Joey* by Rick Salutin and actors of the Rising Tide Theatre plays in the theatre from 11 to 31 January. TWP's third production is Brendan Behan's *Richard's Cork Leg* (25 February to 21 March). The theatre establishes a series of late-night shows to increase its revenue. During the spring, three outside productions rent the theatre – Theatre Passe Muraille's *Crackwalker* by Judith Thompson (1 to 25 April), Jeremy Brett's production of *The Tempest* (12 May to 6 June), and Tom Kneebone's one-man show (8 to 20 June). The final production of the season is Betty-Jean Wylie's *A Place on Earth*, directed by Luscombe (29 June to 11 July).

1982–3

Ken Gass directs the opening show of the new season, *How I Got That Story* by Amlin Gray (14 October to 21 November). A one-man show by Eric Donkin, Charles Dennis's *Altman's Last Stand*, produced and directed by John Banks, runs from 14 December to 2 January, after which Luscombe's production of Ron Weihs's *The Wobbly* (20 January to 13 February) holds the stage. The board of directors appoints Marguerite Knisely as administrative manager. Factory Theatre Lab rents the theatre to stage George F.

Walker's *The Art of War* (23 February to 20 March). In the spring, Luscombe stages *Female Parts* by Dario Fo and Franca Rame (8 April to 15 May). On 27 May, Jaffary steps down as chairman of the board and is replaced by Jerry White.

1983–4

After several delays, Larry Cox's *Names* opens on 20 October and plays until 6 November. It is followed by a revival of *The Wobbly* (15 November to 3 December) and the clown show *Nion* with Ian Wallace (6 to 18 December). Robert Rooney directs David Edgar's *The Jail Diary of Albie Sachs* (29 December to 5 February). Luscombe and Ross Skene produce *The Medicine Show* (14 February to 11 March), during which Knisely resigns. Catherine McKeehan becomes the new general manager. In March, a musical about a South American songwriter, *Victor Jara Alive*, is staged by Ken Gass (20 March to 15 April). It is followed by a revival of *Ain't Lookin'* (24 April to 27 May). In June, the company takes this production to the International Theatre Festival in Quebec City. On 15 August, the company finally secures the deed for the theatre and the land on which it stands with the help of an interest-free loan of $100,000 from the Ministry of Citizenship and Culture.

1984–5

During the summer, Ntozake Shange's *For Coloured Girls*, directed by Charles Gray, runs from 4 July to 30 September. The TWP season opens with *S: Portrait of a Spy* by Rick Salutin and Ian Adams, directed by Ken Livingston, which runs from 18 October to 11 November. Under pressure from McKeehan, Mona Luscombe resigns as administrator. The Canada Council warns the board that it intends to cut back the theatre's grant. McKeehan announces that she plans to resign in February. Gordon Floyd, Jaffary, and Luscombe are named to a long-range planning committee. A third revival of *Hey Rube!* runs from 29 November to 23 December. Robert Rooney returns to direct Raymond Briggs's *When the Wind Blows* (10 January to 4 February). The Prairie Theatre Exchange production of Wendy Lill's *Fighting Days* plays in the theatre from 14 February to 10 March. McKeehan and Floyd refuse to sign Luscombe's application to the Canada Council. Floyd and Jaffary resign from the board. TWP co-produces Gabriel Emanuel's *Einstein* with Theatre Nepesh (21 March to 28 April). Marcia Muldoon replaces McKeehan as general manager. Luscombe travels to Russia as a guest of the Soviet government. On his return, he directs Larry Cox's *Last Hero* (17 May to 9 June). Luscombe convenes a new board of directors, which approves the appointment of Rooney as resident director. The theatre's Canada Council grant is reduced from $125,000 to $95,000.

1985–6

The season opens with Rooney's production of Edward Radzinsky's *Theatre in the Time of Nero and Seneca* (24 September to 20 October), which is followed by Alexandre Hausvater's staging of Joshua Sobol's *Ghetto* (7 to 30 November). Luscombe appeals to the Ontario Arts Council for financial assistance, and in early January a meeting between the Council and the theatre is arranged. The Council offers to pay for a management study by Graeme Page and expresses its opposition to any plans for expansion of the theatre. In early February, the TWP board appoints new officers and launches a fund-raising drive. The theatre is rented out for a production of Shakespeare's *Julius Caesar* (6 February to 23 March). The board appoints Rooney as the new artistic director beginning 1 July. The Market Theatre of Johannesburg's production of *Asinimali* plays from 27 May to 1 June, and Jim Clarkson and Gordon Floyd's production of the musical *Nunsense* moves into the Alexander Street theatre on 29 April and runs until 18 October. On 15 May, the Page report recommends the creation of a board of trustees to supervise the finances of the company. In June, the Canada Council rejects TWP's grant application.

1986–7

On 13 August, a board of trustees is established and a trust agreement signed. A revised application to the Canada Council secures a $25,000 project grant. The Shaw Festival production of *Breaking the Silence* runs at the theatre from 25 October to 30 November. It is followed by the Market Theatre of Johannesburg's production of *Woza Albert* (4 December to 11 January). A second Shaw Festival production, *B Movie, the Play*, runs from 17 January to 15 March, and after that Robert Rooney's first production as artistic director, Ken Mitchell's *Gone the Burning Sun*, moves into the theatre from 19 April to 26 March and then on to China, where it tours from 23 April to 20 May. The season ends with *Mr Jelly Roll* by Luscombe and Larry Cox (30 April to 24 May). The Charlottetown Festival production of *Pump Boys and Dinettes* runs in the theatre from 9 June to 5 July.

1987–8

At a specially called general meeting on 15 September, Luscombe, his wife, Mona, and Larry Cox are dropped from the board. After a rental production of Buddies in Bad Times' *The Postman Rings Once* (30 September to 25 October), the regular TWP season gets under way with Rooney's production of Ralph Burdman's *Tête à Tête* (10 November to 20 December). The musical *Rap Master Ronnie* opens on 5 January and runs to 14 February. During the run, the board fires Luscombe. Rooney's second production of the season, *Something in the Air*, runs from 23 February to 27 March. A co-production, *Pushing Forty* (5 April to 8 May), and the National Theatre School production of Mark Blitzstein's *The Cradle Will Rock* (10 to 14 May) fill the theatre until mid-May. They are followed by the Market Theatre of Johannesburg's *Bopha* (17 May to 26 June), following which the theatre ceases operations and dismisses the staff.

1988–9

In June, Florence Silver takes over as chairman of the board and enters into negotiations with the developer George Vari in an effort to secure a new theatre for the company. On 21 July, the board announces the appointment of Leon Pownall as artistic director. A group of Luscombe supporters calling themselves the 'Committee of Concern' challenge the authority of the board and on 31 September occupy the theatre. Efforts to sell the theatre to a developer fail, and when the Canada Council rejects the theatre's application in early November, the board appeals to the Ministry of Culture and Communications (formerly Citizenship and Culture). Unable to operate the theatre, the board finally votes to sell it to a developer, but on 24 May the sale is blocked by the board of trustees. Negotiations with the Ontario Arts Council, the Ministry of Culture and Communications, and the Toronto Arts Council finally result in the City's purchasing the building at 12 Alexander Street on 26 September.

Notes

Abbreviations

Globe – *Globe and Mail*
Star – *Toronto Star*
Sun – *Toronto Sun*
Telegram – *Toronto Telegram*
Tribune – *Canadian Tribune*
CCA – Toronto Workshop Productions files in the Canada Council Archives, National Archives of Canada
JWP – Jack Winter Papers, William Ready Division of Archives and Research Collections, McMaster University Library
OACA – Toronto Workshop Productions files in the Ontario Arts Council Archives, Archives of Ontario
TWPA – Toronto Workshop Productions Archives, McLaughlin Library, University of Guelph

PREFACE

1 Don Rubin, 'Sleepy Tunes in Toronto,' *Canadian Theatre Review* 20 (Fall 1978), 93
2 Denis W. Johnston, *Up the Mainstream: The Rise of Toronto's Alternative Theatres* (Toronto: University of Toronto Press, 1991), 22
3 Alan Filewod, *Collective Encounters: Documentary Theatre in English Canada* (Toronto: University of Toronto Press, 1987), 78

PROLOGUE

1 Joan Ferry, 'Experiences of a Pioneer in Canadian Experimental Theatre,' *Theatre History in Canada* 8, no. 1 (Spring 1987), 63

2 Joan Maroney Ferry, interview, 23 Apr. 1988
3 Ferry, 'Experiences,' 64
4 Denis Braithwaite, 'New Theatre Group,' *Star*, 21 Mar. 1959
5 Tony Ferry, 'Stratford: Demoralized, Misadventure, Blunder,' *Star*, 27 June 1959
6 David Peddie, 'Stratford Festival Criticism "Blunder,"' *Star*, 4 July 1959, p. 27

CHAPTER 1

1 Details of Luscombe's early life are drawn from interviews held with him in July 1987 and from the manuscript of an unpublished interview by Don Rubin in Luscombe's possession. All quotations not otherwise attributed are from these sources.
2 True Davidson, *The Golden Years of East York* (Toronto: Centennial College Press, 1976), 81

CHAPTER 2

1 George Luscombe, interview, 23 July 1987
2 Details of the history of Theatre Workshop are from Howard Goorney, *The Theatre Workshop Story* (London: Eyre Methuen, 1981), and Howard Goorney and Ewan MacColl, eds, *Agit-prop to Theatre Workshop: Political Playscripts, 1930–50* (Manchester: University of Manchester Press, 1986).
3 George Luscombe, interview, 23 July 1987
4 Ibid.
5 Ibid.

CHAPTER 3

1 Rudolph Laban, *The Mastery of Movement*, 4th ed. (Estover, Plymouth: Macdonald and Evans, 1980), 87
2 Laban, *Mastery*, 17
3 Tony Ferry, '"Don't Think" Director, Students Test Acting Ways and Means,' *Star*, 18 June 1960
4 Quoted *ABC*, 2 Dec. 1978
5 George Luscombe, interview, 20 Jan. 1988
6 'Open Letter from Your Artistic Director,' Arts Theatre Club Newsletter (May 1961), TWPA
7 George Luscombe, interview, 20 Jan. 1988
8 Tony Moffat-Lynch, interview, 6 Apr. 1988

9 George Luscombe, interview, 21 Jan. 1988

CHAPTER 4

1 Nathan Cohen, 'Theatre in the Universities,' *Star*, 9 Jan. 1960
2 Nathan Cohen, 'Reaching a Play's Core,' *Star*, 17 May 1960
3 Tony Moffat-Lynch, interview, 6 Apr. 1988
4 Nathan Cohen, 'Stereophonic Sound and "Lysistrata,"' *Star*, 29 Dec. 1961
5 Herbert Whittaker, 'Luscombe's Merit Shines in Play,' *Globe*, 29 Dec. 1961
6 Cohen, 'Stereophonic Sound'
7 Jack Winter, 'An Experience of Group Theatre,' *Star*, 27 Jan. 1962
8 George Luscombe, interview, 21 Jan. 1988
9 Letter from George Luscombe to the Canada Council, May 1962, TWPA
10 Douglas Livingston, interview, 25 Apr. 1988
11 Jerry Wasserman, 'Buchner in Canada: *Woyzeck* and the Development of English-Canadian Theatre,' *Theatre History in Canada* 8, no. 2 (Fall 1987), 185
12 George Luscombe, interview, 3 Feb. 1988
13 Letter from George Luscombe to the Canada Council, 19 Apr. 1963, TWPA
14 Nathan Cohen, 'A Remarkable Achievement,' *Star*, 17 Apr. 1963

CHAPTER 5

1 Nikolai Gorchakov, *The Vakhtangov School of Stage Art* (Moscow, n.d.), 118
2 William Kuhlke, 'Vakhtangov and the American Theatre of the 1960's,' in E.T. Kirby, ed., *Total Theatre* (New York, 1969), 157
3 Joan Maroney Ferry, interview, 4 Apr. 1988
4 George Luscombe, interview, 10 Feb. 1988
5 Herbert Whittaker, interview, 2 May 1988
6 Ferry, 'Experiences,' 65
7 Nathan Cohen, 'Total Theatre,' *Star*, 13 Feb. 1961
8 Ibid.
9 Herbert Whittaker, 'Success Is Scored by Workshop Actors,' *Globe*, 13 Feb. 1961
10 Tony Ferry, '"Hey Rube" Paid Peanuts, but Created Big Impact,' *Star*, 18 Mar. 1961
11 Jack Winter, 'Music and "The Mechanic,"' JWP
12 George Luscombe, interview, 20 Jan. 1988
13 Herbert Whittaker, 'A Bouncy Hilarious Happening Happens,' *Globe*, 1 Aug. 1964
14 Ronald Evans, 'Mechanic Brings Back Bounce,' *Telegram*, 15 Oct. 1965

15 Herbert Whittaker, 'Comic Business Is a Monkey Wrench,' *Globe*, 13 Oct. 1965
16 Nathan Cohen, 'Much to Admire in "Mechanic,"' *Star*, 16 Oct. 1965

CHAPTER 6

1 Herbert Whittaker, 'Luscombe's Basement Workshop Takes Off with a Poetic, Bawdy Joan of Arc,' *Globe*, 14 Dec. 1963
2 Ronald Evans, [no title], *Telegram*, 14 Dec. 1963
3 Nathan Cohen, '"Before Compiègne,"' *Star*, 19 Dec. 1963
4 Ibid.
5 Ronald Evans, 'The Theatre,' *Telegram*, 4 Apr. 1964
6 Martin Stone, 'Intimate Theatres Preferable to Obsession with Hugeness,' *Tribune*, 4 Apr. 1964
7 Ralph Hicklin, 'Knockabouts Enliven an Unsaintly Joan,' *Globe*, 4 Apr. 1964
8 Kemp Thompson, *K-W Record*, 21 July 1964
9 Nathan Cohen, 'Into the Depths,' *Star*, 15 Oct. 1964

CHAPTER 7

1 TWP brief to the Canada Council, May 1962, TWPA
2 Minutes of the Canada Council meeting, August 1962, CCA
3 Minutes of the Canada Council meeting, August 1963, CCA
4 June Faulkner, interview, 27 Oct. 1992
5 Cedric Smith, interview, 31 Jan. 1989
6 June Faulkner, interview, 27 June 1988
7 Nathan Cohen, 'A Cause for Hope,' *Star*, 24 Jan. 1963
8 Minutes of the Canada Council meeting, 17 Aug. 1964, CCA
9 Letter from George Luscombe to Larry McCance, Actors' Equity, 25 June 1964, TWPA
10 TWP application to the Canada Council, 29 June 1965, TWPA
11 Letter from Peter Dwyer to Brooky Robins, 1 Sept. 1965, TWPA
12 Letter from the Ontario Arts Council to TWP, 29 Sept. 1965, TWPA

CHAPTER 8

1 George Luscombe, interview, 3 Feb. 1988
2 Letter from Brooky Robins to Peter Dwyer, 10 Mar. 1965, TWPA
3 Ronald Evans, 'The Theatre,' *Telegram*, 13 Jan. 1965
4 Nathan Cohen, 'New Version of "Woyzeck" Artificial, Talky,' *Star*, 13 Jan. 1965
5 Don Bell, 'Woyzeck Far from Original,' *Montreal Gazette*, 13 Jan. 1965

6 Herbert Whittaker, 'Luscombe's Theatre Continues Evolution,' *Globe*, 13 Jan. 1965

7 George Luscombe, quoted in *ABC*, 2 Dec. 1978

8 Frances Walsh, interview, 29 June 1988

9 Edward Sanders, interview, 26 May 1988

10 TWP brief to the Canada Council, April 1967, TWPA

11 Milo Ringham Gold, interview, 17 May 1988

12 Frances Walsh, interview, 29 June 1988

13 Nathan Cohen, '"Popular" and "Commercial" Aren't Always the Same,' *Star*, 25 July 1966

14 Herbert Whittaker, 'Golem of Venice Tries Too Hard,' *Globe*, 3 Apr. 1967

CHAPTER 9

1 Cohen, '"Popular" and "commercial"'

2 TWP press release, 18 July 1965, TWPA

3 Victoria Mitchell, interview, 22 June 1988

4 Len Doncheff, interview, 5 May 1988

5 Letter from Victor Polley to George Luscombe, 12 Dec. 1966, TWPA

6 June Faulkner, interview, 27 June 1988

7 Peter McConnell, interview, 8 July 1988

8 Arthur Zeldin, '"Hey Rube" Was a Triumph in the Big City Hall Square,' *Star*, 22 Aug. 1966

9 Letter from Peter Dwyer to Brooky Robins, 15 Sept. 1966, TWPA

10 George Luscombe, interview, 11 Feb. 1988

11 Letter from June Faulkner to Peter Dwyer, 7 Sept. 1967, TWPA

12 George Luscombe, interview, 11 Feb. 1988

13 Nathan Cohen, 'A Musical Cyrano Set with Christopher Plummer,' *Star*, 31 Mar. 1967

CHAPTER 10

1 Diane Grant and Geoffrey Saville-Read, interview, 20 Jan. 1989

2 Notes to *Gentlemen Be Seated*, JWP

3 Erwin Piscator, *The Political Theatre* (London: Eyre Methuen, 1980 [1929]), 207

4 Peter Faulkner, interview, 18 May 1988

5 Diane Grant and Geoffrey Saville-Read, interview, 20 Jan. 1989

6 Jim McPherson, 'A New Play, a New Author, a New Theatre – a Triumph,' *Telegram*, 11 Jan. 1968

7 Martin Stone, *Tribune*, 11 Jan. 1968

8 Calvin Butler, interview, 8 Aug. 1988
9 Herbert Whittaker, 'Mr. Bones – Smashing Documentary,' *Globe*, 23 Apr. 1969
10 Ralph Hicklin, 'Mr. Bones Outclasses Thaw,' *Telegram*, 23 Apr. 1969
11 Nathan Cohen, 'Mr. Bones a Fine Closer for Toronto Workshop,' *Star*, 23 Apr. 1969
12 Nathan Cohen, 'Toronto Workshop Company Rates Special Attention,' *Star*, 15 May 1969
13 Nathan Cohen, 'Bright Faces Invites a Comparison with Feiffer,' *Star*, 29 May 1968

CHAPTER 11

1 Nathan Cohen, 'A Disappointing Turn,' *Star*, 15 Sept. 1965
2 Letter from Cheryl Crawford to Dr Robert Crawford, 18 Aug. 1966, TWPA
3 June Faulkner, interview, 27 June 1988
4 Nancy Jowsey Lewis, interview, 27 Nov. 1988
5 George Luscombe, interview, 11 Feb. 1988
6 Herbert Whittaker, 'Face to Face with a Funny Play,' *Globe*, 29 May 1968
7 Nathan Cohen, 'Bright Faces Invites a Comparison with Feiffer,' *Star*, 29 May 1968
8 Len Doncheff, interview, 5 May 1988
9 June Faulkner, interview, 27 June 1988
10 Letter from Nathan Cohen, 31 July 1969, TWPA
11 Nathan Cohen, 'What Will Success Do to George Luscombe's Theatre Dream?' *Star*, 13 Sept. 1969
12 Nathan Cohen, 'Kline's Play Faces Flops in New York,' *Star*, 17 Sept. 1969
13 George Luscombe, interview, 18 Feb. 1988

CHAPTER 12

1 Correspondence, TWPA
2 Calvin Butler, interview, 8 Aug. 1988
3 Milo Ringham Gold, interview, 17 May 1988
4 Don Rubin, 'Mr. Fratti's Sure Mr. Luscombe Can Make Che Live,' *Star*, 16 Dec. 1968
5 Faulkner–Fratti correspondence, TWPA
6 Letter from George Luscombe to Mario Fratti, 27 Aug. 1968, TWPA
7 Mario Fratti, '"Che Guevara" in New York,' *New Theatre Magazine* 12, no. 2 (May 1972), 2
8 Calvin Butler, interview, 8 Aug. 1988

9 Nathan Cohen, 'Cedric Smith as Che Appears Here Tonight despite Drug Charge,' *Star*, 14 Jan. 1969
10 George Luscombe, interview, 16 Feb. 1988
11 Jim McPherson, 'Entertainment,' *Telegram*, 19 Dec. 1968
12 Herbert Whittaker, 'Mario Fratti Hero-worships Che Guevara,' *Globe*, 19 Dec. 1968
13 Don Rubin, 'A Lack of Focus, That's the Trouble with the Che Play,' *Star*, 18 Dec. 1968
14 Nathan Cohen, 'Che, the Best Play Locally in a Year,' *Star*, 31 Dec. 1968
15 George Luscombe, interview, 18 Feb. 1988
16 Nathan Cohen, 'In Venice There Is Drama in the Streets,' *Star*, 27 Sept. 1969
17 Calvin Butler, interview, 8 Aug. 1988
18 Report of the Canadian consul general, Mary Lynn Reid, 7 Oct. 1969, TWPA
19 Ibid.

CHAPTER 13

1 David Farber, *Chicago '68* (Chicago: University of Chicago Press, 1988), 232
2 Ibid., 229
3 Ibid., 206
4 Ibid., 205
5 George Luscombe, interview, 29 Mar. 1988
6 Steven Bush, interview, 9 Aug. 1988
7 Diane Grant, interview, 20 Jan. 1989
8 Quoted by Herbert Whittaker in 'Chicago 70: A Winner Wooed,' *Globe*, 4 Apr. 1970
9 Rick McKenna, interview, 26 June 1988
10 Martin Stone, 'Chicago "Lynch" Trial on Toronto Stage,' *Tribune*, 18 Mar. 1970
11 Sandy Naiman, 'Press Conference,' *Seneca*, 19 Mar. 1970
12 Whittaker, 'Chicago 70: A Winner Wooed'
13 Herbert Whittaker, 'Chicago 70: Well Matched Absurdities,' *Globe*, 11 Mar. 1970
14 Jim McPherson, 'A One-sided View of Chicago 7 trial,' *Telegram*, 11 Mar. 1970
15 Paul Levine, 'Theatre Chronicle: Chicago 70,' *Canadian Forum* 15 (July–Aug. 1970), 174–6
16 Nathan Cohen, 'Chicago 70 Goes off Track,' *Star*, 11 Mar. 1970

17 Clive Barnes, 'Stage: "Chicago 70" at the Martinique,' *New York Times*, 26 May 1970
18 Martin Washburn, 'Theatre: Chicage '70,' *Village Voice*, 11 June 1970
19 Jack Kroll, 'America Hurrah ...?' *Newsweek*, 8 June 1970, p. 90
20 Calvin Butler, interview, 8 Aug. 1988

CHAPTER 14

1 Nathan Cohen, 'A Look at Theatre in Toronto: The Pace Setters Fall Behind,' *Star*, 5 Dec. 1970
2 John Mortimer, Introduction, *The Captain of Köpenick* (London: Methuen, 1971), n.p.
3 Carl Zuckmayer, Preface, *The Captain of Köpenick* (London: Methuen, 1971), n.p.
4 Herbert Whittaker, 'Captain of Köpenick Is a Tour de Force,' *Globe*, 9 Nov. 1967
5 Nathan Cohen, 'Fitting Finale to Fraser Ave. Theatre,' *Star*, 9 Nov. 1967
6 Martin Stone, 'A Fascinating Play,' *Tribune*, 27 Nov. 1967
7 Martin Stone, 'Spirit of Schweik Captured,' *Tribune*, 5 Mar. 1969
8 Nathan Cohen, 'Theatre in '68 Lacked Social Ferment,' *Star*, 28 Dec. 1968
9 Nathan Cohen, 'Two Folklore Pieces: Schweik Passes Muster,' *Star*, 28 Feb. 1969
10 Maja Ardal, interview, 11 July 1988
11 Jeff Braunstein, interview, 25 May 1988
12 Suzette Couture, interview, 19 Jan. 1989
13 Martin Stone, *Tribune*, 17 Mar. 1971
14 Brian Pearl, *Excalibur*, 25 Mar. 1971
15 Nathan Cohen, 'Toronto Workshop Shows Capacities Aren't Limited,' *Star*, 10 Mar. 1971

CHAPTER 15

1 Peter Hay, 'Cultural Politics,' *Canadian Theatre Review* 2 (Spring 1974), 10
2 Nathan Cohen, *Star*, 31 Mar. 1967
3 Nathan Cohen, 'St. Lawrence Centre Says It's "Your Place" but Is It Really?' *Star*, 2 May 1970
4 Nathan Cohen, 'Regret, Not Panic, Is in Order over New Centre,' *Star*, 7 Mar. 1970
5 See Johnston, *Up the Mainstream*, for the history of this movement.
6 Ken Gass, Introduction, *Factory Lab Anthology*, ed. Connie Brissenden (Vancouver: Talonbooks, 1974), 7

7 Don Rubin,'Creeping toward a Culture,' *Canadian Theatre Review* 1 (Winter 1974), 6

CHAPTER 16

1 Cedric Smith, interview, 31 Jan. 1989
2 George Luscombe, interview, 5 Apr. 1988
3 Grant Roll, interview, 29 June 1988
4 Filewod, *Collective Encounters*, 49
5 Ibid., 22, 183
6 Urjo Kareda, 'Ten Lost Years Beautiful Theatre,' *Star*, 7 Feb. 1974
7 Audrey Ashley, 'Moving Account of Lost Years,' *Ottawa Citizen*, 9 Mar. 1974
8 David McCaughna, 'Ten (Rousing) Lost Years,' *Star*, 1 Mar. 1974
9 Lynne van Luven, 'Ten Lost Years Was Pure Gold,' *Lethbridge Herald*, 8 Nov. 1974

CHAPTER 17

1 'Shrinking Refugee Rights,' *Globe*, 12 May 1989, p. A7
2 'One Year Later: Absolute Order,' *Time*, 23 Sept. 1974, pp. 36–7
3 Roger Keene, 'Fire at TWP,' *Scene Changes* 2, no. 11 (Dec. 1974), 12–13
4 Urjo Kareda, 'Toronto Workshop Loses More in Fire Than Just a Theatre,' *Star*, 6 Nov. 1974
5 Herbert Whittaker, 'Emerging from Ashes Toronto Workshop Back on Three Fronts,' *Globe*, 30 Nov. 1974
6 Herbert Whittaker, 'Return of Ten Lost Years and TWP Both Stirring Events,' *Globe*, 13 Dec. 1974
7 Urjo Kareda, 'Theatre Rises from Ashes with an Elegant Setting,' *Star*, 1 Jan. 1975
8 'Events in Chile Held Up to Clear Glass Window,' *Varsity*, 17 Jan. 1975, 5
9 Kareda, 'Theatre Rises from Ashes'
10 Diane Douglass, interview, 12 July 1988
11 Ross Skene, interview, 26 Aug. 1988
12 Letter from Edward A. Christie to TWP, 8 May 1975, TWPA
13 Urjo Kareda, 'Olympic Drama Flexes Its Muscles on the Wrong Topic,' *Star*, 25 Apr. 1975
14 Joseph Erdelyi, 'New Play by Winter Lacks Force, Finesse,' *Ottawa Citizen*, 28 Apr. 1975
15 Herbert Whittaker, 'Summer '76 More Social Tract Than Drama,' *Globe*, 25 Apr. 1975
16 Ben Duncan, BBC, 11 May 1976, transcript, TWPA

CHAPTER 18

1 See Johnston, *Up the Mainstream*, for a discussion of this change.
2 Agenda of the Canada Council meeting, 21 Sept. 1976, CCA
3 Ibid.
4 Karl Jaffary, interview, 23 Aug. 1988
5 Letter from Allan Sparrow to Committee of Adjustment, 30 Nov. 1976, TWPA
6 Copies of City of Toronto documents relating to the company's long struggle with the developers are included in the TWP archives.
7 Letter from City of Toronto Planning Department to Domingo Penaloza, 18 Jan. 1977, TWPA
8 Report of the Parks Priority Committee meeting, 2 Feb. 1977, City of Toronto Archives.
9 Letter from Domingo Penaloza to June Faulkner, 22 June 1977, TWPA
10 Maureen Peterson, *Ottawa Journal*, 14 Feb. 1977
11 Rick Salutin, interview, 17 Sept. 1987
12 Ibid.
13 Len Doncheff, interview, 5 May 1988
14 Gina Mallet, 'Les Canadiens a Rousing Opening,' *Star*, 21 Oct. 1977
15 McKenzie Porter, 'Les Canadiens Scores for National Unity,' *Sun*, 25 Oct. 1977
16 Bryan Johnson, 'This Year's Winners and Sinners,' *Globe*, 13 May 1978
17 Gina Mallet, 'Playwright Shows How Apartheid Drives Souls Apart,' *Star*, 1 Mar. 1978
18 Robert Wallace, 'Ablaze with Soul,' *Toronto Theatre Review*, May 1978
19 Dick Beddoes, 'Flowers: A Dirty Word,' *Globe*, 17 Apr. 1978
20 Martin Stone, 'Genet Begat Kemp, Kemp Begat What?' *Tribune*, 10 Apr. 1978
21 Kaspars Dzeguze, 'Flowers: Garish, Gaudy, Fetid, Funny, and Unforgettable,' *Sun*, 30 Mar. 1978
22 Peter Faulkner, interview, 18 May 1988
23 Diane Douglass, interview, 12 July 1988
24 McKenzie Porter, *Sun*, 25 Apr. 1978
25 McKenzie Porter, [no title], *Sun*, 28 Apr. 1978

CHAPTER 19

1 Don Rubin, Introduction, *Canada on Stage, 1978* (Toronto: York University, 1979), 7
2 Adele Freedman, 'The Mac-Paps Enter New Theatre of War,' *Globe*, 26 Jan. 1980
3 George Luscombe, interview, 23 June 1988

4 Gina Mallet, 'At Least It Wasn't a Funeral,' *Star*, 1 Feb. 1980
5 Rick Groen, 'Only Some of the Mac-Paps' Parts Good,' *Globe*, 1 Feb. 1980
6 Anton Wagner, '*Mac Paps* Hit and Miss,' *Varsity*, 8 Feb. 1980
7 Gordon Vogt, 'The Politics of Entertainment: George Luscombe and TWP,' in David Helwig, ed., *The Human Elements*, 2d ser. ([Ottawa:] Oberon, 1981), 148–9
8 George Luscombe, interview, 28 June 1988
9 Ray Conlogue, 'This Idealistic Wobbly Sees Things Too Simply,' *Globe*, 21 Jan. 1983
10 Karen Sprenger, *Ryersonian*, 28 Jan. 1983
11 Brian Burch, 'Tools from the Past for Our Timid Times,' *Toronto Clarion*, 12 Feb. 1983
12 Moira Farr, *Newspaper*, 26 Jan. 1983
13 Conlogue, 'This Idealistic Wobbly'
14 Larry Cox, interview, 12 July 1988
15 Gina Mallet, 'A Walk on the Dark Side of Lib-think,' *Star*, 23 Oct. 1983
16 Bob Pennington, *Sun*, 23 Oct. 1983
17 Stewart Brown, 'Play on Witch Hunt Makes for Unnerving Theatre,' *Hamilton Spectator*, 21 Oct. 1983
18 Ray Conlogue, 'Luscombe's Talent Surfaces in Names,' *Globe*, 26 Oct. 1983

CHAPTER 20

1 Consultants' reports, 1981–2, OACA
2 Ibid.
3 Letter from Robert Spickler to George Luscombe, 30 June 1983, TWPA
4 Consultants' reports, 1984, OACA
5 Robert Rooney, interview, 14 Apr. 1991

CHAPTER 21

1 Interim report from TWP to William Lord, 14 Jan. 1981, TWPA
2 Letter from Jack Merigold to Linda Sword, Canada Council, 23 Sept. 1981, TWPA
3 Karl Jaffary, interview, 23 Aug. 1988
4 Toronto City Council Minutes, 1980, 02-9963, City of Toronto Archives
5 Toronto City Council Minutes, 1 Oct. 1980, City of Toronto Archives
6 Catherine McKeehan, interview, 15 July 1988
7 Memo from Gordon Floyd to William Lord, Mar. 1985, OACA
8 Letter from Gordon Floyd to George Luscombe, 22 Mar. 1985, TWPA

9 Letter from Norman Endicott to George Luscombe, 15 Apr. 1985, TWPA
10 Minutes of the TWP board of directors meeting, 1 May 1985, TWPA
11 Letter from Anna Stratton to George Luscombe, 26 June 1985, TWPA
12 Letter from Donald McGibbon to Jerry White, 19 July 1985, TWPA
13 Salem Alaton, 'Ghetto Is Flawed but It Asks Some Useful Questions,' *Globe*, 9 Nov. 1985
14 Marianne Ackerman, 'Ambitious Ghetto a Play That Tackles Universal Questions,' *Montreal Gazette*, 19 Nov. 1985

CHAPTER 22

1 Unsent letter from Walter Pitman to George Luscombe, 12 Feb. 1986, OACA
2 Minutes of the TWP board of directors meeting, Jan. 1986, TWPA
3 Memo from Graeme Page to Walter Pitman, 23 Jan. 1986, TWPA
4 George Luscombe, 'Proposal to the Funding Agencies, and the Province of Ontario,' 24 Jan. 1986, TWPA
5 Letter from Walter Pitman to George Luscombe, 28 Jan. 1986, TWPA
6 Minutes of the TWP board of directors meeting, 31 Jan. 1986, TWPA
7 Report from Graeme Page to Anna Stratton et al., 3 Mar. 1986, TWPA
8 Graeme Page, Report to the Ontario Arts Council, 30 Apr. 1986, 3–5, TWPA
9 Consultants' reports, 1986, OACA
10 Minutes of the Ontario Arts Council meeting, July 1986, OACA

CHAPTER 23

1 Robert Crew, 'Toronto Workshop's Luscombe Says He's Just "Moving Aside,"' *Star*, 27 May 1986
2 Frances Walsh, interview, 29 June 1988
3 Peter McConnell, interview, 8 July 1988
4 Nathan Cohen, 'Total Theatre? Yes It Is – But Some New Text Wouldn't Hurt,' *Star*, 26 Nov. 1966
5 Herbert Whittaker, 'Hey Rube! Back Bigger, More Appealing Than Ever,' *Globe*, 8 Dec. 1972
6 Joseph Erdelyi, 'Workshop's Hey Rube! Is Still a Hit,' *Peterborough Examiner*, 8 Dec. 1972
7 Don Rubin, CBC, 11 Dec. 1972
8 Matthew Fraser, *Globe*, 1 Dec. 1984
9 Henry Mietkiewicz, 'Hey Rube a Dazzler but It's Barely Theatre,' *Star*, 30 Nov. 1984
10 Victor Paddy, 'Baseball Play Is Well Worth Catching,' *Globe*, 30 May 1980

11 Kevin Boland, 'Ain't Lookin' Hits Home Run,' *Star*, 30 May 1980

12 Gordon Vogt, *CBC Stereo Morning*, 30 May 1980

13 Gordon Vogt, 'The Politics of Entertainment,' 155

14 Susan Puff, interview, 7 Feb. 1989

15 Ray Conlogue, 'Jazz Loses Its Sparkle in Mister Jelly Roll,' *Globe*, 1 May 1987

CHAPTER 24

1 Minutes of the TWP board of directors meeting, 5 Feb. 1988, TWPA

2 Robert Pennington, *Sun*, 30 June 1988

3 Robert Crew, 'Theatre, Developer Differ on Its Future,' *Star*, 30 June 1988

4 Robert Crew, 'Leon Pownall Named Workshop's Director,' *Star*, 21 July 1988

5 Anne Bermonte, interview, 7 June 1991

6 Tom Butler, interview, 4 June 1991

7 Letter from Leon Pownall to the Ontario Arts Council, 17 Dec. 1988, TWPA

8 Notes from the consultants' meeting, 23 Jan. 1989, OACA

9 Agreement of Purchase and Sale, 4, TWPA

10 Letter from William Scoular to TWP, 23 May 1989, TWPA

11 Minutes of the TWP board of directors meeting, 23 May 1989, TWPA

12 Ray Conlogue, 'Toronto Workshop Theatre Board Rejects Bailout Offer from Toronto,' *Globe*, 16 July 1989

Index